A Journey of Voices
Stewards of the Land

Diane McAdams Gladow

Cover image: Philip Crume's land in the Shenandoah Valley, Virginia. Photo by Dean Gladow.

"A Journey of Voices: Stewards of the Land," by Diane McAdams Gladow. ISBN 978-1-62137-0-758.

Published 2012 by Virtualbookworm.com Publishing Inc., P.O. Box 9949, College Station, TX 77842, US. ©2012, Diane McAdams Gladow. All rights reserved. No part of this publication may be reproduced, stored in a retrieval system, or transmitted in any form or by any means, electronic, mechanical, recording or otherwise, without the prior written permission of Diane McAdams Gladow.

Manufactured in the United States of America.

Dedication

To my husband, Dean, without whose assistance and interest, this book would not have been possible. You are my research assistant, chauffer, photographer, tombstone reader, map maker, proofreader, and report writer -- my partner in family book projects as well as in life. This one is for you.

Table of Contents

Chapter 1
　Introduction 1
Chapter 2
　The Immigrant to America 5
Chapter 3
　The Shenandoah Valley Years 8
Chapter 4
　Moving to Kentucky 26
Chapter 5
　New Endeavors in Different Places 47
Chapter 6
　The Spirit of Adventure 62
Chapter 7
　Crume Valley Years 65
Chapter 8
　The Passing of Crume Valley 79
Chapter 9
　Civil War 92
Chapter 10
　Slavery and the Crume Family 103
Chapter 11
　Going to Texas 109
Chapter 12
　Pine Town's Crume Family 125
Chapter 13
　The Birth of Maydelle, Texas 136
Chapter 14
　Enduring Inheritance 153
Chapter 15
　A Family on the Move 155
Chapter 16
　The Challenge of West Texas 171
Chapter 17
　Achievement Through Struggle 189
Chapter 18
　The Great Depression and the Dust Bowl Years 203
Chapter 19
　Living Apart 219
Chapter 20
　The Effect of Hard Times 234
Chapter 21
　New Beginnings 236

Chapter 22
    World War II 250
Chapter 23
    Coping with Endings 267
Chapter 24
    Gus Crume's Family 280
Chapter 25
    Living History 289
Epilogue ....
    Breckinridge County, Kentucky..
    October 2009... 292
Author's Notes... 297
Family Charts 300
Notes and Sources 312

Note: *Please use the generation charts at the back of the book beginning on page 300 to clarify the names of individuals and their families as you are reading.*

Introduction

"Gladys Prune, Gladys Prune," my mother was mimicking some kid from her childhood in a high, sing-song voice. When she was young, Mom was not too happy with her family name. Crume was a fine, Scottish-Irish name with a rich history, but it was too easy to rhyme it with something unfortunate or misspell it to make it Crumb. She had to endure many teasing incidents as a kid.

Hesitant to comment much for fear of encouraging my mom to start talking about our family history, I ventured to ask a question, "How did you handle the teasing?"

Mom quickly replied, "I mostly tried to ignore it. It was either that or smack that kid every time he opened his mouth."

"When did you change your mind about your name?" I was curious enough for the moment to ask.

"Well, of course, my name changed when I married your dad, but before that when I started teaching, respect for my name was expected. Also, my parents, your grandparents, were always respected members of the community, so when I became an adult, I took my place beside them. I really became proud of the name after I started researching it."

My mother's research into the family was very familiar to me by this time, and this was why I hesitated to get my mother started talking about family and the past. At my young age, her enthusiasm had not yet captured my imagination. Her research had begun with the opening of an old, weathered, hump-backed trunk and the discovery of the Crume family treasures, including old letters, pictures, and artifacts saved and passed down through the generations. Related to the Crumes were the Jordans, Fergusons, Withers, Lincolns and other families who had immigrated to America from the British Isles – Scotland, Ireland, England, and Wales. Upon reaching the new world, they grouped themselves together with other families from the home countries, their children married the other families' children, and they spread out across America together, mostly seeking a better life on new land. The names of America's cities and towns, mountains, rivers, and lakes reflect the large number of cultures that came together in America, including the native peoples who were already present when the "new people" arrived. Those names tell their own story about where people chose to live in this vast land, rich in opportunity.

As a child of a mother on a quest, I had already become accustomed to seeing trunk treasures scattered about: a Civil War vintage letter lying on the dining room table ready to be transcribed, an old "last" used for constructing shoes during the Civil War serving as a door stop, and genealogical records and old pictures in piles covering the dining room desk. However, of all the objects preserved in the old trunk, the pliers used to pull teeth fascinated me the most. Old family stories related that the pliers had been used by ancestor land owners to "cure" their workers' toothaches. The pliers had most likely belonged to my great grandfather Crume. In addition, antiquated eyeglasses and pipes, straight razors, watch chains, Bibles, school books and slates, and even a paint set became familiar objects to charge the imagination.

Mother tried her best to get me interested in her research project and in the old family treasures, but it just didn't happen to any great degree until much later when finally my curiosity and love of history pushed me into picking up where my mother had left off in her research. Shining light on my family's past was my heritage, and it could only be delayed so long. After my mother died, my father brought me the old trunk, and my fate was sealed. I was to be the next "keeper" and researcher. My brother and father also got involved, traveling around the United States and even to the British Isles, collecting information, especially concerning my father's side of the family. I also did some traveling and collecting of records, but my greatest interest was in the letters and old papers found in the trunk. Many were not in very good condition – mouse-chewed, faded, the handwriting barely legible, not to mention the fact that the spelling and sentence structure belonged to an earlier time. But the voices I discovered in the old letters called to me, and my desire to know the people behind the voices grew as I read and transcribed the letters.

My grandmother, Lanora Belle Ferguson Crume, had not been born a Crume but had married into the Crume family, making her a Crume for most of her adult life. She began to learn about the family even before she married into it because her father, John T. Ferguson, had married a second time late in life and to a much younger woman, Ada Belle Crume, the sister of the man Lanora was later to marry. Her stepmother became also her sister-in-law! In visiting with the Crumes before her marriage and after, Nora, as she was known, discovered that her husband came from a family with a rich history, but it did not occur to her to delve very deeply into the family's past. In those days, most people were too busy to worry about what happened years before their time. However, Nora carried into her marriage an old trunk full of Ferguson and Jordan keepsakes, and to this collection she added many Crume letters, documents, and pictures. As a result of her doing this, her voice became an important one in my journey to discover more about my family. Before I could do this, I, as my mother had done before me, had to go backwards in time nearly to the beginnings of America when the first Crume arrived on the east coast of the "new world," possibly between 1700 and 1715. Mother's research, her quest, had found what was then known about this man as well as the others in her long Crume line.

"Mom, just last week I was studying about the first settlers to come to America. Do you suppose that our Crume ancestors were like them?"

"Our ancestors were not among the first settlers to arrive in this country, and so when they came, they had some assurance that the American colonies had developed some semi-civilized towns and settlements. They didn't have to be totally fearless as the first settlers were. I cannot even imagine what courage it took for those people to cross the Atlantic, not knowing what they would find at the end of their journey if they could even complete the journey," Mom enthused. She always liked to encourage her children's interest in history. "Our family came by ship to the settlements on America's eastern shore, fortified themselves, and then moved out to the land that they were seeking which eventually turned out to be in Virginia's wilderness country. They were farmers, stewards of the land, and finding good land for this occupation was their ultimate goal."

"Do you think that they knew what they would find and that they would be successful?" I asked one final question.

"I think they knew what they wanted, and with God's help, some luck, and their own hard work, they felt they could build a life for themselves, a life on the land. They must have asked themselves, 'What more could we want?' They didn't lack courage or determination, and their success was in their own hands."

The Immigrant to America

A man, merely a dark silhouette, stood at the rail of a ship that was fast making its way towards its destination. The bright light from the moon revealed quiet seas, nothing but water for as far as the eye could see. Although the breeze was brisk but not fiercely cold, the man had thought to bundle himself in an outer coat which swirled around him, rather like large wings. The only sounds to be heard were the rushing water and the flapping sails as the ship made its way onward -- and occasionally, a shout from one of the sailors manning the ship. A few tendrils of fog were enshrouding the ship, occasionally blocking out the multitude of stars and the moon, giving an eerie, somewhat lonely feeling to the night. The man was without a doubt thinking of the future and what lay ahead at the end of his journey across the seemingly endless ocean. He had left his home in the British Isles behind and was risking everything, including perhaps his present or future family, on the promise of a new land and a new start. Had he made a mistake? It was too late to worry about that now. Instead, a small shiver of excitement ran down his spine when he thought about what lay ahead.

"New is the right word," he thought as he stood at the ship's rail, "and it is a good word, full of hope for all that the future might hold." There was nothing to stop him but his own fear or lack of ambition and hard work. Those things were not going to be a problem. As he stood watching the water pass by the ship as it hurried on its way, he felt strong and capable and ready to get started. A Crume was coming to the American colonies in the new world. And thus it began for him as it had begun for countless others – on a ship surging towards a new future in a new land.

The family stories and traditions concerning Daniel Crume, the most likely first Crume man to come to America's shores, are varied, but actually very little is known conclusively about him and his origins. What is known is that a Daniel Crume was married to Elizabeth Brooks either in the British Isles or in Virginia and had at least one son, Philip, born on August 9, 1724, in Virginia. Many years later Philip Crume listed in his family Bible his parents' names, Daniel and Elizabeth Brooks Crume. Other than these facts, many theories exist which have been developed over the years by various researchers and family members with little or no factual evidence or sources provided to support them.

According to some, Daniel was supposedly born September 1, 1680, in Scotland, the son of Daniel Croom, known as "the old." Other researchers have proposed that the elder Daniel was the immigrant to the colonies, bringing with him his three sons, one of whom was Daniel born in 1680. One account has Daniel, the immigrant, as an ambassador from the king on official business in America, and another account says that he came to America to fight in the Indian wars. Many believe Daniel sailed from Edinburgh and originated from Kilmonarch, Scotland. Others propose he may have come from Ireland or England and perhaps have come to America by way of Barbados. Two members of the Crum family, Henry and Lucinda Crum Coger, lived in the same counties as Daniel's son Philip and could be related, but again, no evidence has been found to confirm this. Other relationships to people living in Philip's time period in Virginia have been pursued, including a DNA link to a Daniel Croome in Henrico County, but thus far, nothing has been proven. It is even possible that Philip as a young man was the immigrant to America and his father Daniel never left the British Isles.

A long-held story in the family concerning Daniel's death says that he left the colonies to return to Scotland to settle an estate and was lost at sea, leaving his family in America to continue on without him. If this occurred, it would have been after 1724 when his son Philip was born. Another version of this story has Daniel's father, "the old," being the one who returned to the old country. Still another version of this story has Daniel with twenty-eight children immigrating from Scotland in 1702 with fourteen of them. When he returned to Scotland to retrieve the other fourteen, he was lost at sea, leaving Philip in charge of the children in America.

No family accounts have been found which were written by either Philip or his children or grandchildren who would have possibly known Philip's background. Philip's grandson, Jesse, wrote a diary late in his life, but other than the parental relationship between Philip and Daniel, nothing about the early family was recorded there. Someone else, in a different handwriting, added to the diary his or her theory about the early Crume history. This could have happened much later than the date of the diary, and the researcher did not provide sources or evidence for what he or she wrote. Furthermore, very few public records in Virginia exist which would be old enough to provide proof of the immigrant's identity or whereabouts, because of fires of one kind or another in the county courthouses over the years. Daniel Crume, therefore, remains a figure of mystery, but his place in family lore as the immigrant to America, or one of the immigrants along with his father, seems firm. If nothing else, he stands as the symbol and embodiment of the courage and conviction that brought the Crume family to this country. In every Crume descendant's imagination, he was the man who stood by the ship's rail, listening to the call of a new land and resolving to grasp his future with both fists.

The Shenandoah Valley Years

In 1746, Philip Crume, son of Daniel and Elizabeth Brooks Crume, was twenty-two years old, unmarried, and more than ready to start making his own big ambitions become reality. On March 18, 1746, he was appointed by the county court to work with some local landowners on surveying a road in Augusta County, Virginia.[1] This appointment was meaningful for him because the court was accepting him as an established member of the community even though he may not have owned his own land yet. Land ownership was his first goal, however, in the plans he was making to become a successful planter and livestock producer in the Shenandoah Valley, his chosen place of residence. By the years 1749-1752, Philip had reached his first goal because according to land and court records in Augusta County, some of which spelled his surname as Crum, he was a land owner on Flint Run, a tributary of the south branch of the Shenandoah River. He was on his way, and his drive and energy were boundless.

Philip's land was located in the Shenandoah Valley which not only contained the river but the rich, fertile soil that the river and its tributaries created. The Valley was adjacent to mountains covered in forests, a breath-taking backdrop for the farmland and an awe-inspiring view from the high ground of the mountains themselves. Although it was absolute wilderness and more than likely had to be cleared of timber in most places to create the fields and pasturelands that he wanted, Philip had chosen a spectacular place to live. His 400-acre parcel of land was granted to him with a warrant and a survey report. The actual deed to the land would be recorded later.[2] The Shenandoah Valley was located in Augusta County, Virginia, when Philip began working his land. However, Frederick County was adjacent to Augusta, and when the border was adjusted in 1753, Philip Crume's land fell under the jurisdiction of a new county.[3]

Shenandoah River and Valley

Philip discovered early in his land ownership that he did not have to physically move to get a new address. The county lines seemed to move on a regular basis. It would happen again in 1772 when a large part of Frederick County became Dunmore County and then once again when Dunmore County became Shenandoah County. All of Shenandoah County, which included Philip Crume's land, was a part of the "Northern Neck of Virginia," which was originally Lord Fairfax's large domain. Thomas Lord Fairfax, Baron of Cameron, was an old friend of George Washington, and he had been granted by the British Crown a huge tract of land in the colony of Virginia. The southwestern border of the Northern Neck was a seventy-six mile artificially drawn and surveyed line known as the Fairfax Line.[4] Therefore, all of Philip's original land patents, as well as those of his neighbors, were issued by Fairfax, no matter what the county name was.

In those early days, Philip could not have chosen a better place to live and a better friend and mentor than Ralph Withers, a landowner in the Valley and successful farmer who married four times in his lifetime and eventually lived to be over a hundred years old. He had been living in Frederick County on Crooked Run and/or several other parcels of land since at least 1716, one of his land parcels being near a small settlement called Front Royal and only a few miles from Philip Crume's land. He bought and sold land to his advantage all of his long life.[5] It is not known when or under what circumstances that Ralph Withers and Philip Crume met, but it is possible that Ralph Withers may have facilitated Philip Crume's start in farming by having him farm some of Wither's land in an overseer or sharecrop agreement.

As a bonus, in the course of his business dealings with Withers in Frederick County, Philip had the opportunity to meet Ralph's daughter, Sarah. A relationship developed between them, and at age twenty-five, Philip married Sarah Withers, age nineteen, in Frederick County, Virginia, on December 23, 1749.[6] Their first child, a son named Ralph whom they undoubtedly named after Sarah's father, was born a year later on December 12, 1750. In the ten years after their first son, Ralph, was born, Philip and Sarah had a busy life building a home in the wilderness, getting their farming and livestock operation started, and adding five more children to the family, Philip Withers Crume (also named for his grandfather) on August 31, 1752; Susanna on July 10, 1754; Mary on March 15, 1756; Daniel (probably named for Philip's father) on January 27, 1758; and Jesse on January 16, 1760.[7]

During the years 1754 – 1763 while the Crumes were settling in on the land in the Shenandoah Valley, the colonies in America were in a state of turmoil with two European giants, England and France, fighting to gain control over the land east of the Mississippi River where almost all of the established colonies in America were located. Hostilities had broken out over England building forts in the Ohio Valley of Pennsylvania and France taking them over as spoils in battles until finally actual war was declared in 1756. The struggle in America was in reality a part of a much larger conflict being waged in Europe among the countries of England, France, Austria, Prussia, and Sweden called the Seven Year's War. In America the fighting was called the

French and Indian War. Although France had the upper hand in the beginning, it was England that ultimately prevailed and gained control of all the land east of the Mississippi River except the New Orleans area in what would later become the state of Louisiana. The conflict was ended in 1763 with the Treaty of Paris.[8]

No significant battles were fought in the area where the Crumes were living, although it is possible they may have had increased trouble with the Native Americans during this period. In 1795 when the last of the Crumes left the Shenandoah Valley on their journey to Kentucky, they passed through the area in Pennsylvania where an early battle in the French and Indian War was fought in 1755. Major General Edward Braddock on the British side was killed and his forces defeated about ten miles east of Fort Duquesne. This was also the area where a young George Washington, a soldier in the British army in Virginia, blazed a road which was later named for Braddock. Washington also learned during this period from his native American friends about guerrilla methods of warfare, which would later serve him well as the commander of the American colonists during the Revolutionary War. The battle location was known as Braddock's Fields and could be seen from both the roads or trails in the area and the Monongahela River which flowed nearby.[9] The Crumes may have seen it from both places. Although the British won the French and Indian War, it was so costly financially for the British that it led to taxation of the colonies which in turn led to the American Revolution ten years later.[10]

After the French and Indian War was settled, life in the American colonies became more routine again although tax issues (taxation without representation) continued to keep the citizens stirred up. Philip and Sarah Crume were living in the wilderness of the Valley, away from the major towns in the American colonies, and were able to avoid much of the turmoil. Their home was most likely a well-built log house of reasonable size to accommodate a growing family, and it may have been expanded several times over the years to make room for new family members. Outbuildings and some fencing were constructed to help care for their animals. Living in the wilderness was a constant learning process, and the security of an extended family (the Withers) nearby proved to be very helpful. Essentially all of the family's necessities had to be grown or made at home; there were no fully-equipped local stores nearby. There also were no banks in the wilderness; people mostly kept very little cash and lived by the promissory note that was only as reliable as the man who issued it. These facts for rural America would remain true for many years until a sound banking system and trading posts followed by retail stores in small settlements could be fully established.[11]

Philip Crume's Land on Flint Run in the Shenandoah Valley

Philip was learning the skills he would need all of his life in his chosen career of farmer/livestock producer and landowner. Until his sons could grow older, larger, and more capable of helping with the multitude of jobs involved in maintaining the farming operation and other businesses Philip envisioned, he either had to keep his land holdings relatively small so he could manage them or hire help. There is no evidence that he hired help or used indentured servants, but it was possible. Eventually he had all the help he needed from his family, and he slowly increased his land holdings. Whether it was implementing the newest farming techniques, dealing with the Native Americans, handling illness, or finding markets for his crops, animals, and timber, every day brought new challenges and opportunities for him to grow in experience. He was also learning to be a father as the children kept arriving every two years on schedule. During this ongoing growing and building period, 1762 was to be an important year for the Crumes.

In 1762, Philip finally had the deed recorded for his 400 acres in Dunmore County (formerly Frederick), which later became Shenandoah County.[12] The land grant was the first sizable one for him, granted by the British proprietor, Lord Fairfax. In this year, Philip and Sarah also had another child, Elizabeth (perhaps named for Philip's mother), on April 19, 1762.[13] It was a very good year. Thus began the Crume's long succession of land purchases and successful business ventures in the Shenandoah Valley of Virginia that would continue until after the American Revolutionary War. By 1762, Philip was not only an accomplished farmer and animal producer, but he showed an aptitude for buying and selling land which added to his income and his holdings, providing opportunities for his growing family. His mentor and example in these endeavors was undoubtedly Ralph Withers who had operated in the same manner with his land holdings. In 1767 Philip received another grant for 200 acres. In 1771, Philip patented 168 acres on Flint Run, with the final deed being recorded in 1777.[14] By this time he and Sarah had added two more children to the family, William on April 2, 1764, and Moses on February 27, 1766. Up until 1776 when the Revolutionary War began, Philip continued accumulating land and also adding children to the family. Isaac was born on March 17, 1768; Sarah was born on March 11, 1771; and Eunice was born on December 7, 1776.[15]

When Eunice was born, Philip's oldest son, Ralph, was already twenty-six years old and had married Mary "Polly" Riggs on August 4, 1772. Two other children of Philip and Sarah had also married by this time, and with their marriages, two large families in the area were united. Susanna Crume married Eleazer Birkhead on July 26, 1773, and apparently on the same day her sister, Mary, married Abraham Birkhead.[16] Philip's married children continued to live near him, on land that he deeded to them, or land close by that they purchased, helping him manage his large agricultural and timber operation. Because Philip had twelve children, he was beginning to see that more land would be necessary to support them all. Three of his children were already married and starting families of their own, and soon there would be more families that the Crume land would have to support.

Perhaps this was one reason why Philip became interested in other land ventures outside of his Shenandoah Valley holdings. In the early 1770's the citizens of Augusta, Frederick, and Shenandoah Counties developed a great interest in land purchase and possible emigration, and the object of their interest was southwestern Virginia in the wilderness country of Washington County. Washington County had been named in 1776 for George Washington, the then commander-in-chief of the Continental Army. This area, although still populated by Native American tribes, was the doorway to the new territory of Kentucky. It contained the southern route to Kentucky through the Allegheny Mountains popularized by Daniel Boone in his attempt to establish settlements in the new territory.[17] In the years 1769-1771, Boone and five other men established a trail across southern Virginia, through the few gaps that were present in the Allegheny Mountains, and into Kentucky. In 1775, when large amounts of land were purchased from the Cherokee by American land speculators, Boone was commissioned to mark the trail that he had already discovered to be the fastest way through the mountains to Kentucky. It would become known as the Wilderness Trail, and by the end of the Revolutionary War over 10,000 pioneer settlers had traveled it. Before it fell into disuse in 1840, hundreds of thousands of people had used it to get to the new lands in the West.[18]

Philip Crume purchased or claimed land in two parcels along the Clinch River in Washington County in Southwestern Virginia, perhaps as early as 1776. This land was very near the Wilderness Trail and had become of interest to the citizens of the Shenandoah Valley for its mining possibilities as well as its farm land. Although Philip's land purchase was not recorded until 1782 and 1783, a note with the record stated that actual settlement occurred in 1776.[19] Perhaps Philip sent some of his sons or went himself to inspect the land and make a few improvements on it in that year.

Although beautiful land, it probably did not meet with favor because of the Indian situation which was still not settled plus the land itself was wooded and rough. Neither Philip nor any of his family ever lived there permanently. Many of the early settlers of that area during these years lost their lives and property at the hands of the Native Americans who did not want to give up their territory.[20] Perhaps Philip had thought that it would be a good investment because of the public's great interest in it and because it might make a good stopping off place on the way to Kentucky along the Wilderness Trail, but Philip never wanted to be the first to settle in a place which was in violent contention. He always waited for the dust to settle. Eventually, with Philip's absolute commitment to Kentucky, and after his residence there, the Clinch River land was sold in 1797.

Clinch River in SW Virginia

Philip was concerned about his land situation in the early 1770's, but he was also facing a much larger problem. In 1776, the British colonies in America declared their independence from the mother country, and shortly thereafter, war was the dominant issue in every citizen's future. It was useless to pretend that the people of the back country could remain uninvolved and impartial. Much was at stake, not only in the way business would be conducted in the future and what markets would be available for raw goods, but also in how the government that ruled individual lives in the colonies would be constructed and how the questions surrounding the unification of the colonies into a single country would be answered. Every man and woman that lived in the colonies was being asked to decide where they stood – with the mother country that they knew or with the colonies and a bold new future. For many, this would prove to be very difficult. With the escalation of violence and destruction during the war, the decisions became easier for some. Life was intolerable under the present rule; even starting a new country would be preferable. But many did not hold this view. No matter what choice people made, death and/or the loss of property were very real possibilities.[22]

What was Philip Crume's stand? For several years, he and his family had probably been discussing and dealing with the growing difficulties with Great Britain that had finally disintegrated into violence in 1775, so perhaps in one way the momentous Declaration of Independence in 1776 was a relief. A decision had been made. Now citizens had to make their choice and fight to make the side that they chose be the ultimate victor. Perhaps the decision had already been made for Philip and his family because Philip's father, or perhaps just he alone, had chosen to physically leave the old country behind, gambling on a future in the new land. Philip's children had never known anything but the new land with all of its dangers but also its promises of a good life. Perhaps Philip felt that economically he would be in better condition with the independent colonies if they could form a viable government than with Great Britain and its heavy tax structure. This independence and war was just the next step, but it was not taken lightly. They had much to lose.

Every county in Virginia and the rest of the colonies had a militia, and this had been true long before the American Revolution began. These militias were necessary for protection against trouble with Native Americans and other serious threats to peace. The colonies in America were dependent upon what Great Britain could provide in troops and often it was not enough to handle day-to-day protection. These county militias composed of ordinary citizens had laid the groundwork for the army that would be needed to win the upcoming war.[23] The militias were not highly respected by the British army, but they were tolerated when men were needed for fighting purposes or boring tasks that the British soldiers did not want to do.[24] Apparently, part of the militia's duties in each county involved taking a census of residents, especially noting men above the age of sixteen who would be able to join the militia. A census was taken in 1775 in

Dunmore County (later Shenandoah County) that included Philip Crume, Ralph Crume, and Eleazar Birkhead. Ralph Crume was a member of the militia at this time, serving as a lieutenant under John Netherton, and was shown on the census to have two children. Philip was shown with ten children (excluding Ralph and Eunice), and Eleazer had two children.[25]

Philip's sons Ralph, Daniel, and Philip Jr. served in the militia along with Eleazar Birkhead[26], and Philip Sr. contributed to the war effort in other ways. At the close of the war Philip submitted a claim to the Court of Shenandoah County for some beef that he had provided to the American army.

> A copy of the records of the Court of Shenandoah County, Virginia on file in this office shows that on May 31, 1782, the Court considered the claim of one Philip Crume for 375 pounds of beef and one-half day wagonage.[27]

The above evidence that Philip Sr. had given assistance to the American cause resulted in many years later in 1967 his being designated as a "Patriot" by the Daughters of the American Revolution.[28] Ralph had attained the rank of Captain in 1782, and by the end of the war, he held the rank of Lieutenant Colonel.[29] He was 31 years old. Of the estimated 55,000 to 60,000 Virginians who fought at some time in the American Revolution, 35,000 were militia. They were part time soldiers, appearing when needed and disbanding when the danger passed.[30]

In the midst of war, life went on in the Crume households. Philip Withers Crume, Philip Sr.'s son, married Sarah "Sally" Trot in 1778, Jesse Crume married Elizabeth Collins in March of 1779, and Daniel Crume married Mary Dodson in the early 1780's[31]. Philip Sr. continued to buy land during the war to accommodate his growing family. He also continued to sell it at various times, typically in 100 acre plots to family members. In 1779 he acquired by grants ninety-nine acres, and in 1780 another twenty-four acres.[32] In 1781 he bought 400 acres from Will Edwards of Culpepper County, Virginia.[33] All of Philip's land lay along both sides of the eastern branch of the Flint Run tributary of the Shenandoah River in the

Round Mountain on Philip Crume's Land in Virginia

Shenandoah Valley, close to Long Mountain, Round Mountain, and about 17-18 miles from the Manassas Gap, a wind gap and the lowest point for crossing the Blue Ridge Mountains in Virginia. Round Mountain was actually on Philip's land. However, his land was not all connected. It was laid out in two sections separated by miles of timberland. Another piece of Crume land belonged to Philip's son, Philip Jr., and was located on Crooked Run, deeded to him in 1779 by Ralph Withers.[34] It was located near the town of Front Royal, a few miles to the north of Philip Sr.'s land.

Fortune was with the Crume family during the war. In spite of wartime hardships, all of the members of the family survived. By 1785 after the war was over, Philip and his children owned an estimated 1400 acres of land in the Shenandoah Valley of Virginia. The Shenandoah Valley was known as the breadbasket of the country in the 1780's because of the grain that it produced.[35] It would still have this reputation during the Civil War almost a hundred years later, prompting the Union armies to target it for destruction to keep it from supporting the Confederate cause.

The American Revolution ended in 1781, and it had been won by the Colonists in part because of their knowledge of back-country guerrilla fighting. This type of warfare was something the American colonists had learned while attempting to build and

A Journey of Voices: Stewards of the Land

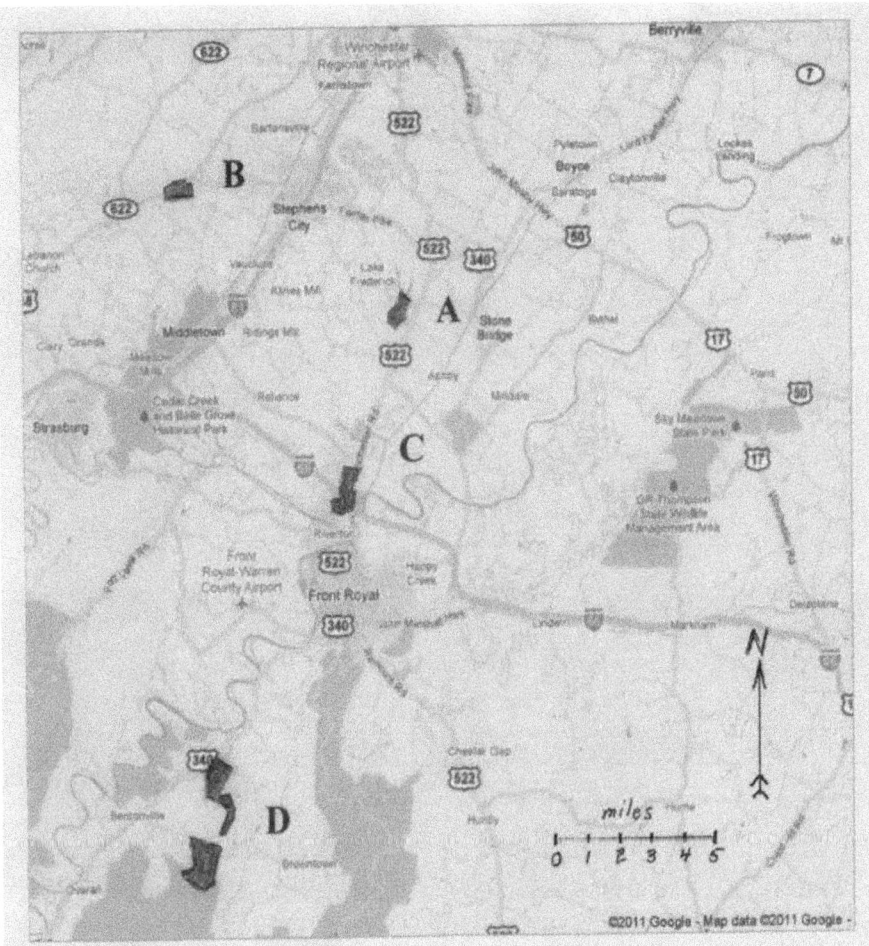

CRUME & WITHERS LAND IN NORTHERN NECK OF VIRGINIA
A. Initial 300-acre tract of Ralph Withers on upper Crooked Run
B. 390 acres of Ralph Withers on Cedar Creek
C. Combined 435 acres of Ralph Withers on lower Crooked Run (140 acres to Philip Crume Jr
D. Combined 1291 acres of Philip Crume Sr. on Flint Run

D. Gladow Feb 2011

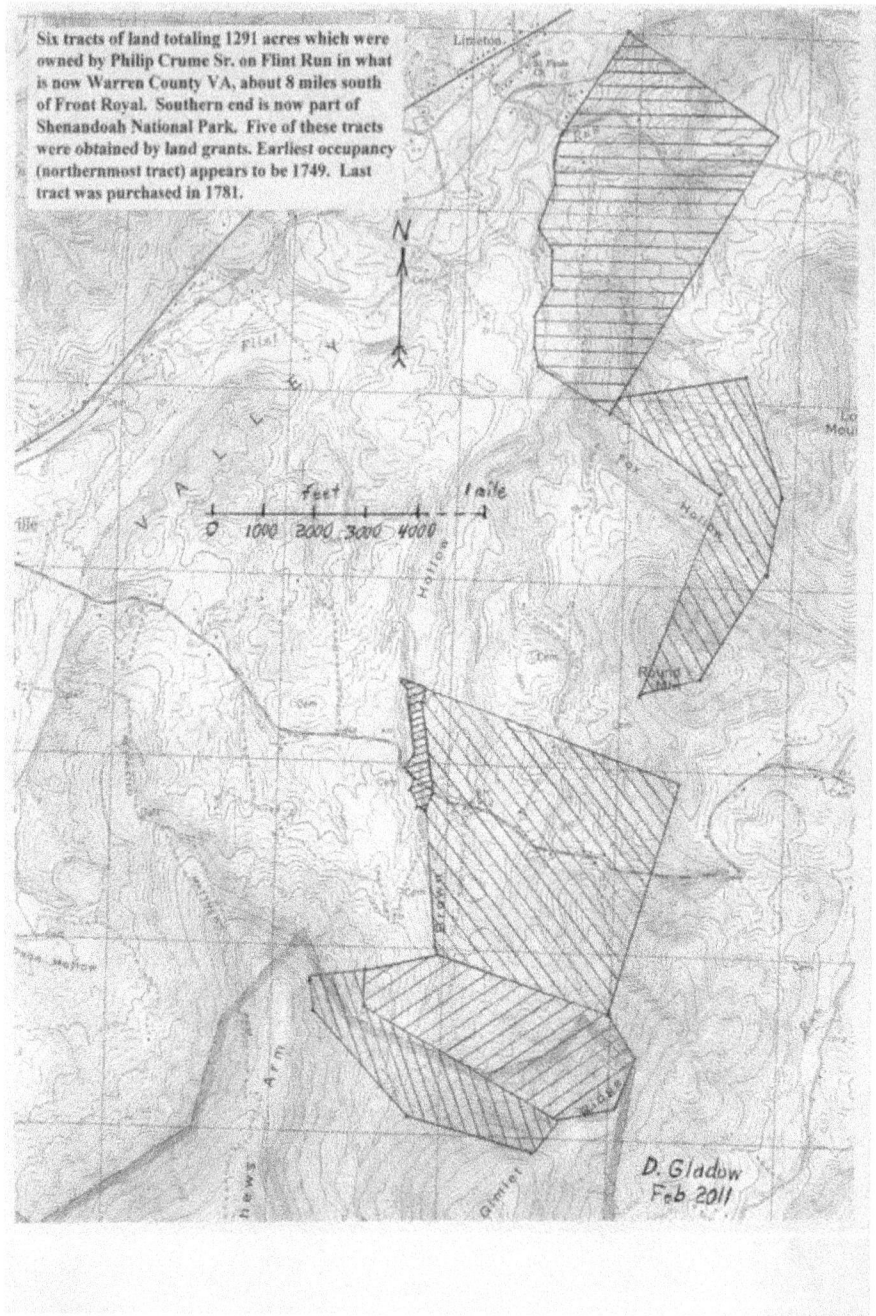

protect farms and estates in the new world and which the British soldiers knew little about. Throughout the war, it bought the Colonists the time they needed to mold themselves into a trained army that could compete in the large battles of the war when they occurred. Where the guerrilla fighting occurred, however, it was brutal and very hard on the civilian population. It is not known whether it touched the Crume family in the Shenandoah Valley, but it is not likely because the American Revolution was fought for most of the war in colonies other than Virginia, and when the war did finally come to Virginia, it was fought on the eastern side of the colony. The Revolutionary War was mostly fought on land and sea as a delaying action, an expensive, time-consuming, casualty-causing irritant to Great Britain with the purpose in mind to hold on until Great Britain got tired of it, gave up, and negotiated a satisfactory (to the colonies) peace. It worked. The war ended for all practical purposes at Yorktown,[36] and the aftermath of decisions pertaining to political questions was the next order of business. What Philip and his family might have contributed to this period of forming a new nation is not known.

What is known is that the marriages of Philip's children were continuing. His daughter Elizabeth married James Harrell on March 25, 1783[37], and as each of his children married and moved into a home of his or her own, the need for more land grew. At the age of 61, Philip had begun to feel cramped on the land that he had acquired in Virginia and farmed for so long, and perhaps the turmoil in the newly-formed nation was disturbing to him as well. Civilization and more people were creeping into the Shenandoah. During this period, the government of the new United States of America was issuing grants for the land farther west in Kentucky to those who had served during the war, as well as others. Philip was probably not contemplating moving at that time, but he may have felt it was a wise move to obtain some of the new land.

Why did Philip choose Kentucky and not the closer land in the Allegheny Mountains? First of all, the Kentucky land was plentiful and affordable. Secondly, to choose the land in the Allegheny Mountains would mean to condemn his family to poverty for generations. This land, although beautiful, was not good for farming, and those who chose it struggled to make a living.[38] Philip, with his excellent "land sense," knew that the Allegheny Mountains were an obstacle to climb over, not a place to inhabit. Therefore in 1785, he was granted by Treasury Warrant one thousand acres on the north side of the Beech Fork of the Salt River in Jefferson County (later Nelson County), Kentucky.[39] His son Daniel had been granted five hundred acres nearby on the southeast side of the Beech Fork in 1780.[40] A few years later in 1790 Philip obtained another 201 acres adjacent to his son's land on the Beech Fork, also by Treasury Warrant.[41] He was steadily moving towards a way out of the Shenandoah.

The Kentucky 1000 Acres

The Kentucky land grants were the beginning of a period of about ten to fifteen years when the family was split in two locations. It was necessary, according to the stipulations of the Treasury Warrants that Philip and his son, Daniel, had secured, that the lands in Kentucky be surveyed and either inhabited or some improvement made on them within three to five years of the date of the Treasury Warrant issuance.[42] Therefore, because several of Philip's sons wanted to go to Kentucky to see the new land, assess its possibilities, and perform the necessary legal obligations while there, Philip saw this as a way to keep the land without having to be there himself. It is not known whether the men took their families with them in the beginning and settled there or whether they traveled back and forth alone, primarily by horseback, for a period of time. If they did settle there with their families, it is hard to determine exactly when this occurred. Daniel Crume, Ralph Crume, and a young Moses Crume are known to have made the trips, and it is possible that most or all of their brothers and brothers-in-law may have traveled back and forth as well. These early explorations were very useful in preparing the land for future occupation by the entire family.

On January 9, 1787, the same year in which the Constitution for the United States of America was written, Philip and his family suffered a large shock. Sarah Withers Crume, the wife and mother of the family, died in Virginia.[43] After almost forty years, Philip was left alone with only the last child, Eunice, then age ten, to raise. His remaining sons who were not married were old enough to take care of themselves. Sarah, like many other pioneer wives living in the wilderness of a beautiful but dangerous new land, had for many years been the strength and support for the family she loved. Her twelve children were representative of her strengths as well as her husband's and her determination to build a life on the land with her own hands and succeed at whatever she tried. She would be greatly missed.

Sarah died in January and two of the last five children married in March and April. Were these weddings already planned or was there a sense of urgency in the children to leave a home that did not seem the same with no mother present on whom to rely? Whatever the circumstances, Philip's daughter Sarah married George Marks on March 29, 1787, shortly after her sixteenth birthday, and Moses Crume married Sarah Marks on April 16, 1787, about three weeks later.[44] These marriages cemented a long association between the Crume and Marks families. In 1786 Philip had sold a tract of 100 acres of land to William Marks, and William Marks and his wife would make the trip to Kentucky with the Crumes when they were ready to emigrate. There were several families of Marks, and the Crumes may have had connections to all of them. No connections among the Marks families have been proven conclusively, only presumed as probable. [45]

Moses was one of the Crume brothers who did settle in Kentucky with his wife after he married in 1787 because most of his children were born in Kentucky. Some sources indicate that Moses was in Kentucky as early as 1783 with his brothers and certainly by 1786 when he and his brother built a grist mill at the mouth of the Chaplin River. Moses would have been twenty years old at the time. If these stories were accurate, he must have returned to Virginia to marry in 1787. Some records have Moses converting to the Methodist church in 1787, others have 1785, but all have the location as being Virginia.[46] A young Moses Crume, according to family stories, built the first flatboat for travel on the Beech Fork to the Salt River to the Ohio River to the Mississippi River and down to New Orleans. Moses was definitely not the first man to flatboat on the Salt River to connect to the Ohio, but he might have been the first to try it on the Beech Fork.

Also according to family stories, in 1788 he established a boat yard business that remained for many years and carried his name.[47] How active or extensive this business was is not known. Assuming it existed, it may have just been a business within the family. Floating flatboats on the Beech Fork was not exactly simple. Most of the time flatboaters had to wait until the winter months when the river was flooding to have enough water for boating.[48] In the years that followed, this flatboat business would have been very handy for the Crume family in getting their crops and products to markets down river from Kentucky. Because the Beech Fork was so difficult, it is more likely they transported their goods to the Salt River at least part of the time and started from there or perhaps even went directly to the Ohio.

Other Crume businesses may have begun at this time as well because Ralph and Daniel knew how to build mills – both saw and grist. Daniel and Moses built a mill during these years at the mouth of the Chaplin River where it ran into the Little Beech River forming the Beech Fork.[49] In 1784 two members of the Crume family in Virginia, Ralph and Jesse, had taken on bonded servants – young men who wanted to learn the trade of blacksmithing – which would indicate that this was a family business as well and likely also to have been transferred to the new country along with Ralph and Jesse.[50] Blacksmiths were needed not only to shoe horses and mules but to make tools, pots and pans, kettles, fittings for doors and machinery, or anything requiring metal. The Crumes also knew how to distill whiskey, or they learned once they arrived in Kentucky. Most of Kentucky sits on a natural limestone shelf, and therefore the water in Nelson County and other Kentucky counties was ideally suited to make fine whiskey due to its high calcium content. In the years to come, Nelson County would become known for its large distilleries and fine bourbon.[51] The Crumes quickly saw the lucrative possibilities of this business.

Ralph was another son who brought his family to settle in Kentucky before 1792 because he appears on the tax list in Nelson County, Kentucky, in that year, and by 1792 Jesse had joined his brothers in Kentucky. He probably had his family with him because his wife died sometime between 1794 and 1795 and he remarried in Kentucky in 1795.[52] Daniel's family situation during the early years in Kentucky is difficult to determine. His last two children by his first wife, Mary Dodson, may have been born in Kentucky, placing the family in Kentucky as early as 1785. Ultimately however, in spite of all of this activity in Kentucky, the principal headquarters of the Crume family remained in Virginia, spiritually and probably physically as well, with Philip Sr. His sons were competent to handle affairs in Kentucky and begin the family occupation of the land there, but Philip was still the head of the family.

Moving to Kentucky

Receipt for Stilling Whiskey

First dip your tub clean.
Then put in one gallon of cold water if the weather is very cold and if very warm, put four gallons to proportion it according to the weather.
Then put in five buckets of hot slop.
Then put in one bushel of meal.
Stir it five minutes.
Then put in gin, more buckets of hot slop.
Stir it well together. Then let it stand thirty-six hours.
Then put in a gallon of rye meal and a half gallon of malt meal.
Then draw in eight gallons of cold water.
Stir it well. Let it stand two hours.
Then fill it up. Put in one half gallon yeast.
[Slop was grain residue from a previous stilling session]
--Jesse Crume from his diary 1859[1]

Philip took some time to recover from the loss of his wife and then began to consider finding a new one. The search ended with his marriage to Anna Barret on September 9, 1788.[2] He was 64 years old and she was 18. He was starting over again and must have felt very strong and invigorated with new lands to conquer in Kentucky and a new wife to share his life. The secret to Philip's success had always been stimulating his boundless energy by building something new. He was now continuing the pattern. Anna was joining a very large group of tight-knit families who were all united as one family with Philip at the head

– a somewhat daunting task at her age, but Anna's place by Philip's side was assured. Anna and Philip began a family almost immediately. John Crume was born November 26, 1789, Margaret Crume was born June 14, 1791, and Nancy Crume was born December 20, 1792.[3] By all accounts, Philip's two families got along well, even though Anna was younger than most of Philip's children, only five years older than Eunice, the last of Philip's children by Sarah.

Late in the decade on February 16, 1789, Philip's son William married Mary Thomas.[4] William bought sixty acres of land[5] and lived close to his father's holdings, just as his brothers and sisters before him had done. At this time, there were only two unmarried children left from Philip's first marriage, Isaac and Eunice. Isaac was pretty much on his own at age twenty-one, but Eunice was only twelve. Late in 1789 or perhaps early 1790, another traumatic event took place in the family. Ralph Withers, Philip's father-in-law through his first marriage, died at the age of 108 years![6]

Over the years, Ralph had been generous in gifting Philip, Sarah and their children with land and other personal property. As an example, he arranged in 1779 to sell to his grandson, Philip Withers Crume, the son of Philip Sr. and Sarah, some land in exchange for Philip Jr.'s care of him and his wife in their old age.[7] Ralph Withers made a deed of gift of much of his personal property to Philip Sr. in 1786,[8] but then before he died, he made out a new will in 1789 rescinding his gift of personal property to Philip and instead leaving it to his fourth wife, Patience.[9] Why he did this is not known. He may have been influenced by his wife to do so, or he may have been unhappy with the death of his daughter, Sarah, in 1787 and Philip's second marriage to a much younger woman in 1788. In any event, Ralph died before his daughter's family moved to Kentucky, a move in which he would not have been able to participate at his advanced age and also which would have meant the loss of his grandchildren. He had dedicated the best years of his long life of 108 years to Virginia, and her soil would be his final resting place. To this point, the Crume family had been very fortunate to have lost only two family members. They had lived through wars, suffered illness from time to time, and endured many hardships in the early days of living on the land in a virtual wilderness, but they had managed to keep the family intact and to keep it growing. In 1791 this good fortune was to change.

Isaac Crume became ill and died on February 7, 1791.[10] He was 22 years old and unmarried; he would remain forever young. His possessions, as listed in his estate settlement, were "one bay mare, one man's saddle and bridle, 13 ½ bushels of wheat, one man's hat, three yards of brown linen, one pattern of deer skins and trimming, two shirts and two stocks, two waistcoats, one pair of britches, one old coat and waistcoat, two pair stockings, one pair mittens, one pair old shoes with buckles, one pair leggings, one scythe and cradle, upper leather for one pair shoes, and one old hat."[11] It didn't seem like much, but it was more than many people, especially young people, had been able to accumulate who lived in the back country of Virginia. He was, more than likely, buried beside his mother on the Flint Run farm in the Shenandoah Valley. Furthermore, this was not to be the only change for the family with the beginning of the new decade. By 1794, a short three years later, Philip, at the age of 71, had finally decided to make the move to Kentucky. The days for the Crumes in the beautiful Shenandoah Valley were numbered.

In 1792 Philip sold a small tract of land of 40 acres to Thomas Marks, which was typical of his normal land transactions, but this time it was more significant. It was the beginning of many land sales in the three years following that would place the Crume family on the road to Kentucky. The Native Americans had mostly been pushed into the Northern Territories of the United States above the Ohio River, leaving Kentucky and Tennessee open for settlement and United States statehood. This circumstance may have affected Philip's decision to move. Kentucky became the fifteenth state in the union in 1792, and Tennessee was the sixteenth in 1796.[12] The new state of Kentucky was now a safer place for Philip's family. Part of the family was already there, but close to fifty people remained in Virginia. Identifying the remaining family members is difficult because the families of some of the men in Kentucky may have still been in Virginia, but Philip Sr. and his new family with Anna were certainly in Virginia, which included four children under the age of seven. A new child, Keziah, had been born on February 17, 1795, to Philip and Anna.[13] Philip's son Philip Withers Crume and his family, Eunice Crume age nineteen, and William Crume and his family were all still in Virginia.

This plan to move to Kentucky must have been agreeable to all of the Crumes, with the possible exception of James and Elizabeth Harrell. No definite proof has been found that they emigrated to Kentucky, but it is likely that they did, perhaps before the Crume trip of 1795. There were names that matched those of James's family in Nelson County records before 1795 and on the census records in that county for 1800 and 1810, and Elizabeth was mentioned in her father's will in 1801. Even without Elizabeth and her family on the 1795 trip, the number of people who made the trip swelled due to relatives of some of the people who had married into the Crume family.[14] It was a monumental undertaking and would take careful planning. Why an individual in his seventies would want to attempt such a trip is almost incomprehensible, but the Kentucky land and the rest of his family were a powerful draw for Philip. He wanted his family all together in a new location which would provide enough land for all of them and those family members to come in the future.

The planning was the first step. It was first determined that they would use the northern route to Kentucky via the Ohio River rather than the southern route on the Wilderness Trail. Perhaps the northern route to Kentucky was considered faster or less hazardous, but travelers could still find trouble with the Indians along the Ohio River, trouble with the flatboats on the rivers, and trouble dragging wagons over steep mountains. It is not known how the first half of the family got to Kentucky, but they may well have determined the preferred route for this large group to take in 1795. The Crumes were going to have to cross the Allegheny Mountains, part of the Appalachian chain which extended from New York to Tennessee, and they were leaving after harvest in late October which would mean traveling in winter weather. They would trek overland, through the mountains, to the Monongahela River, float north to Pittsburgh where the Monongahela flows into the Ohio River, and thence

The Crume Emigration Trip to Kentucky 1795-96

float down to Kentucky on the Ohio, leaving the river at Limestone (later Maysville), Kentucky. They did not want to chance encountering trouble with Indians, known to be present in large numbers at the big bend of the Ohio near Cincinnati. Then they would travel by wagon overland to Lexington, and finally turn west to reach the Beech Fork River in Jefferson County (later Nelson), Kentucky.[15]

It can be noted that these plans utilized well-established roads or trails, larger towns which were well-supplied with food and other necessities, and the best boatyards for constructing flatboats. It was not an easy trip, but everything possible was planned to make it successful.[16] Forty-nine people had committed to make the trip, and it must have been quite a project organizing the horses, oxen, and/or mules to draw wagons loaded with household goods, not to mention any farm animals and stock that accompanied the families. Even if each family only brought along a minimum amount of supplies to get started in Kentucky, there were still forty-nine people, and that meant a large amount of goods.

The second step was to complete the sale of all the Crume land in the Shenandoah Valley. This land was the only home the Crume family had ever known; therefore, the move was going to cause some sadness as well as fear - of the unknown new land and the trip itself with all of its dangers. This fear, however, had been mitigated somewhat by fifteen years of traveling back and forth by family members and the family as a whole learning about the new place. The bulk of the Crume land was sold in 1794 to Joseph Stover, a merchant from Strasburg, Virginia, and the rest was sold in 1795, including the piece held by William Crume and the Crooked Run land Philip Jr. inherited from Ralph Withers.[17]

Finally, everything was done that could be done, and the Crume family set out on October 28, 1795, from the Crooked Run farm of Philip II (Philip Withers Crume) in the Shenandoah Valley just north of the town of Front Royal. Philip Crume Sr.'s grandson, Jesse, who was sixteen years old at the time and the son of Philip Withers Crume, many years later recorded his memories of the trip in his diary of 1859.

Account of the Emigration trip of 1795 in Jesse Crume's Diary Written in 1859

There was Forty Nine persons of us we Bought a Bief and Three Firkins of Butter to last us over the Mountains Some very Dangerous places the passway down one hill was about a Mile down and about a foot wider than their waggon track and very sideling Now if the waggon had missed the track all the horses that did not hang in the forks of trees would have to go 300 feet or more before they would touch ground Some teams had onct with that kind of luck before us this was down the hill to the South Branch of Poto= mac thence over the Mountain and lastly down the Laurel Hill to Log Town next Bresontown thence to Redstone old Fort where we Stayed Three weeks to get two Boats Built Started down the river Monongahala Boats hung on Sawyers the first Night hindred 4 days

1859

In 1795 leaving Virginia and coming to Kentucky in those days was considered a very hazardous journey. I will give you a sketch of our traveling. We started October 28, 1795, from Crooked Run, Frederick County, Virginia. We got about ten miles the first day, pitched our tent and slept on the ground the first time in my life. We traveled two or three days. We passed Winchester and Rumney and entered Morefield in the Allegheny Mountains. Our provisions gave out. There was forty-nine persons of us. We bought a beef and three firkins of butter to last us over the mountains. Some very dangerous places. The passway down one hill was about a mile down and about a foot wider than the wagon track and very sideling. Now if the wagon had missed the track all the horses that did not hang in the forks of trees would have to go three hundred feet or more before they would touch ground. Some teams had met with that kind of luck before us. This was down the hill to the south branch of the Patomack [Potomac] thence over the mountain and lastly down the Laurel Hill to Logtown, next to Beesontown thence to Redstone Old Fort where we stayed three weeks to get two boats built. We started down the Monongahela River. Both boats hung on sawyers the first night, hindered four days. Continued down to Limestone. Father's brother and cousin died. We moved four

Monongahela River outside of Redstone Old Fort PA

miles out and camped the eighth day of December 1795 for winter lodgings. Made 200 pounds of sugar and started the fifteenth of March for Nelson County, Kentucky where we raised corn and in the Fall moved to where I now live. (A small sketch of our travel from Virginia here.) [18]

A grandson of Jesse's, who could remember his grandfather telling the above account many times, further elaborated on the trip. This letter was written on March 9, 1928, by Jesse W. Crume.

Grandfather [Jesse Crume] was born in Frederick County, Virginia July 9, 1779. Came with his father [Philip Withers Crume], uncles, and cousins to Kentucky in 1795. Have heard him tell of this trip so often, and they stopped on the Monongahela River just above Pittsburg and made flat boats to float down the Ohio. I crossed the same river the 10th of January last while at Pittsburg. The whole Crume family came at the one time in 1795, over the mountains, and would cut trees and tie to the rear axle as brakes coming down the mountains, and that had been done so often that they would have to cut a way through them at the bottom. After making their flat boats, they drifted down the Ohio to Red Banks, now Maysville. The Indians were troublesome then, and they were afraid to go by Cincinnati. Sold their boats at Red Banks, loaded up the wagons, and started toward Lexington, through the woods. They ran into a large tract of sugar trees, made camp, slung the kettles, and tapped the trees and made sugar enough to take them through the year. An amusing incident happened here. There was a lot of Buckeye trees close, and as the wood was soft and easy to cut, some of the men made a lot of the sugar troughs from these trees, and as the water would drop in them, it would soak out as fast as it came in, and they had all their work for nothing.[19]

Both of these accounts gave some of the details of the trip but not all. Because the information in the first account came from the memories of a sixteen-year-old boy, since grown old, the most harrowing details were what was remembered and recounted. The second account by Jesse's grandson has numerous mistakes in it because as he tried to remember the story from his youth, the grandson was old and his memory was not as sharp. Jesse, the sixteen-year-old adventurer, actually did better in his old age at remembering the details and place names of the trip than his grandson. Of course, he lived it, and for him, it must have been one of the greatest adventures of his life. Regardless, it was a long and very difficult trip by wagon over the mountains near Romney, West Virginia, across the south branch of the Potomac River, and along the old Braddock Road which had been blazed by George Washington in the French and Indian War. They had more mountains to cross at Laurel Hill, Pennsylvania, passing Beesontown (now Uniontown, Pennsylvania) and finally arriving at Redstone Old Fort (today Brownsville), Pennsylvania.

Barge Yard at Brownsville, Pennsylvania

Redstone Old Fort was a bustling town with many businesses and industries and also known for its boatyards and supplies for traversing the great rivers which surrounded it. The area contained an ancient history even in 1795 with evidence of Indian rock carvings and also battles between the Indians and the white man. Rich in natural resources and fertile farmland, the area had advanced in building bridges, roads, and manufacturing plants.[20] The Crumes undoubtedly restocked their supplies here while their flatboats were being constructed and then began the long float trip down the Monongahela and Ohio Rivers, worrying about trouble with the Indians for the entire journey. Also, it was then December, the water and the weather were icy cold, and they were navigating large rivers, making the floating sometimes a rough experience. The rivers contained sandbars and occasionally dangerous rapids and falls which could snare the flatboats if the boatmen were not careful.[21]

Mural at Maysville, Kentucky showing barge arrivals in 1790

They could not finish the entire journey to Kentucky before winter weather set in completely but had to stop near Limestone (now Maysville), Kentucky, where they had made landfall from the Ohio River. The travelers had to provide some kind of shelters to tide them over until the worst of the winter weather was over. The Limestone area, including a small town a few miles inland called Washington, was thriving in 1795 due to the river traffic and influx of new settlers. Even though Jesse reported that the family camped out, they probably were not lacking in many necessities. They may have made crude shelters from the lumber in the flatboats or sold the flatboats and camped out in their wagons. The land at this location included a large cane break, and this is more than likely where the Crumes made their two hundred pounds of sugar.

They continued on by wagon in March south to Lexington along an old buffalo trace and Indian trail[22] which was wooded

Mural at Maysville, Kentucky showing the Buffalo Trace

according to Jesse Crume's grandson. His story about the sugar trees may have been remembered correctly but perhaps not. Lexington was at that time the largest and most flourishing city in Kentucky with many fine homes and businesses.[23] The Crumes probably enjoyed a rest here and a chance to restock before moving on west to the present-day Bardstown, Kentucky, area in Nelson County[24] where the rest of the family waited in great anticipation. The celebration upon arrival must have been heartfelt and jubilant for both the resident Crumes and the newcomers. It is entirely possible that some of the family members had not seen each other in many years. Journey's end was indeed a welcome place to be, especially after such a long and hazardous trip with young children to supervise! They were undoubtedly glad it was over.

However, the trip was not without its casualties. Philip Sr.'s son, William, and an unidentified cousin of Philip Jr. both died on the trip. According to Jesse's account, their deaths apparently took place either on the river or shortly after the family reached Limestone, before the group made their camp for the winter. This must have been a great source of sadness for the family. They had been so optimistic about getting the trip to Kentucky accomplished with the family intact and well. William left a wife, Mary Thomas Crume, and two children, Sarah and Phoebe. His estate could not be settled until after the Crume family reached their destination in Kentucky, the court finally ruling on it around 1800. Philip, William's father, included his son's wife and children in his division and distribution to his children of his 1200 acres in Kentucky in 1797. Moses Crume was appointed guardian of the children to insure that the girls received their inheritance from their grandfather.[25] As usual, in good times or bad, the family held together.

Upon arrival in Kentucky, there was so much work to be done building cabins and getting settled at the new place that the family's sadness became relegated to the background of their thoughts. Jesse wrote in his diary of 1859 about building his cabin and clearing thick, tangled wildwood for a site on which to build.[26] The land itself contained gently rolling hills with wide stretches suitable for pasture or farming cut through with rivers and streams and some wooded areas. There were some large hills and knobs that were suitable only for the lumber business.[27] By the time the final group of Crumes arrived, the area was already taking on an inhabited look. With a family as large as the Crumes, there were plenty of people to help the newcomers build homes to their satisfaction. Thus the years in Kentucky began for the reunited Crume family, totaling over one hundred people. Half of the family had already begun farming and building businesses, and more industry would follow with the new arrivals. They were self-sufficient, industrious, and prosperous, a force to be reckoned with along the Beech Fork River.

The houses that the Crumes built in Kentucky were large log cabins with huge fireplaces, sometimes six or seven feet wide and typically located at both ends of the cabin, and puncheon floors which were small logs split in half lengthwise and joined together with a broad axe with the flat side of the logs facing up. The lumber used could be ash, maple, or oak, depending upon what was available. The homes were usually located near a water source, either a spring or small stream.[28] The needs of the family living there determined the size of the cabins, the number of stories in them, and how elaborate the construction was. So many of Philip's children were grown and had families of their own that the number of log homes had to have numbered more than a dozen, closer to two dozen. Philip's sons and sons-in-law who had arrived early in Kentucky had obtained more land for themselves besides the original land owned by Philip; therefore the Crumes were spread out over a large area on both sides of the Beech Fork River.

Life in these homes was largely self-sufficient with very few store-bought goods. Almost everything was made by hand – from the food on the table, to the clothes people wore, to the furniture, to the tools people used. Meat was just as likely to be wild animal as it was domesticated cattle or hogs.[29] Jesse Crume in his diary of 1859 wrote of one hunting trip that he went on shortly after arriving in Kentucky.

> I with five others went into the then wilderness part of Kentucky, now Henry County, to hunt and look at the land. We killed bear, deer, turkey, raccoons, and some duck. We found plenty of honey and saw two Indians. We had a fine time of it. This gave me a great fondness for hunting. I killed many deer and other game up to the time I got married and many more since. In 1804 I hunted in Indiana, rather unsuccessful hunt, killed one deer. Saw a great deal of Indians. They killed most of the game and left the place.[30]

A "short" list of the chores which needed to be done by a family living along the Beech Fork was recorded by a descendant of one of Philip's younger children:

> Making home-made soap from rendered fat and lye; hominy making from large, perfect grains of dry corn; black walnut shelling; making dye from walnut hulls, tree barks, polk berries, and other vegetables; carrying innumerable

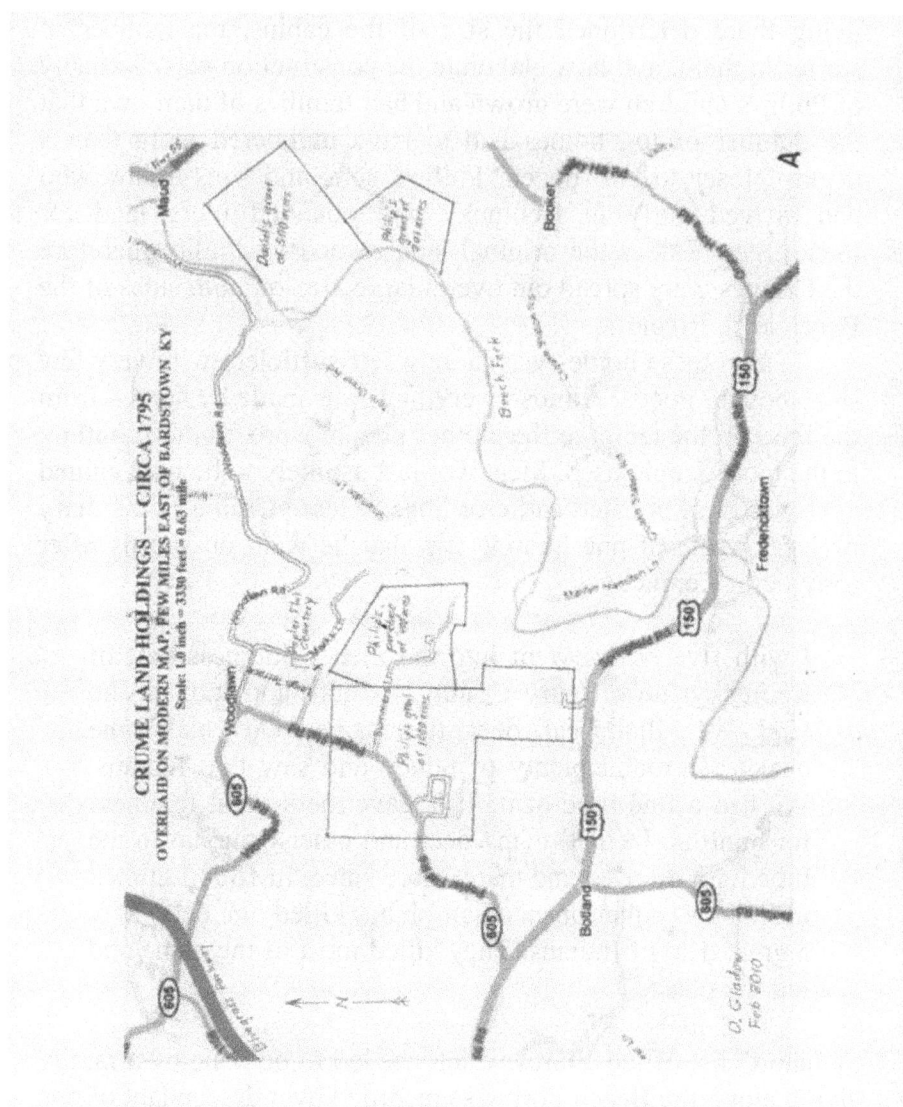

buckets of spring water up the hill to the house; shredding flax; picking and combing cotton; combing wool after sheep shearing; making souse, sausage, cheese heads; curing and smoking meats; drying apples, peaches, pears; drying herbs for seasonings and medicine; gathering wild blackberries and drying them; spinning flax, cotton, and wool into thread; weaving materials; knitting socks, gloves, mittens, and mufflers for everyone; shelling dried beans, peas, corn; drying wool carefully so as not to make it harsh; weaving blankets; weaving under petticoats; sewing at night by candlelight; making over old garments for the children or for carpets using braiding or a carpet loom; and scrubbing floors with wet sand or lye soap.[31]

All of this work was done as well as putting regular meals on the table and taking care of children, but it did not get done without a cost. One early Crume matron was said to have commented, "That's why my one eye is blind and I can't see far out of the other – work hard all day and then sew until eleven or twelve by candle light."[32] It took many hands to accomplish the work, and this was perhaps one of the reasons why some of the Crumes eventually became involved with slave ownership which had become more commonplace in society over the years.

A place to worship God had also been established by the time all of the Crume family settled in Kentucky. Joseph Ferguson emigrated to the area of Poplar Flat in Jefferson County (later Nelson County) from Fairfax County, Virginia, in 1784 and by 1790 had built a church on his land. His land was about six miles east of the settlement of Bardstown. The first church building was a round-log house with a clapboard roof and was known as Ferguson Chapel. It was the second church building constructed in Kentucky. In 1816 a second structure of hewn logs was constructed about fifty yards away, and in 1844 a brick building was built, again about fifty yards distant. The name had changed to Poplar Flat Methodist Church by this time, and the name of the cemetery beside the church also became Poplar Flat. The name came from a large grove of poplar trees located nearby. Eventually the church moved to Woodlawn, about a mile away, and the growing cemetery took over the tree-covered knoll where the early settlers, including the Crumes, had worshipped.[33]

The newly arrived family began to pursue their own business interests. Philip Withers Crume built a saw and a grist mill which produced flour and lumber, and he distilled whiskey just as his brothers were already doing.[34] His son Jesse, author of the diary, later built and ran these kinds of businesses as well. In much later years, John and Squire Crume, youngest sons of Philip, also distilled whiskey in a place called Whiskey Hollow.[35] Much of what the family could produce in the way of excess crops and products was floated down river on flatboats to Natchez or New Orleans. Upon arrival there, the boats were sometimes broken up and sold along with the goods they carried. With this system, those individuals in charge of the boat then had to make their way back home by horse or foot or perhaps wagon if they bought supplies. Because the men returning home were carrying a goodly amount of money and/or store-bought goods, a thriving business in relieving them of that money or goods by force arose along the roads leading north and east from Natchez or New Orleans.[36] The most famous of these roads was known as the Natchez Trace, first used as an Indian trail, and much later preserved in the twentieth century as a paved historical drive. However, it is not known whether the Crumes or their agents encountered any difficulty with highwaymen during these years or traveled the Natchez Trace. During the early decades of the 1800's, the advent of the paddle wheel steamships eventually made a large difference in the transportation of goods to market and the growth of river port towns. New Orleans became a very large hub of activity in the river system of America, being both a seaport and a river port.[37]

In the early days of Kentucky, Louisville and Lexington had become well-established towns, and Frankfort would soon follow them. These towns would eventually grow into large metropolitan cities. However, the settlement that was closest to the Crume land was Bardstown, begun around 1780 and incorporated as a town in 1790. Some of its early buildings were made of stone and brick in the colonial style, and there were many homes and businesses of rough-hewn logs. The town was

Old Talbot Tavern at Bardstown, Kentucky

Old Jail at Bardstown, Kentucky

laid out in streets extending from a central square, which contained the county courthouse in later years. Bardstown never grew into a large city, but it did grow to a medium sized one, and over the years when it modernized to suit the times, it still maintained its 1790's colonial flavor in the older sections of the city. The Crume family members undoubtedly shopped there, established businesses there, relaxed there at the Old Talbott Tavern (built in 1779), and conducted court business there. Perhaps one or two unwillingly visited the old county jail, which was built in 1819.[38]

Upon arriving in Kentucky in 1796, Philip Sr. bought an additional 400 acres from John Lewis which adjoined Philip's 1000 acre tract and was located on Sunfish Creek, a branch of the Beech Fork. He built a two-story wood home for his wife and young family, situated possibly near Willow Spring and also near to the meeting house known as Ferguson Chapel which later became the Poplar Flat Methodist Church and Cemetery. Some descendants recall that the Philip Crume home place was called Riverside, and it included several outbuildings, a corn crib, and meat house. However, the name Riverside is not recorded in any of the land deeds, so perhaps later generations named the home to suit themselves.[39] Another son was born on July 17, 1798, named Squire, giving Philip five children by Anna.[40]

Philip had reached a point in his life, and perhaps had been there for quite some time, even in Virginia, where he could afford some finer things and a larger, more finished home in which to live. He was also a slave holder; several slaves were a part of his estate when he died.[41] It is possible his ownership of slaves began in Virginia, and they came with him to Kentucky, but public records in Virginia up until 1785 did not indicate that he owned slaves.[42] It may have been something new for him in Kentucky because his older children were taking care of their own families and business interests and his younger children were too young to help him.

The Crumes were always looking for new opportunities. Settling in one place was fine, but when news came of other places, the Crumes often went to investigate the new areas that were being opened up for settlement. One account of such a trip was written in a letter of March 9, 1928, from Jesse Crume's grandson, Jesse W. Crume, who could remember his grandfather telling the story.

I [Jesse Crume's grandson] heard him [Jesse Crume] tell often of going to Missouri, with his father [Philip II] and Uncle John Crume, and they went on horseback through Illinois, crossed the Mississippi River at St. Louis, when it was a small town on the bluff, bought provisions, including a mackerel, and went on out into the wilderness, and camped for the night, made coffee and cooked the mackerel. His [Jesse's] father [Philip, II] waked up in the middle of the night nearly crazy for a drink, and he took the coffee pot, and went back along the road to a small creek. He washed out the pot and as he raised up, a big Indian waded into the creek, and passed him at a swift walk, and said 'How.' Grandfather said it scared him quite a bit, as the Indians had killed a man near this place a short time before. Now Grandfather [Jesse Crume] did not like Missouri, as it was swampy at the places they visited it and the mosquitos were bad, so they came back.[43]

Jesse Crume (picture above taken in older years) in his own account of the trip reported seeing twenty-seven canoes loaded with Indians and furs at St. Louis - all kinds of skins.[44] The country and sights he saw were wild, untamed, and free, but not always appealing to him as places where he wanted to settle. Thus ended another family adventure and the prospects of the family moving to Missouri, at least for another decade. Life still seemed good in Kentucky, and the family was content to stay there.

New Endeavors in Different Places

"I was surrounded with plenty in the midst of want. I was happy in the midst of dangers and inconveniences. In such a diversity it was impossible I should be disposed to melancholy. No populous city, with all the varieties of commerce and stately structures, could afford so much pleasure to my mind, as the beauties of nature I found here."
"I need more elbow room."
-- Daniel Boone[1]

From the 1790 Census and 1792 tax list, the early Crume residents of Nelson County, Kentucky, included Ralph Sr. who owned 673 acres of land, Daniel who had obtained 500 acres by treasury warrant as early as 1780, Jesse, and Moses.[2] It is possible that one (or more) of the Birkhead families was there as well, and also the Harrell family (Philip Crume's daughters). This was prior to the large Crume trek in 1795-6. The Beech Fork River formed the boundary for Nelson and Washington Counties, and the Crumes owned land in both counties, doing business on two sides of the river.

Even in the earliest days, the neighborhood where the Crumes settled was beginning to fill up with hardy, pioneer people from Virginia. This was a natural occurrence not only because of the rich river bottom land, but during the Colonial American period, Kentucky was a territory of Virginia and a logical place for expansion. Daniel Boone, the famous trailblazer of the Wilderness Road, and Captain Abraham Lincoln, the President's grandfather, were two such pioneers. They brought their families with the intent of settling the new territory, even though the Indian situation had not been resolved and the dangers were many. Both Boone and Lincoln had lived in the Shenandoah

Valley in the Linville Creek area of Rockingham County, Virginia, which was to the south of where the Crumes were living at Flint Run. Did they all know each other? There are no records to show it, but it is a possibility. Boone was exploring Kentucky as early as 1769 and established his settlement at Boonesborough in 1775 after blazing the Wilderness Trail.[3] These early farms had to be located close to forts or be walled fortifications themselves due to troubles with the Indians. Why did Boone and others keep pushing into areas where the native people who were there first did not welcome them? The answer was the lure of rich land, the challenge of making it produce, good hunting and fishing, and the lack of people in great numbers – or as Boone put it in his famous line, "elbow room." [4]

Captain Abraham Lincoln, veteran of the American Revolutionary War, also explored Kentucky after the war, obtained some sizable parcels of land, and moved his family in 1782. His land was near Hughes Station, and the family lived in

Capt. Abraham Lincoln's Gravesite at Long Run Baptist Church ruins

one of the eight cabins there until they built one on their own land. This land was near Long Run Creek, present-day Middletown, Kentucky, an eastern suburb of Louisville. In 1786, while Lincoln was planting corn, he was attacked and killed by a small band of Wyandotte Indians. The family, although devastated, remained on the land for another year but eventually moved sometime before 1788 to Washington County and the Beech Fork River area. Relatives and friends there helped the family get settled on a new farm. Bersheba (sometimes Bathsheba) Lincoln never remarried and raised her family, Mordecai, Josiah, Mary, Nancy, and Thomas by herself. The cabin that Captain Abraham had worked so hard to build was turned into a school and finally the Long Run Baptist Church. When a new building was needed for the church, the cabin was torn down and the new church covered Captain Abraham's grave.[5]

The Lincoln family lived a few miles south of the Beech Fork River until the children were grown, and they occasionally interacted with the Crumes who lived close by on both sides of

Replica of Bersheba Lincoln's Cabin where Mary Lincoln Was Raised

the river. Daniel Crume, Philip Sr.'s son, in particular, had land on the same side of the river as the Lincolns, and he served as a witness, along with the Lincoln sons, on land and other business transactions in that time period. Other families such as the Berrys and Brumfields moved to Nelson and Washington Counties – friends and relations of the Lincolns – and many had known each other or been connected in some way in Virginia.[6] By this time, towns and settlements were growing, and farms and related businesses were becoming prosperous – civilization had arrived.

By the year 1801, Philip Crume had amassed a large number of grandchildren. From his sixteen living children, he already had fifty-two grandchildren. There would be many more to come because one of his children by Sarah and five of his children by Anna were not married. His oldest son Ralph had eight children, was fifty-one years old,[7] and was proving to have the same skills as his father in buying and selling land, making it produce, and building successful businesses. Daniel, Philip Jr., Moses, and Jesse were doing much the same. Philip had passed his strength and skills along to his sons, and he must have been proud of their accomplishments. They were even surpassing him in some areas that had come about because of new inventions and innovations. Some of his grandchildren were grown and starting their own families and homes. Thus the dynasty that he had created was continuing on, growing larger and more far-reaching, perhaps more far-reaching than even he could ever have imagined. More than the land that he owned, his children were his legacy for the future. However, every life, no matter how strong or successful, eventually must wind down and end. This was the case in 1801 for Philip.

On April 20, 1801, Philip died at the age of seventy-seven years,[8] his wife and children undoubtedly by his side. He had accomplished everything and more that he had set out to do as a young man in a new land. Philip's advantages had been the sheer amount of land available in America and the number of opportunities presented to those who were willing to grasp them and build something of great worth. Just imagine buying thousands of acres of land, selling it, buying thousands more in a different place, giving that away to one's children, and buying more land once again, knowing each time that the land would be available, affordable, and richly productive. America seemed like a paradise compared to what most European immigrants had known in their native countries – tiny, ill-producing farms, if land was available at all, or dirty, overpopulated cities. It is no wonder they fought for a new life in America, and, in like manner, the Native Americans fought to keep what they had. All Philip (and others like him) had needed was personal strength and skill in land management, both of which he had in abundance.

Even in the last years of his life, Philip had planned for the future. He probably sensed that he would not be able to manage immense land holdings for very much longer. Perhaps he realized even in the late 1770's when he bought the Kentucky land that it would be for his children to conquer and manage. He had devised a plan to divide his original Kentucky twelve hundred acres among his children by his first marriage so that they would all have something of his to use as they so chose. Before he left Virginia, he began the process in 1788, in the time period between his two marriages, by granting his power of attorney to his son Ralph Sr. and a neighbor in Kentucky, Richard Parker, to divide the land. Richard Parker was to receive part of the land as recompense for assisting with the division, probably including surveying. In 1797, after Philip had arrived in Kentucky, he completed the division and distribution with land deeds issued to his children and Richard Parker. Only one child did not receive a land deed, Elizabeth Harrell. However, she was mentioned in Philip's will, so perhaps he provided for her in another way.[9] Upon his death the remaining 400 acres on Sunfish Creek, where he was living in Kentucky and which he had bought upon his arrival in the state, was divided among his second wife and his two sons by her. His daughters by his second marriage received household goods and slaves.[10]

From him came sixteen family lines, eight of which bore the Crume name. He had been fortunate in good health for himself and his family, but he had made his own fortune in everything else. His story was the American story in so many ways. He was the embodiment of the opportunities that the free enterprise system created, the self-made man, and the rags to riches

Philip Crume's Bible in which he recorded his family's vital records shortly before he died in 1801.

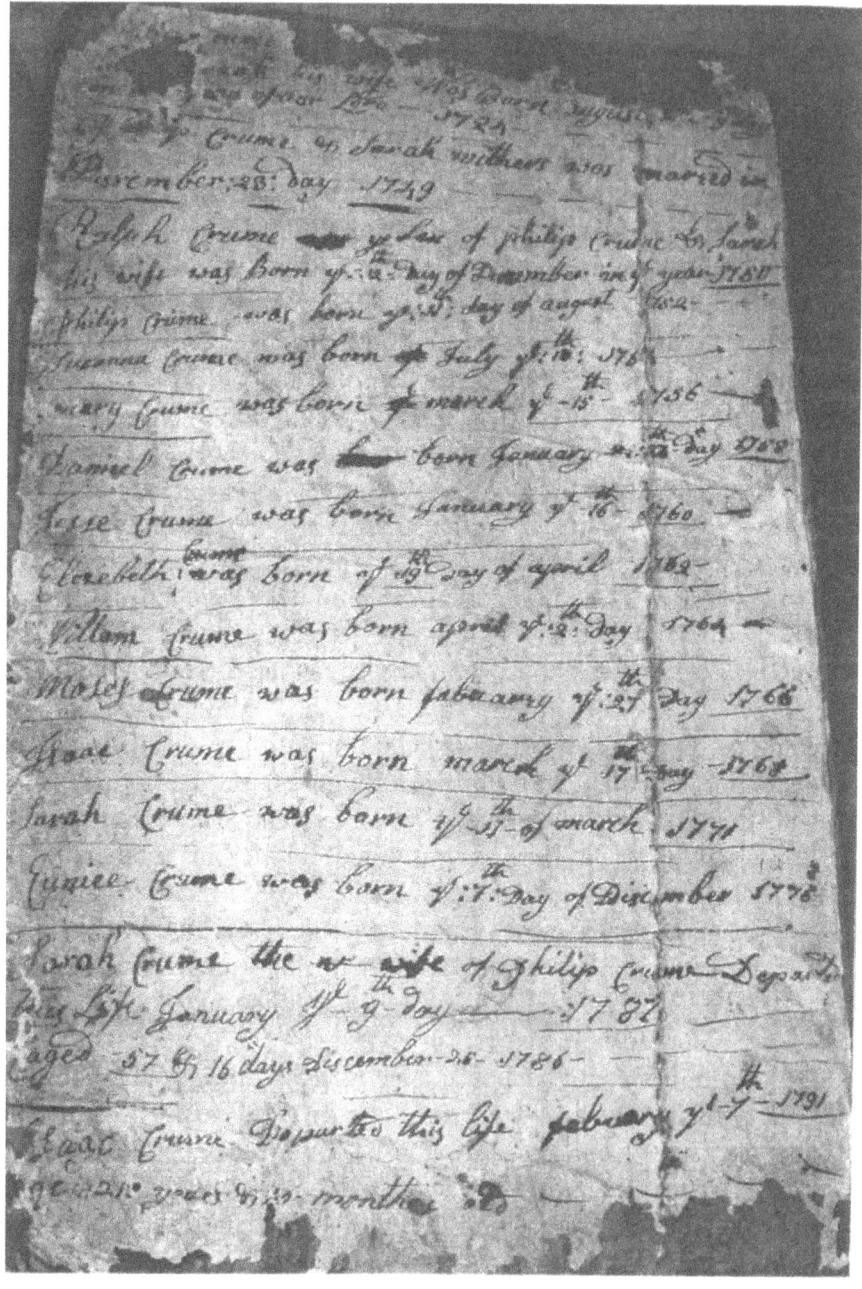

individualist. But perhaps more significantly, he and the generations that followed him represented the great stewards of the land who dominated American society in its early days up through the first part of the nineteenth century. He was buried in the Ferguson Chapel meeting house burial ground which was close to his house and which would later be known as Poplar Flat Cemetery.[11] A stone marker identified his grave for all the generations to come, a lasting testament to what he had accomplished. In 2010, his descendants placed a new stone marker beside the old one which had become unreadable, insuring that he would not be forgotten.[12]

Once the head of the family was gone, changes for the family as a whole were in the wind. Philip's sons, especially those who had been in Nelson County, Kentucky, for sixteen years or more, were feeling the urge to move on to new places that were less settled and had more land available. In the Crume family, there must have existed a great strain of restless energy or desire to live in wild, sparsely-populated areas. Within two years of Philip's death and after his estate was settled, Daniel, Ralph, and Moses were ready to go. The family of William Crume, who had died on the Crume emigration trip to Kentucky in 1795, had already left. Mary Thomas Crume had remarried to Samuel Horsley, the family had moved to Tennessee, and eventually they went to Arkansas.[13] Daniel Crume and Moses were headed north to southwestern Ohio with their families and Ralph was going west to Breckinridge County, Kentucky. Even Jesse Crume headed to Ohio with Moses, but he would later return to Kentucky to live out his life there.

Daniel Crume had perhaps been in Kentucky longer than any of his brothers. He had received a treasury warrant from the Commonwealth of Virginia for land in 1780 and could have gone to look at it any time after that, or he could have explored the land before 1780 and then sought the treasury warrant for it. He most certainly was there by 1785, and his family was with him. Daniel had first been married to Mary Dobson in Virginia. She had given him four children but then died in Kentucky. The date of her death is not known, but it was sometime after the birth of her last child in 1790. There are no public records to show Daniel's marital situation from the time of her death to 1801. Some accounts in the family, supported by family letters and records, family names, and proximity in location of family members, say that Daniel during this period formed a frontier (or common-law) marriage with young Mary Lincoln, daughter of Captain Abraham and Bersheba Lincoln, which resulted in two daughters. Whether or not this relationship actually occurred in the years after Daniel's first wife died, these daughters originally bore the Crume name and two large lines of descendants came from them. Sarah Crume married James Hasty, and Elizabeth W. Crume married Robert Davis.[14]

Daniel married again on January 12, 1801, complete with a marriage license, to Hannah Springer Askins without needing a divorce (no record has been found), and Nathan Crume was born on October 25th of that year.[15] Hannah Askins had been married before and had children from that marriage. Sometime around 1805, Daniel took his family, including all of his children by his two or possibly three marriages, and moved to Butler County, Ohio. Later in his life he moved to Dearborn and Decatur Counties in Indiana. He had nine children by two wives, perhaps two children by another relationship, and some stepchildren by his last wife. He became a part-time preacher in his later years as well as a farmer.[16]

Moses Crume had returned from Virginia to Kentucky after he married Sarah Marks in 1787. The early dates in Kentucky proposed for Moses do not all agree, one indicating he was in

Kentucky in 1783 at the age of seventeen and another indicating he was there in 1786 to build a grist mill, but his marriage date is a matter of record in Virginia. In the years before his father died, he and his wife had produced one child in Virginia and five children in Kentucky, and he had built multiple successful businesses. His work with the Methodist church had grown, and he was considered a leading light of that faith in Nelson County.[17] However, sometime between 1803 and 1805, he moved his family to Butler County, Ohio to a place called Cotton Run, northwest of Hamilton.[18]

In Ohio he added two more children to the family and began to practice one of his careers in earnest. While in Kentucky he had been licensed to preach by the Methodist Church in 1793 (some sources have 1791), and he had been fulfilling the ministerial duties of preaching and performing marriages since then, along with his many other careers. Apparently he had been greatly impressed as a young man with the preaching of men such as Father Wiley and Father Hathaway in Virginia, and thus wanted the career to be a part of his life.[19] After he moved to Cotton Run, he became an itinerant minister or missionary for the Methodist Episcopal Church, serving the white settlers as well as the Indian villages in his large district. He also supported the small church at Oxford as well as the school and postal service.[20] He was described by those who knew him in Ohio as "a portly, dignified man of intellectual appearance who rode a large, black horse." He lived for many years at Oxford and eventually died there on April 1, 1839. His first marriage ended in 1829 with the death of Sarah, and he remarried to Anna Morehead in the same year.[21] All three of these Crumes were buried in the Oxford Township cemetery.

Because both Daniel and Moses became Methodist ministers, it can be noted that the only requirement to become a minister in the Methodist Church, and also the Baptist Church, in the early years was the desire to become one. It was sort of a learn-as-you-go type of career. It was even said of Moses Crume by one of his eulogizers that he did not have "the advantage of much education, but he possessed a strong mind and a sound judgment." Another eulogizer commented, "His manner of presenting the truth was such as to impress the minds of those who heard him that he felt and believed what he taught the people."[22] The Methodists, in the early years of settling Kentucky, Tennessee, and the Northwest territories where many lived on the frontier, devised a truly effective method of reaching these people with religious services, the circuit rider. These men conducted all of the services usually obtained at a local church, but they had to ride hundreds of miles each month into wilderness areas to find their parishoners.[23] "The devotion and indefatigability of these circuit riders became proverbial. Kentuckians remarked of a day of foul weather that no one would be abroad in it 'but crows and Methodist ministers.'"[24] The dramatic growth of the Methodist and Baptist churches was a result of these churches' willingness to be creative.

Ralph Crume had brought his family to Kentucky by at least 1790, but may have arrived there as early as 1787 after another of his children was born in Virginia. In 1788, he was appointed Captain of the Militia for Nelson County, and this was also the year he obtained his father's power of attorney to divide the Crume land in Kentucky.[25] Also worthy of note is the fact that George Marks signed the power of attorney as a witness, indicating that he was in Kentucky, possibly with his wife, Sarah Crume Marks, daughter of Philip Sr. Ralph could also have traveled back and forth for several years before he moved his family to the new lands, as could any of the Crume men. He and Mary had one more child born in Kentucky.

200 Year-old Snug Harbor

Ralph had eight children by the time his father died, and he was coming to the end of his middle years in age. He probably felt it was time for him to see how far his land management skills would take him, so when his father died, he began to buy and sell property in preparation for the move out of Nelson County. He sold some of his land to Cyrus Talbot, a former sea captain, who in turn built a fine home on it that he named Snug Harbor.[26] The land and home came back into Crume family hands several generations later around 1900.

Ralph and his son Ralph Jr. sought to buy land in Breckinridge County – a less populated, wilderness area farther west in Kentucky. To say that Ralph Sr. was a "chip off the old block" was putting his situation mildly. He had inherited every bit of his father's skill at buying and selling land, and he had learned much from his father about the successful use of the land. He knew how to build, and he was intent now on boldly doing just that in a new part of Kentucky. He and his son, Ralph Jr., bought land in 1803 and moved their families to Breckinridge County shortly thereafter.[27]

Prior to the move, Ralph Jr. married Mary Lincoln, daughter of Captain Abraham and Bersheba Lincoln, on August 5, 1801. Mary's marriage bond was signed by Mordecai Lincoln, her brother. This was the same Mary Lincoln who has been reported by some family members to have been in a marital relationship with Daniel Crume, Ralph Jr.'s uncle, for at least some of the years 1790 to 1801. Mary did not need a divorce in order to marry Ralph Jr. (no record has been found), and her brother signed the bond for her, which indicated she was eligible to be legally married.[28] This could have indicated she was never in a relationship with Daniel Crume; however, this would have been the case in a frontier or common-law marriage situation as well. It is interesting to note that Daniel married his second (or third) wife, Hannah Askins, in January of 1801, and Mary married Ralph Jr. in August of 1801 – perhaps a little "tit for tat" here, but there is no hard evidence of this. Mary just might have wanted to get on with her life. Ralph Jr. was four years younger than Mary and twenty-two years old. He apparently had enough money to buy land in Breckinridge County, however, because he was buying it at the same time as his father and later his brothers.

The marriage of Ralph Jr. and Mary Lincoln forever after linked the Crume and Lincoln families. Ralph Jr. and Mary's three children were first cousins to Abraham Lincoln, the sixteenth President of the United States. President Abraham Lincoln's father, Thomas, was Mary's brother. Any children that Mary had in other relationships would also be first cousins to the President. In 1801 when Mary began her marriage to Ralph and moved to Breckinridge County, the next federal census record in 1810 showed that she had no children living with her other than Ralph's, one girl and two boys. Census records after the 1810 record continued to show this until she and Ralph disappeared from the records after 1830.[29] If there were any children of hers by any other relationships, they were at least primarily raised by their father and not Mary.

The beginning of the final breakaway of family members from the Philip Crume family in Nelson County came on December 20, 1804, when Anna Crume, Philip's second wife, married for the second time to Jacob Marks. Philip's son by his first marriage, Moses, married the couple in Nelson County, Kentucky. Jacob was twelve years younger than Anna.[30] She was definitely going in a different direction with this marriage in regards to the age of her husband. The last of the stepchildren from Anna's first marriage, Eunice, had married Michael Klinglesmith December 4, 1802[31], and Philip's five younger children by her were ages ten to nineteen and mostly too young to marry. Eunice and Michael lived for most of their married lives in Hardin County, Kentucky, occasionally in Nelson County, and had seven children.[32] Perhaps because of the ages of Philip's younger children by Anna, the Jacob Marks family stayed in Nelson County for a few years.

Margaret Crume, Anna's oldest daughter by Philip, was the first of Philip's younger children to marry, and she married John Ridgeway on October 21, 1807[33] at the age of sixteen. Margaret and John moved back and forth from Breckinridge County to Ohio County until around 1827 when they moved to Harrison County, Indiana, and John died there. They had eleven children, the last of whom was born in 1828 at Parke County, Indiana. Margaret eventually went to live with her son in Jefferson County, Iowa where she died.[34] She had possibly been named by Anna for Anna's mother, Margaret Coffman Bonehart. Margaret

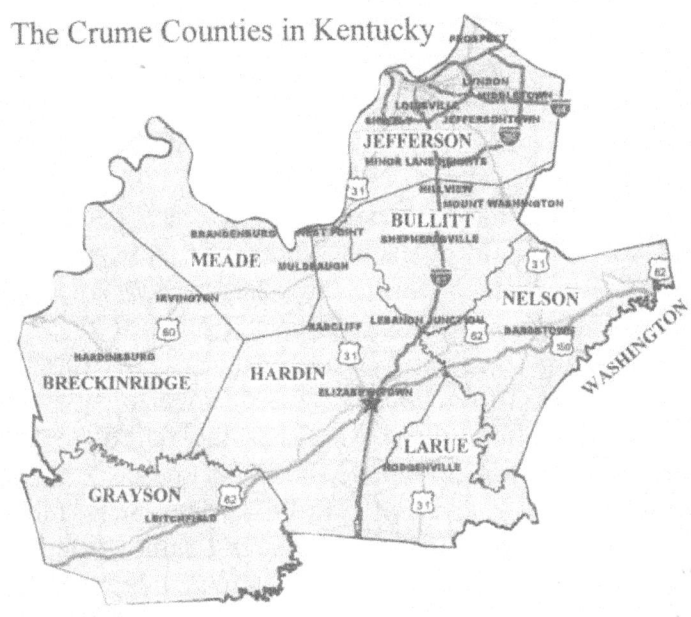

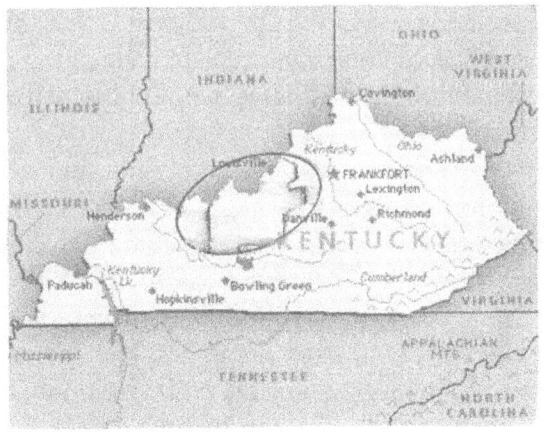

and her husband John were Anna's parents even though her surname was Barret when she married Philip Crume. Margaret and John had married a few years before Anna and Philip, so obviously John was Anna's stepfather, but where did the name Barret come from? No explanation has been found for this. The Boneharts moved to Nelson County in Kentucky probably when the Crume family came in 1795. In December of the same year that Margaret Crume was married, 1807, John Bonehart committed suicide by hanging.[35] Also, earlier in that year Anna had her first child by Jacob Marks, Thomas, born on March 5, 1807[36] The year 1807 was obviously a very emotional one for Anna. Thomas was quickly followed by James Marks on October 19, 1808, and Elizabeth Marks on August 17, 1810. [37]

Also in 1810, Jacob and Anna decided to try a new location and chose to follow the Ralph Crume family to Breckinridge County. They bought 450 acres on Calamese Creek, a branch of the Rough River, adjacent to Ralph Crume, Sr.'s land and moved there shortly after 1810.[38] Margaret Crume Ridgeway (Anna's daughter by Philip) and her family moved as well. A final child for Jacob and Anna, William Marks, was born on March 21, 1812, in Breckinridge County.[39] At this point, Anna was the mother of nine children and eleven stepchildren, although the stepchildren must have seemed more like brothers and sisters to her.

Anna's son John by Philip married Elizabeth Cotton on March 26, 1811, at age twenty-one in Nelson County.[40] He may have stayed behind on the home place, which would eventually be his, when Anna moved to Breckinridge County because he knew that at age twenty-one he could marry and claim his inherited land from his father. He was certainly old enough to be on his own. He stayed in Nelson County, Kentucky, all of his life, siring eleven children by two wives.[41] His younger brother, Squire, may have stayed with him in Nelson County rather than moving to Breckinridge County with his mother, because John was Squire's legal guardian. By 1814, Anna's brood needing supervision had diminished to two unmarried children by Philip, Keziah (age 18) and Squire (age 16) and her four children by Jacob Marks, Thomas (age 7), James (age 6), Elizabeth (age 4), and William (age 2). [42] She and her husband Jacob seemed to like Breckinridge County and the land they could call theirs alone, not a parcel inherited from Philip.

Philip Crume Sr.'s family was now split in many directions, and it would remain that way, but the Crume name would be carried to new parts of the country and become well known there. The children that remained in Kentucky, in mostly Nelson County but other counties as well, were Ralph, John, Squire, Jesse (after his return from Ohio), Philip Jr., Susannah Birkhead, Mary Birkhead, Sarah Marks, and Eunice Klinglesmith. When Squire came of age, he was either in Nelson County or Breckinridge County, but regardless, he claimed the land his father had left him in Nelson County and began farming. Philip's son, Jesse, had eleven children by two wives during his lifetime, Philip Jr. had three, Susannah had ten, Mary had ten, and Sarah had three.[43] The sons and daughters of Philip were by all accounts strong, capable, and forward-looking people. They carried the genes of their father into new areas of endeavor, while they continued his interest in agriculture and his love for the land. One son in particular seemed destined to stand in his father's shoes and become another great steward of the land. Ralph, the first-born son, was intent on carving out a place for himself and his family - a big place - in a new part of Kentucky.

The Spirit of Adventure

"Mom, after hearing about Philip Crume and his children and their adventures, I guess the question I have to ask is 'Why?' Why would an older man who had everything he could ever need or want risk it all to start over again in a new place? What was he thinking?"

"Well, of course we can't know what he was thinking for sure because he didn't write it down." Mom was doing some thinking of her own in order to figure out this puzzle. "I think it had something to do with the character traits that made up the man and his children also. He seemed to always be looking for ways to improve his lot in life, he wasn't satisfied, and he had this tremendous energy and drive. He also wasn't overly comfortable with cities and civilization. He liked his creature comforts, but he seemed to truly enjoy the beautiful, wild places to be found in America, the outdoors and the land. He was not bothered by change. In fact, he embraced it and used it as a tool to further his interests. He had a spirit for adventure. Risking tremendous losses only made the gains of rich new lands even sweeter."

"Yes, but that Shenandoah Valley land was beautiful with those high mountains for a backdrop and the rich rolling farm and pastureland. Who among them could resist just mountain-gazing while they worked the land? Perhaps the large family needed more space for larger farms, though."

"Perhaps, but deep down, I think Philip liked a challenge, and a change of location provided that challenge. I think if he could answer your 'why?' question, he would say 'why not?'"

"He surely laid his family on the line with that move, though," I mumbled. "I get the shakes just thinking about dragging a wagon over those mountains and floating down the frigid rivers watching for Indian canoes – Indians with war paint on their faces!" I had just seen the movie, How the West Was Won, and was thinking how much the Crumes reminded me of the family in the movie which traveled down the Ohio River in a flatboat and lost some of their family members in the process.

"In fairness, though," my mom said, "you have to give part of the responsibility for the family having to brave those perilous conditions to the family members themselves. They were willing to make the trip, so they were just as guilty as Philip of having that streak of wild, reckless adventure in their veins."

"Yeah, I guess," I allowed. "I wonder if it was truly unanimous to make the trip. Surely, out of that many people, there were some who didn't want to go."

"Would you have wanted to stay behind if your entire family was leaving and you wouldn't ever see them again?" Mom asked.

"Well, no, I guess not. Some may not have liked the idea, but they were going anyway. It takes real courage to move to a new location in any time period, but in those early days, their very lives were at stake. Two men died on that trip; if they hadn't gone with the rest, they might have lived out long lives."

"Well, I think the answer to that is the word 'might.' If they hadn't gone on the trip, they might have stayed in Virginia and died of disease. There were so many ways to die in the wilderness. It is useless to assume that their decision to go to Kentucky made their deaths more likely."

"Did the family think the trip was worth it when they reached Kentucky? I hope they did."

"Kentucky offered rich land, and it was beautiful in its own way. I'm sure with that big family all together in one spot in one of God's prettier green locations, they felt at peace in their new home. And another thing - leaving Virginia and the Shenandoah prevented their descendants from experiencing the trauma of the Civil War up close – real close, as in large battles in the backyard."

"Yes, that is true. It kind of reminds you of the Jordan family that left Louisiana and moved to Texas in the middle of the Civil War to get out of the way of the Union troops.[1] Although they were losing something, they were gaining a lot more. The Crumes may also have felt they were gaining something as well as giving up something, but they didn't have very long to enjoy being together as a family in Kentucky. Philip died within a few short years, and the family split up to go in separate directions."

"Yes," Mom mused, "but that is what happens when the family members don't mind change and do like a challenge."

Crume Valley Years

John Fentress of Ohio County, Kentucky, to Ralph Crume,Sr. $120.00, 120 acres on Clear Fork of Calamese Creek being part of Mathew Walton 11,300 acre survey. Dated January 12, 1810. Witnesses: Charles Crume, John Ridgeway.[1]

    Breckinridge County, Kentucky, was rolling, hill country with good soil for farming and plentiful sources of water. Occasionally the hills would reach an elevation as to provide a nice overview of the countryside, but there were no high mountains. The towns that sprang up to support the multitude of farms remained small communities. The roads curved and wrapped themselves around the hills and farms, giving the impression that they were not in a hurry to get anywhere else. Even as the years passed, no large cities existed in the county. A few of the towns grew to a moderate size, but for the most part, the county retained its untouched, sometimes rough, sometimes pastoral flavor. Ralph Crume Sr. was satisfied with finding a place to build his farming operation and other businesses. When he arrived, there were few roads and no towns, just beautiful, wild country that spoke to him as the Shenandoah Valley in Virginia had in his youth.[2]

    All of the Crume land taken together, counting Ralph's land, his sons' land, his sons-in-law's land, and eventually his stepmother's land comprised Crume Valley, a wide swath of rolling fields, thousands of acres, which stretched out for miles across what is now known as Fairfield, Kentucky. Ralph Crume and his son, Ralph Jr., began it all in 1803 with the purchase of land along the Calamese Creek, a branch of the Rough River, in

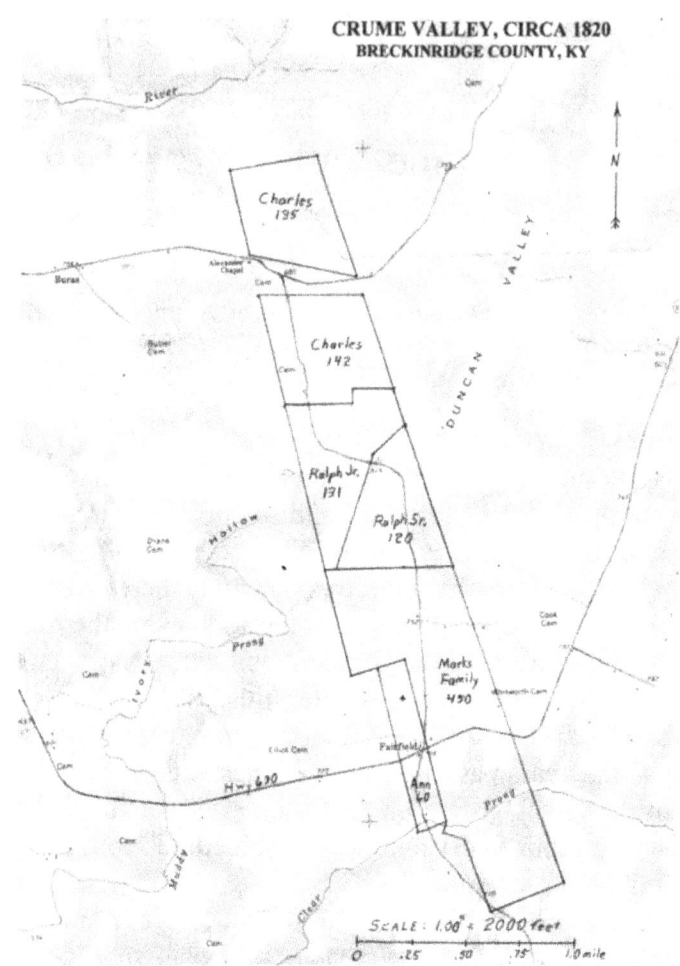

Breckinridge County. This land was part of the ten thousand acre tract owned by William Hardin, a land developer and early pioneer of the county who was interested in selling land and populating the area. The Crumes' first land was eventually sold after the purchase of better land from John Fentress in 1810.[3] These 1810 land purchases began the large number of acquisitions by the Crumes which would form the core of Crume Valley, or as it was called in some land and court records, the Crume settlement. Ralph, his sons, and his sons-in-law were buying and selling land continuously from 1803 through 1828.[4] They were duplicating and enlarging upon what Philip Crume, Sr. had done in Nelson County, Kentucky, and before that in Shenandoah County, Virginia.

Breckinridge County, Kentucky

The Ralph Crume children, each head of his or her own family, were Rachel Crume Lucas and Benedict Lucas, Ralph Crume Jr. and Mary Lincoln Crume, Charles Crume and Mary Snelling Crume, Sarah Crume Horsley and Levi Horsley, William W. Crume and Susannah Luvernia Jones Crume, Mary Crume Pile (later Ruchman) and Thomas Pile, Silas Crume, and John Crume and Permilia Shrewsbury Bratcher Crume. All of the children except the youngest one, John, were born in Virginia, and four of the children were married in Nelson or Washington County, Kentucky. Charles married on December 29, 1794, Rachel about February 24, 1797, and Sarah on September 27, 1797 in Nelson County, and Ralph Jr. married on August 5, 1801, in Washington County. William W. married on August 1, 1805 in Breckinridge County, Mary on March 10, 1812, Silas never married, and John married sometime before 1824 in Hardin County.[5] The first four children made Philip Crume, Sr. a great grandfather before he died in 1801, had well established families, and were able to join Ralph Sr. in buying land in the years after 1810. The other children did their part as well after they married and started families of their own.

On February 27, 1812, in Breckinridge County, Nancy Crume, daughter of Philip Crume, Sr. and Anna Crume Marks, married the Rev. Charles Jordan, nicknamed "Brick." She was twenty years old. He descended from a long line of Jordans in Virginia and North Carolina, was a Methodist minister, and apparently became an abolitionist at some point because he carried the distinction (at least in family lore) of being the first citizen in Kentucky to free his slaves. Over the next forty years, the Jordans would sire thirteen children, most of them in Breckinridge County but the last few in Vermillion County, Indiana, and eventually they moved to Kansas. Nancy, however, died in Illinois, probably after moving back to live with one of her children.[6]

Although the farming business had been good in Breckinridge County, the Crume families had prospered, and their health had been strong, the year 1812 was to bring an unwelcome change. In 1812 William W., and probably his wife Susannah, died. The circumstances of their deaths are not known, and there is even one theory in the family that Susannah did not die at this time but remarried and had another family. This theory does not explain why she did not raise her four children by William, however, because there is no census evidence that the children were living with their mother and a new husband after their father died or that their mother had more children. There is also no explanation for Susannah not being listed as one of

William's heirs if she were alive, both in land purchase documents for the orphans and the estate settlement documents for Ralph Sr. In 1813, Ralph Crume Jr. was appointed the children's guardian by the courts, mostly to administer William's estate until the children came of age, but the children did not live with Ralph Jr.'s family, at least during the census years. However, there were many possibilities among the Crume families for homes for the children, and it is likely that they lived with Ralph Jr. part of the time.[7]

The Crume family was still reeling from this blow when they were hit with another unexpected event. Jacob Marks died suddenly in 1814 at the age of thirty-three.[8] Anna Crume Marks was left a widow again, but this must have been much more of a shock than her first husband's death, because of the large difference in her two husbands' ages. Who would have thought that a thirty-three-year-old man in his prime would die? She was left alone to raise her four small children by Jacob and the youngest two of her children by Philip Sr. After much thought, she decided to stay in Breckinridge County, although she had the choice of going back to Nelson County if she wished. She had family support in both places.

While the Crumes were trying to cope with the unexpected deaths of family members during 1812 and the years which surrounded it, they also had to be concerned about national events. America was at war with Great Britain - again. This did not seem to affect the Crume family directly, either in Breckinridge County or Nelson County, Kentucky, or the various other places family members lived such as southern Indiana, Illinois, and Ohio. There was no fighting or destruction on the widespread families' own soil or even close to it. Most of the battles of the war were fought along the Canadian border with the United States and along the eastern seaboard, including the notable occasion of the sacking and burning of the nation's capital, Washington, D.C. There was a small amount of fighting in the Northwest Territories and more along the lower Mississippi River, which included the Batttle of New Orleans, the last battle of the war that made a hero of Andrew Jackson. Although there were other issues, the one that most concerned the

Crumes in this war was probably the question of the Indians living in the Northwest Territories (future states of the United States to the north of the Ohio River). The war's end and peace settlement, in addition to the Indian treaties that followed, eventually moved the Native Americans further west on the continent, leaving the Northwest Territories open for settlement by the United States government. Many American settlers were already there by the time the final agreements were made.[9]

There were three known members of Philip Crume Sr.'s immediate family involved in the war as soldiers. John Ridgway served a little over two months in 1814 as a sergeant in Dudley's Mounted Battalion Kentucky Volunteers. He was married to Margaret Crume, daughter of Philip and Anna, at the time.[10] James Howey, before his marriage to Keziah Crume, daughter of Philip and Anna, served first as a sergeant in Captain William Walker's Company, 13 (Gray's) Regiment, Kentucky Militia. He was promoted to the rank of ensign (a rank in the militia equivalent to second lieutenant in the regular army) on January 5, 1815, and stationed at Baton Rouge, Louisiana, where he served on the staff of General Andrew Jackson as an orderly. One of his most unforgettable memories of the service with General Jackson was his witnessing British General Packenham's fall from his saddle when a rifleman, at the suggestion of Jackson, took careful aim and fired. He was mustered out of service in 1815 when the war ended.[11] There was also John D. Crume, son of Philip Withers Crume (Philip II or Jr.), who served as a private in the Second Regiment (Thomas) Mounted Kentucky Volunteers, and an Isaac Crume - who has not been positively identified as a family member - who served as a private in the Second Regiment (Cotgreave's) Ohio Militia.[12]

By 1810 Ralph Crume Jr. and Mary Lincoln Crume had three children, Ann (born between 1801 and 1804), William Cox (born in 1804), and Ralph Lincoln (born in 1809).[13] Ralph Jr. was forty-one years old and had accumulated a significant amount of land in Crume Valley in Breckinridge County through judicious buying and selling. He was active in county affairs, especially court service and land witness obligations. He also took part in the planning and surveying of a north-south road that bisected Crume Valley.

May 15, 1820
Ordered that Benedict Lucas, Charles Jordon, Ralph Crume, Jr., and Charles Crume or any three of them being duly sworn do view and mark a road from James Barkley's shop to intersect or join a road leading to the mouth of Salt River by Thomas Stiths, and make report thereof agreeably to law. [14]

His brothers and sisters had likewise done well and were involved in many of the same pursuits. Rachel and Benedict Lucas had seven children by 1810 and would eventually have eleven in all. Benedict was greatly admired by his father-in-law, Ralph Sr., and had been liked by Philip Crume Sr. as well. He seemed to be just as astute in land management as Ralph or Philip, and he was the only grandchild or in-law of a grandchild to be given any of Philip's land, other than the children of Philip's son, William who had died on the Kentucky emigration trip. Benedict was also land rich after 1810. Charles Crume, Ralph Sr.'s first-born son, had seven children before 1810 and had obtained a large tract of land. Sarah "Sally" Crume and Levi Horsley had eight children, and Levi had also been able to obtain a nice parcel of land. Ralph's younger children, Mary "Polly", Silas, and John came into their own in later years.[15]

In 1816, Mary Lincoln Crume and Ralph Crume Jr. had occasion for special contact with her brother Thomas Lincoln. In the years after 1801, Mary's sister Nancy Brumfield and family, her mother Bersheba, and her brother Thomas had been living in Hardin County, Nancy and her mother in the Mill Creek area and Thomas at Knob Creek.[16] Hardin County was adjacent to Breckinridge County; therefore, it is likely that the Lincolns stayed in touch with Mary Lincoln Crume in the years between 1801 and 1816. As well as being a farmer, Thomas Lincoln practiced the carpenter trade, constructing large buildings and mills as well as crafting furniture. He made his sister Mary a nice corner cabinet in which to store her dishes.[17]

However, in 1816 Thomas had been evicted from his Knob Creek farm due to a lawsuit over the land title and had decided to move to Indiana. He sought help from Ralph Crume Jr. for the move, perhaps borrowing some wagons by one account. At the

Mary Lincoln Crume's Cabinet

Cloversport, Kentucky Crossing Point for the Ohio River

very least, it seems certain that Thomas stopped to see his sister when the family passed through Hardinsburg in Breckinridge County on their way to a crossing point on the Ohio River at Cloverport.[18]

Perhaps a seven-year-old Abraham Lincoln had a chance to play with his cousins William, Ralph, and Ann, children of Ralph Jr. and Mary Crume. Thomas Lincoln never returned to Kentucky to stay for any length of time, making only short trips on business. Indiana and then Illinois were his new home. He did return in 1819 after the death of Nancy Hanks, his first wife, to Elizabethtown, Kentucky, to marry Sarah Bush Johnston and bring her and her children by a first marriage (to Daniel Johnston) back to Indiana.[19] Whether he enlisted help from Ralph Crume Jr. again is not known. It also seems possible that Thomas used his brother-in-law's help another time in 1830 when he moved to Illinois from Indiana because Ralph Jr. was in Indiana at that time.

In 1819, Keziah Crume, daughter of Philip and Anna, married James S. Howey, most probably in Hardin County but perhaps in Breckinridge County. The Howey family had moved from Virginia to Kentucky in 1796 to Hardin County and lived there for several generations. Keziah and James had eleven children in Hardin County, but after James died, Keziah went to live in Tippecanoe County, Indiana to be close to her half-brother, Thomas Marks, son of Anna and Jacob.[20]

In 1820 Keziah's brother, Squire Crume, last son of Philip, married Sarah Ann Cotton on October 5 in Nelson County, Kentucky. He was twenty-two years old, and finally of age to receive his father's land. Because his brother John was his guardian, he may have lived with him in Nelson County after his mother and Jacob Marks moved to Breckinridge County. He, his brother John, and mother Anna shared the piece of land that Philip Crume Sr. had bought on Sunfish Creek and which had been divided by Philip's estate settlement into three parts. He remained on his part of this land all of his life, adding to it, building a fine home that his family named Seven Cedars, and siring thirteen children.[21]

John, Squire's older brother, who had married Sarah's sister, Elizabeth Cotton, in 1811, had set about making his land prosper. He was living on his father's (Philip Sr.) home place because his mother was in Breckinridge County, but he was also managing his own land. He sired nine children by 1822, but Elizabeth died in 1823. He remarried in 1824 to Elizabeth Wood and added two more children to his family. He lived a long life, witnessing the near destruction of the country his father had loved, but he saw the end of the Civil War before he died in December of 1865.[22] John and Squire, after they came of age, walked in their father's footsteps, just as their older brothers had. They each managed large plantations successfully; however, their holdings never reached the vast extent of their father's or that of their older brother Ralph's family.

Seven Cedars and Snug Harbor (the home built by Cyrus Talbot that eventually was bought by Crume family descendants) were not too far from each other and were connected by a private road in later years built by a descendant of Squire, John R.

McIntyre. The houses weathered the long years into the future, remaining standing into the twenty-first century.[23] Philip Crume Sr.'s only home in Kentucky, the two story log house that he built upon his arrival in the state (or perhaps acquired from John Lewis), was located on the parcel of land belonging after his death first to Anna, his wife, and then to her son, John, after her death. It stood for many years, fairly near the old meeting house, Ferguson Chapel, which became the Poplar Flat Methodist Church, and had several owners including the Woods, Duncans, and Reynolds, before it was finally torn down around 1948.[24]

Anna Crume Marks was left as a widow in Breckinridge County with just the four Marks children to raise, but in 1819 she bought a small parcel of land of 60 acres for herself, perhaps because she wanted her children to eventually have and divide most of the Marks land among themselves. This sixty acres of Anna's was located adjacent to the Marks land in Crume Valley,[25] and it would become very important in the future, mostly because of the cemetery that was created on it. Anna may have had another reason for purchasing the land, and this reason became apparent in the 1820 census for Breckinridge County that showed she was married again for the third time.[26] Sometime before the census and after the land purchase of 1819, Anna married Rev. William Morris, a local land owner and Baptist minister. He had five children by his first marriage, all of them grown. This time Anna had married a man somewhat older than she was, but not extremely so. He was 64 and Anna was 50. Perhaps age had ceased to be important to her after the shock of losing Jacob, a man in his prime.

Anna's children by Jacob Marks were still young at this time, with the oldest being twelve, so Anna would once again have help raising her children. During her lifetime, she had nine children and seventeen stepchildren. Rev. Morris had purchased his land in Breckinridge County in 1815, and he sold it off in parcels to his children in 1818. He bought a tract of land adjacent to the town of Hardinsburg with his son Jonathan in 1819, mainly as a business venture. He may never have lived on it or lived there only a short time prior to his marriage to Anna. After their marriage, he lived with Anna on her land.[27]

When Ralph Crume Sr. and his family first started living in Crume Valley, there was no crossroads at Fairfield and no place named Fairfield. The road that the Crumes were asked to help with in 1820 became more than likely the Fairfield-Buras Rd of modern times which intersects with state road 690 at Fairfield, Kentucky.[28] From the wilderness of forest that they first found in Breckinridge County, Ralph and his family carved beautiful farms and pasturelands, a testament to hard work and a way of life that brought satisfaction and a sense of accomplishment. They bought and sold thousands of acres of land to grow their enterprise, and they nurtured the land they kept to make it work for them.

Crume Valley from the Fairfield Buras Road near the Fairfield Intersection

Not much is known about Ralph's other businesses in Breckinridge County (his occupations in Nelson County), but it can be assumed that he continued to use the skills that he had learned, including mill construction and operation, blacksmithing, perhaps whiskey distilling and horse breeding. However, getting his crops and other products to the Ohio River for transport to other markets was probably handled differently. He may have carried his goods overland to Hardinsburg and then to Cloverport, which was a river port on the Ohio. This would have been his closest river port, or perhaps he used nearby Rough River to float his goods up to the mighty river. At any rate, at least three generations of Crumes, connected to Ralph Sr. in some way, lived in Crume Valley up until 1828, working together, always looking to improve upon what they had built.

If Ralph practiced his blacksmithing trade, one can almost imagine what he looked like – stocky, muscular and powerful. He had also been a military man, so he probably carried an air of command. He served in various positions of authority in the county, but he was not above settling a dispute with his fists. There was at least one instance where he was charged with assault, but he was part of a group who were charged and eventually acquitted of the charge.[29] However, just as Philip Crume Sr.'s life could not go on forever, son Ralph Sr. was collecting years, and his life was dwindling down.

In 1827, an unexpected death occurred in the family. Elizabeth Marks, Anna and Jacob Marks' daughter died at the age of seventeen, October 14, 1827.[30] Her probable burial on Anna's sixty acres established a new Crume Cemetery although that was probably not the intention of the family at the time. Other Crumes had died before this time and possibly been buried in Crume Valley, including Ralph's son William and his wife and Anna's husband Jacob Marks, but Anna seemingly wanted to bury her daughter on her sixty acres as a single grave. A scarce eighteen months later, another burial place would be needed in the Crume family, and the decision concerning its location would prove pivotal to establishing a final resting place for many of the Crume family.

Ralph Crume Sr.'s long life came to an end in Crume Valley in February of 1829.[31] He was 79 years old. He and his family had been in Breckinridge County, Kentucky, for a little more than twenty-five years, and they had repeated and improved upon the success of Philip Crume. Ralph was every bit the pioneer and empire builder that his father was – another great steward of the land. He had also been a soldier who had served his country well. The Crume family decided to bury Ralph Sr. in the same area as Elizabeth Marks rather than on his own land.[32] Anna obviously offered the land, but why did the family decide to proceed in this location? Perhaps Ralph had chosen the spot before he died, but another possibility might be the decision had something to do with the upcoming estate settlement.

Oddly enough, Ralph died intestate and left no will, and this meant all of his property would be sold and the proceeds divided among his wife and eight children or their heirs. Perhaps he died suddenly, but in his failure to provide for the distribution of his estate, he was different from his father. It is also possible that his remaining estate was not as sizable as it had once been, and the lawful division of estates provided by the state of Kentucky perhaps suited his wishes. The estate would not be finally settled until 1842 when everything was sold and the proceeds divided.[33] Perhaps his widow, Mary, had a premonition of this and wanted to bury him on Marks or Morris land where the land was less likely to be sold. Unfortunately, Mary was also dead (before 1839 and possibly as early as 1832) by the time the estate was settled, and she was almost certainly buried beside her husband.[34] In the space of a few short years, the Crume Cemetery was begun with three members of the Crume family to be followed quickly and unexpectedly by others.

Ralph Sr.'s wife, Mary Riggs Crume, and children were left to carry on in his footsteps, but great changes were about to occur. What had happened in Nelson County was about to repeat itself in Breckinridge County. After the death of the patriarch, the family split in many directions. Mary, of course, died within ten years of her husband's death. Of Ralph Sr.'s eight children, only three stayed in Crume Valley until their deaths and left descendants there to continue the Crume presence in the county. Thus Crume Valley disintegrated, and the land became the property of others. The three that remained were Rachel Crume Lucas, Sarah Crume Horsley, and Ralph Crume Jr. Rachel and Sarah and their families purchased as many shares of the proceeds from the sale of their father's estate, in advance of the sale, as they could from their departing siblings. Charles Crume moved to Illinois before his father's estate was settled, Ralph Crume, Jr. died early before the estate could be settled but did leave descendants in the county, William Crume had died before his father but also left descendants in the county, and Silas Crume never married, disappeared from public records, and probably died before the estate settlement.[35]

Ralph Crume, Sr.'s son, John, accumulated a large part of his father's land, either from his father directly or from his brothers

Breckinridge County Kentucky Overlook

and sisters before the estate settlement. It was all sold out of the Crume family when John moved to Missouri around 1844 and eventually to Texas to live with one of his sons where he died. Over the years, he sired eleven children.[36] Mary "Polly" Crume, Ralph Sr.'s daughter, first married Thomas Pile in 1812, and after his death married a second time to James Ruchman. The Ruchmans sold their portion of Ralph Sr.'s estate and moved to Vermillion County, Illinois, around 1842, and Mary had at least nine children, possibly more.[37]

Of Ralph Crume Sr.'s children who could carry on the name in the county, William, who had died early in 1812, had children who stayed in the area but not always in Breckinridge County. Two of these, William Washington Crume and his brother Silas Crume, settled in other nearby counties, while their brother, James B. Crume, stayed in Breckinridge County. Ralph Jr. had one child and two grandchildren who stayed in the Crume Valley area, at least for one more generation.[38] Although Ralph Sr. had passed the estate-building genes of his father on to his children, it would not become apparent in some of the family lines for another generation or two. Within four generations, the Crume name was virtually gone from Breckinridge County. However the Crume presence remained in the county through the Lucas families, the Tucker families, and possibly the Horsley families.

The Passing of Crume Valley

Sometime between 1829 when Ralph Crume, Sr. died and 1830, Ralph Crume Jr. and his family decided to go to Vermillion County, Indiana.[1] Part of the attraction of this place may have been that other members of the Crume and Marks family had moved to Indiana and may have touted its advantages. As well, Ralph Crume Jr. had helped his brother-in-law, Thomas Lincoln, move to the state and at that time may have gotten a good look at the Wabash River country of western Indiana. Ralph and Mary's children were all grown and some were starting families of their own. William Cox Crume had married Mary Susannah Hoskinson on February 7, 1825, in Hardin County, Kentucky, which was one of the home counties for the Hoskinson family.[2] The Hardin County/Breckinridge County line was very close to both Crume Valley and the Hoskinson land, so the Crumes and the Hoskinsons more than likely did business in both counties.

Susannah's (she was known by her middle name) father was Rev. David Hoskinson, a Methodist minister who practiced his profession for many years in Hardin County, marrying numerous couples, including several in the Crume family. He was also a landowner and one of a group of Hoskinsons who had emigrated from Maryland to Kentucky. Some of these Hoskinsons had served in the Revolution and had arrived in the area as early as 1780. The Hoskinsons had generally been Catholic in Maryland, but apparently they changed religions after the move to Kentucky. The Rev. David Hoskinson was married in Washington County, so perhaps he had interests there as well as Hardin and Breckinridge Counties. Hoskinson had a large family, as was evidenced by his estate settlement in 1855.[3]

William and Susannah Crume had three children by the time of the Crume family's move to Indiana, Silas Moses age 5, John Daniel age 3, and Ann age between 1 and 2.[4] Ralph Lincoln Crume was as yet unmarried in 1830, but his sister Ann had married Charles Hoskinson, brother of Susannah, on February 23, 1827.[5] The Hoskinsons had two daughters.[6] Because of the impending move, Ralph Jr.'s obligations as guardian to his brother's (William who died in 1812) four children had been transferred to others at the children's request. Mary Crume, the youngest, married in 1831 to Thomas Drane with her oldest brother Silas signing the bond and her brother William Washington Crume listed as her guardian.[7] There is no evidence in public records that any of the William Crume orphaned children accompanied the Ralph Crume Jr. family to Indiana. On the other hand, all of the members of Ralph Jr.'s immediate family went to Indiana. Ralph Jr. and Mary did not stay long, however. They returned to Kentucky by 1831, perhaps because their only intention in going to Indiana was to help the young people get started, perhaps because economic conditions were not conducive to their buying land, or possibly because they suffered the loss of loved ones there. Ralph's son, William C. Crume, and his family may also have returned to Kentucky with the elder Crumes because they are not on the tax records in Indiana after 1831.[8]

While in Vermillion County, Indiana, only one parcel of land was purchased from the government, and it was in Ralph Lincoln Crume's name.[9] The document actually shows him as a resident of Parke County, Illinois, which was located just across the Wabash River from Vermillion County. No one else in the family purchased land. This land was located on the west bank of the Wabash River, so it could offer rich, river bottom soil for farming as well as a dock for a ferryboat business. Apparently competition was pretty stiff in the ferry business in the area along the Wabash as many got licenses and tried it. In spite of this, Ralph Lincoln and Charles Hoskinson, his brother in-law, made application for a ferryboat license, received one after some legal appeals were made, and stayed in the county, working together on the land and in the ferry business until around 1834. At that

A Journey of Voices: Stewards of the Land   81

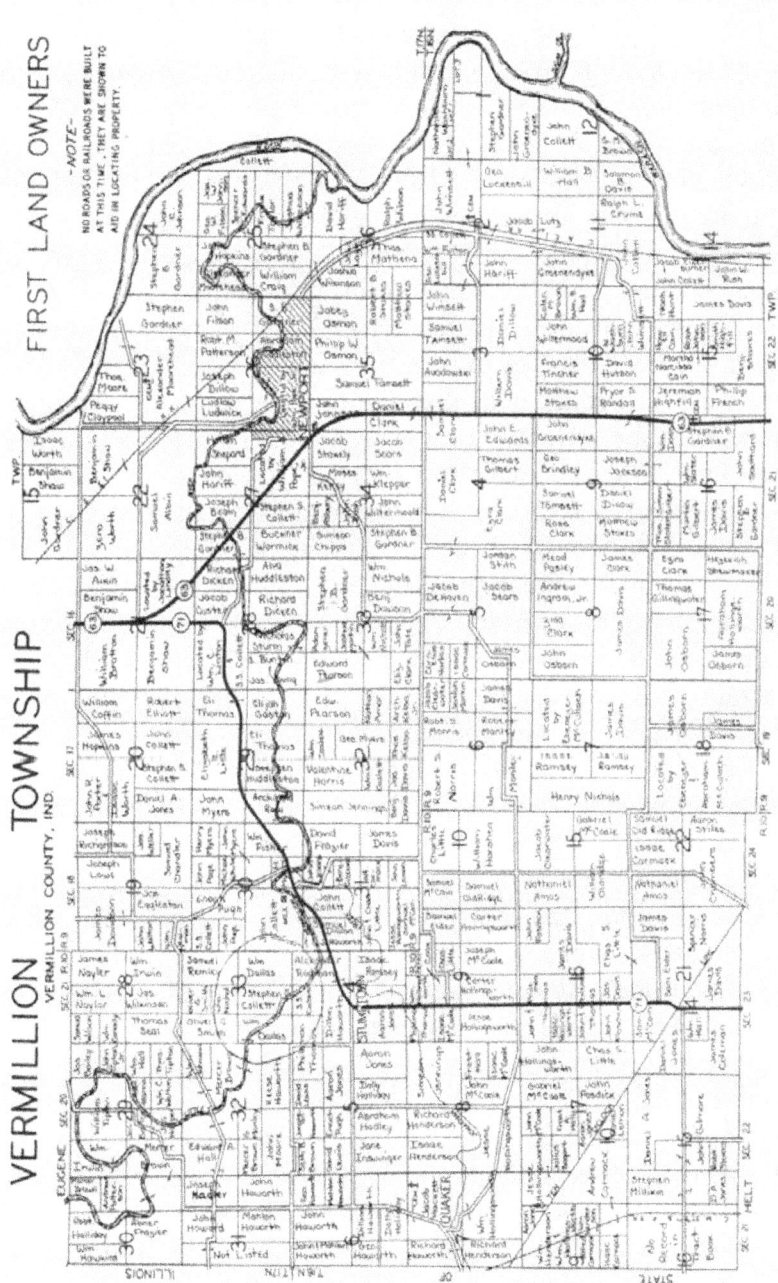

time Ralph Lincoln Crume returned to Kentucky to either Breckinridge County or Hardin County.[10]

In 1832, the youngest child and orphan of the William Crume who died in 1812, Mary, and her husband Thomas Drane sued the Ralph Crume Sr. estate to recover money owed to Mary by her guardian of 1828, Ralph Crume, Jr. The amount was $145.45 plus interest since 1829 (Ralph Sr.'s death and the beginning of court jurisdiction of the estate). The contention was that Ralph Crume Jr. never paid Mary what was due her from her father's estate when he relinquished his guardianship around 1829 when Ralph moved to Indiana and Mary chose her brother William for her guardian. At the time she changed her guardian, Mary was too young for the distribution, and she therefore became the only one of the orphans who did not receive a portion of her father's estate, which included a portion of her father's share of Ralph Sr's estate.[11] In the confusion of the move to Indiana and the move back to Kentucky, Ralph may have forgotten about the situation or believed he was not responsible since he was no longer Mary's guardian or intended to release the money to her because she had married in 1831, but shortly after his return to Kentucky, most likely in 1831, he died suddenly. Perhaps if Ralph Jr. had not died, there would not have been a suit. He might have made things right with Mary. The reason why he did not turn over her share of her father's estate to her new guardian in 1829 is not known. Perhaps the answer lies in the dates of her court transfer of guardianship. Her date was 1831 while her brother, James's date was 1829. Did she wait until 1831 to legally change her guardian?

Mary Drane may have felt she had no other recourse than to sue Ralph Sr.'s estate to obtain her inheritance. She may have been encouraged in this action by her husband and interested heirs of the Ralph Crume Sr. estate who were looking to buy any shares of the estate that were available for sale. Mary eventually sold her share of her father's part of Ralph Sr.'s estate to Henry Lucas, son of Rachel and Benedict Lucas, other heirs to the estate. When the Drane/Crume case was heard in 1832, not all of Ralph Jr.'s heirs appeared in court to make their depositions and Ralph was deceased; therefore, the court judged in favor of the plaintiffs, Mary Drane and her husband. Ralph Jr. could not be present to explain his actions, and his children, if they knew anything about the matter (which they may not have), were either still in Indiana or unavailable to appear. It is possible Mary Lincoln Crume appeared at the 1832 court hearing for the Drane suit along with her son William C., depending upon how the court document is interpreted. [12] However, the end result of the court's ruling was it would now never be known whether Ralph Jr. was negligent by deliberate intent or careless oversight, or would have made things right.

The court decided to force the sale of the Ralph Crume Sr. slaves in order to raise the cash to split among Ralph Sr.'s heirs and pay the debt to Mary Drane from Ralph Crume Jr.'s share. Because the slaves had been given to Mary Riggs Crume in a dower settlement in 1829, agreed to by the other heirs to Ralph Sr.'s estate, this may have meant that Mary Riggs Crume was deceased; however, the slaves may have still been considered part of the estate. Her actual death date is not known except that it was between 1832 and 1839. [13] This lawsuit was an unfortunate occurrence within the family ranks, but nothing is known about its lasting effects or if there were any. Perhaps the family as a whole just wanted to see Mary receive what was due her, and so they had no hard feelings. Obviously they wanted the matter settled. The 1832 court document was significant in that it revealed the death of Ralph Crume, Jr. in a public record, allowing for an approximation of his date of death. It can be noted here that the Crumes never hesitated to sue each other to settle questions of land and money. It would happen several times in Nelson County after Anna Crume Marks Morris died.

Ralph Jr. would have been about fifty-three years old at the time of his death, and the cause of death is not known. He more than likely died suddenly because he did not leave a will. Furthermore, his wife, Mary Lincoln Crume, may have died at the same time as Ralph did or within a year or two. She is not listed in the homes of her children or siblings in the 1840 census or as living alone. Ralph was buried in the Crume Cemetery next to his father where they share a tombstone, and it seems almost certain that Mary Lincoln lies beside him. For many years she was reputed to have been buried at the Mill Creek Cemetery in Hardin County, Kentucky, (later owned by the Ft. Knox military reservation) with her mother and sister, but that Mary Crume was Ralph Lincoln Crume's wife.[14] Ralph Jr. was not to have the long, successful life that his father had enjoyed. He died intestate as his father had, but his estate was not nearly the size of his father's. It may have been quite small because Mary Drane sued Ralph Crume Sr.'s estate and not Ralph Jr.'s. Ralph Jr.'s heirs were listed in the 1832 court document as William C. Crume, Ralph Lincoln Crume, and Ann and Charles Hoskinson, thus substantiating the conclusion that Ralph and Mary had only three children together.[15] In their family line, the torch had been passed to the next generation earlier than would have been expected.

Also during this period, Ralph Jr.'s daughter-in-law, Mary Susannah Hoskinson Crume, wife of William C., died and could well have been buried in the Crume Cemetery. Within a few years, her daughter Ann followed her.[16] This period must have been very hard to bear for the Crume family. Family members were either leaving the county or dying prematurely; the family was being torn asunder. What was the cause of death for all these Crumes? Was it a plague of some sort? Was it heart disease? Perhaps, but maybe it was just coincidence that they all died in the same brief time period. All of this happened even before Ralph Sr.'s estate could finally be settled and in the same time period as another death, that of Mary Riggs Crume, Ralph Sr.'s wife (possibly as early as 1832).

Ralph Crume Jr.'s children were left to continue on. William Cox Crume and his two boys were in Breckinridge County where William had started to accumulate land in Crume Valley. Charles and Ann Hoskinson bought the Vermillion County, Indiana, land from Ralph Lincoln Crume in 1836 while Ralph was living at Hardin County but still not married.[17] Ralph Lincoln may have been feeling a money pinch which had been revealed earlier in a mortgage agreement initiated to pay off his debts in Breckinridge County in 1835.[18] The Hoskinsons kept the land in Indiana until 1837 when they sold it and moved.[19] They may have been unable to keep the farm and ferry business going by themselves. Nothing more was known about them or their whereabouts after this sale

Vermillion County, Indiana Crume Land by the Wabash River

until Charles appeared as an heir to his father's estate in a settlement action in 1855. Ann was not mentioned.[20]

Ralph Lincoln was in Hardin County and trying several things to make a living when on July 1, 1837, he married Mary Brumfield, his first cousin on his mother's side. Mary's mother was Nancy Lincoln Brumfield, sister of Mary Lincoln Crume, Ralph Jr.'s wife, and her grandmother was Bersheba Lincoln.[21] It is interesting to note here that three successive generations of Ralph Crumes married women named Mary, forever after creating consternation for family record keepers who made repeated mistakes. Ralph Lincoln Crume eventually settled down with his family in Hardin County in 1843 where he rented land from Samuel Haycraft and farmed in the Mill Creek area where the Lincolns and Brumfields were living.[22]

William Cox Crume, as well as being a land owner and farmer, was also a medical doctor. Whether he actually had a medical education or a license to practice is not known. These credentials would not become requirements to practice medicine until the 1840's at the earliest,[23] but for most of his life, he was known as "Dr. Billy," so he must have practiced some form of medicine, at least in his early years. While William was growing up and in the twenty years or so thereafter, most people relied on home remedies and herbal recipes because doctors were scarce, especially on the frontier. Some of the "doctors" that did exist were bad to the point of being dangerous.[24] If he was known as Dr. Billy for most of his life, his clients must not have been too dissatisfied with his work. Some examples of home remedies can be found in Jesse Crume's (grandson of Philip Crume Sr.) diary written in 1859. Since they seemingly weren't lethal, they may have worked or at least didn't do any harm. It is not known whether Dr. Billy used any of these or similar ones.

Cyatic Drops or Birkhead Medicine [Came from the Birkhead family?]
½ ounce oil of hemlock
¼ ounce oil of wintergreen
¼ ounce oil of anniseseed
(This will cure cholic or pains.)
teaspoonful of cayenne pepper dissolved in a pint of alcohol
A spoonfull in a half glass of water is a dose. If it makes you sick, cease giving it. Give every fifteen minutes.

To Cure Flux
Give salts first, work it off well. Put a handful of Sweetgum bark, a handful of Mullein roots and a handful of Blackberry roots in a gallon of water. Boil down to a quart. Strain it and add a teaspoonful of salt petre. Give a wine glass full for a grown person 4 to 5 times a day. A dose for an infant is a teaspoonful as often. If it pains gripe, give a teaspoonful of paragoric. Twice a day drink slippery elm tea or ground ivy tea and mutton soup for food. Indian doctor

To Cure Rheumatism
Heat strong vinegar. Rub the part as hot as can be born.
Wrap brown paper round it wetted with vinegar twice a day. Take a dose of Calomel before breakfast. In the evening take a spoonfull of sulpher in molasses. Repeat.[25]

After Mary Susannah Hoskinson Crume died around 1832, William stayed unmarried for a while, but he decided to make a change in 1837. On July 27 he married Mary Ann Lucas Norris, a daughter of Ignatius Lucas Jr. who was a probable relation of Benedict Lucas, husband of Rachel Crume (Ralph Sr.'s daughter). Benedict and Ignatius probably had another relation, Zachariah, because all three of these men had come at the same time to Kentucky from Maryland. Mary Ann had first married Thomas Norris, and she had two children from her first marriage, Harriet (age 9) and William (age approximately 11).[26]

William's two boys by his first marriage, Silas Moses and John Daniel, would have been around William Norris's age. However, they had lost so many family members and had been without a mother or any siblings for five years, making the transition to a new family not easy for them. The following year on May 11, 1838, William and Mary added a baby girl to the family, Eliza Jane. Two years later Ralph Mark was born on April 23, 1840, and three years after that, Susan Mary was born in April of 1843.[27] William was the father of five children and two stepchildren, eight children overall counting the one daughter from his first marriage, Ann, who had died. His farming business seemed to be operating successfully also. His brother, Ralph Lincoln Crume, and Ralph's wife, Mary Brumfield Crume, had two children during this same time period, Nancy Lewis Crume around 1843 and Ann Mary Thomas Crume around 1847.[28] Ralph was still renting land, which he farmed in the Mill Creek area of Hardin County.

Anna Crume Marks Morris, Philip Sr.'s second wife, suffered another loss in November of 1837. Her third husband, Rev. William Morris, died at the age of 82. In his will he directed that all of his property be sold and the proceeds divided among Anna and his children by his first wife. She was to receive half and the children half, a generous settlement for her, but the children had already received land from their father before he married Anna. However, this time Anna was not left with children to raise alone because all of the Marks children were grown.[29] Anna was 68 years old. Did she continue to live on her own land and receive help when needed from her son, William, who lived on the adjacent land? Did she live with William? Not much is known about this time period in her life except that she eventually did live with her son William for a few years, perhaps due to her ill health, before she decided to make a change in 1844.[30]

In 1842 in Breckinridge County, the Ralph Crume Sr. estate was finally settled. Various heirs to the estate had sold their portions to other heirs, so that now the portions were mostly in the hands of Lucas and Horsley family members and John Crume. In 1842 a commission was appointed to sell Ralph Crume's land at auction. Because Ralph Sr.'s wife was no longer living, most of his personal property and his slaves had already been sold to meet various debts and obligations. A land holding business bought the remaining land in 1842 and resold it to William P. Pool. At this time John Crume sold his land to Pool as well in preparation for his move to Missouri. The heirs to Ralph Crume Sr.'s estate received the proceeds of the auction sale, and the land was gone, out of the family. [31]

Two years later in 1844, Anna Marks Morris and her family decided it would be best to sell their property in Breckinridge County, mostly because the Marks children were married and living elsewhere and Anna was interested in moving back to Nelson County to live with her sons, John and Squire on the land the three had inherited many years before from Philip Sr. Sons Thomas Marks and James Marks had married Howey sisters, Lydia and Jane respectively, [nieces of James Howey, husband of Keziah Crume (Philip Crume Sr.'s daughter by Anna)] and moved to Indiana. William Marks and his family, including his wife, Catherine Greer, moved to Meade County, Kentucky, after the Breckinridge County land was sold.[32] In preparation for the land sale, William Marks gained power of attorney from Anna and his brothers, and then the Marks 450 acres and Anna's 62 acres were sold to Philip Thurman and thus out of the family.[33]

In selling the 62 acres, Anna was also selling the Crume Cemetery. That may have concerned her, but she was 75 years old by this time and just wanted to go home to Nelson County. Perhaps her health was not good, and she was already thinking about her own final resting place. It was probably wise that she settled the question of her land holdings in Breckinridge County and moved back to live with her sons by Philip Crume Sr. in 1846 because this meant a simpler existence for her. She died two years later on December 27, 1848, in Nelson County, Kentucky, and she was buried close to Philip in the Poplar Flat Cemetery.[34] She had lived a long and full life, raised her children the best that she could in sometimes trying circumstances, and charted her own destiny with the choice of her husbands. She had been a part of building huge land holdings in bold new lands and establishing close to twenty family lines. She, like the wife and mother of the Crumes who came before her, Sarah Withers Crume, typified the frontier women of America's early years whose courage and hard work sustained their families.

In Breckinridge County, the Lucas family, the Horsley family, Dr. William Crume's family and James B. Crume, son of Ralph Crume Sr.'s son William were left to make their own mark on the county, even though Crume Valley was no more. According to some family stories, Dr. Billy and his wife Mary Ann in Breckinridge County had difficulty melding two families together after they married and started having children of their own. Silas Moses was twelve when his father remarried, and he had been without the softening influence of a mother for about five years. In that time period he had lost his mother, his grandparents, and his sister. This served to harden him at an early age and make him more independent of family influence. He had a strong personality and apparently did not get along very well with his stepmother. As soon as he was able, he wanted to leave home to make his own way in the world.

Silas had big ambitions, very similar to his great, great grandfather Philip and his great grandfather Ralph Sr. He wanted to be like them and accomplish what they had. Although he was only four years old when Ralph Sr. died, he was well aware of the accomplishments of his ancestors because of family stories and from just living in Crume Valley. He had watched the slow disintegration of his family's holdings in the Valley and did not see much there to help him with his future plans. His father was preoccupied with new children, some of them boys, and so even though Silas was the first born son of Dr. Billy, he probably concluded that he did not really have a place in Breckinridge County. It is not known when he made the decision to leave, but it may have been as early as age eighteen. At some point during the middle to late 1840's, he moved to Meade County, Kentucky, and stayed with a relative, William Marks (son of Anna Crume Marks Morris) who had moved to Meade County around 1845 after the Marks land was sold in Breckinridge.[35] Silas Moses was still paying taxes on land he owned in Breckinridge County in 1848 and 1850,[36] but by 1850 (possibly as early as 1848), he was working as an overseer for the John Findlay Williams Sr. family in Meade County.[37] He already knew a lot about farming and raising livestock, and he was learning more. He was on his way to making his vision of a successful future on his own land into a reality.

In 1846, Dr. Billy and Mary had their last child, a son named James F.[38] When this occurred, Silas may have already been gone from home, if not to Meade County. William's other son by his first wife, John Daniel, did not seem to have as much of a problem with his father's second marriage and the new children that came from it. He lived at home with the Crumes until 1851 when he married Melinda Jane Nottingham, a neighbor girl .[39] As soon as he was able, John began to purchase land and farm, but he was also a tavern keeper which made a nice second income for him.[40] Often tavern businesses were operated out of an individual's home which may have been the case here. John D.

and Jane, as she was known, had three children, Susan Adeline Crume, in 1851, Silas Moses (probably named after his uncle) in 1853, and Mary Catherine on April 2, 1857.[41] After the birth of his third child, his wife Jane died five days later of childbed fever.[42] Within five months he had married Julia Butler on September 27, 1857.[43] He had been unfortunate in losing his first wife at so young an age; moreover, his own life was not to be a long one either. He died of now unknown cause sometime in 1863 at the age of 36.[44] Julia remarried in 1864, and Ralph Mark Crume, Dr. Billy's other son, became guardian of John Daniel's children in 1865.[45] John Daniel's life had flared out in a hurry, but in contrast, his children lived long lives and had many children.[46] Before his death, he had showed the family aptitude for purchasing and selling land, but his life never reached its full potential. He was gone too soon.

Civil War

Mother and her sisters and brothers were not allowed to talk about the war between the states as Grandmother Mary Ann's brothers had not seen alike, and some were for the North and some for the Confederacy.
---Orrie Beam Kellogg[1]

Dr. Billy Crume continued to farm and raise livestock as well as dabble in medicine, but in 1851, he made a decision that he had been thinking about for some time. He approached Philip Thurman about purchasing some land, and the reason for his interest in this particular piece of land soon became obvious. It was rich land in what used to be Crume Valley with good sources of water, but its main attraction was a certain cemetery that lay on it. Dr. Billy's father, mother, grandparents, and probably his first wife and a daughter were buried there, as well as some other Crume family members. The cemetery had been out of the family long enough; he wanted it back. Barely had he acquired it and the 122 ½ acres on which it lay, when, unfortunately, he needed it.[2] His youngest son, James, died at the age of six on April 5, 1852, from a worm ailment.[3] He was buried with his forebears, a small comfort for Dr. Billy and Mary Ann.

Ralph Lincoln Crume, Dr. William Crume's brother, had married his first cousin, Mary Brumfield and had two daughters in the years 1847 to 1850 in Hardin County, Kentucky. He and Mary also had a son, John William, around 1850 who probably died as an infant, either in 1849 or early 1850 before the 1850 census was taken.[4] Not much is known about him or where he was buried, perhaps in a now unmarked grave at the Mill Creek Baptist Church Cemetery. The next year, Mary, who may have been in ill health since the birth of John, died on June 15, 1851, and was buried in the Mill Creek Baptist Church Cemetery next to her grandmother, Bersheba Lincoln, and her mother, Nancy Lincoln Brumfield.[5]

With two little girls to raise, Ralph Lincoln remarried six months later to Rebecca Ann Carr on January 12, 1852, and moved to Breckinridge County.[6] However, something was not quite right with the family because in 1855, John Daniel Crume, nephew of Ralph Lincoln, was appointed guardian for the two girls, and they henceforth lived with the Brumfield and Nall families, their mother's relations.[7] Perhaps Rebecca Ann died, but no records have been found which would confirm it. After John Daniel died around 1863, a new guardian had to be appointed, perhaps one of the Brumfields or Nalls. Nothing more is known about Ralph Lincoln and Rebecca except for one tax notice which appeared in the Breckinridge County newspaper around 1890 when they would have been quite elderly. Being a tax notice, it only mentioned Ralph Lincoln.[8] The two daughters eventually grew up, and Mary married her first cousin Ralph Mark Crume. Nancy moved to Missouri to live with a cousin, and many years later when she died, she was discussed in a newspaper article as being a double cousin of the slain President because both of her parents were first cousins of Abraham Lincoln.[9]

By the 1860's in Breckinridge County, all of Dr. Billy's younger children were grown, and unfortunately, they reached adulthood just in time for the Civil War crisis and all the chaos that it caused in America. There were changes within Dr. Billy's family during this decade as well. His two daughters, Eliza Jane and Susan Mary married within months of each other at the beginning of the Civil War. Eliza Jane married William Hall Hudson on September 18, 1861, and Susan Mary married John Berry Tucker on December 19, 1861.[10] Eliza's husband, William, entered the Civil War in 1863 in Blackford County, Indiana, where they had moved after their marriage. He served until the end of the war as a sergeant in the 130th Indiana Infantry, and while he was serving in the war, Eliza returned home and lived with her father. After the war the Hudsons stayed in Breckinridge County for seventeen years to have their children and then began roaming and living in the West, part of the time in New Mexico and part of the time in Nebraska.[11] Susan Mary and John Berry Tucker lived all of their lives in Breckinridge County, Kentucky, had nine children, and farmed for a living.[12]

Susan Mary Tucker and grandson Leland

William Hall and Eliza Jane Hudson and son Marion

Ralph Mark, Dr. Billy's son, entered the Civil War from Breckinridge County in 1861 and served in the 27th Kentucky Infantry, Company F, as did others from the county, until the end of the war. Most of the unit's battles were in Kentucky and Tennessee, but they also fought around Atlanta and some in Alabama.[13] Both William Hall Hudson and Ralph Mark Crume fought for the Union, and like many other fighting units in the war, they lost more men to disease than to fighting. When Ralph Mark was mustered out of the army in 1865, he married his first cousin, Mary T. Crume, daughter of Ralph Lincoln Crume on August 31, 1865.[14] He was the fourth Ralph Crume to marry a Mary in four generations, further perpetuating the tradition and creating everlasting confusion for future family researchers.

The Civil War was truly a house divided for the Crume family as a whole. The men who served were 2/3 Union and 1/3 Confederate. The 1/3 Confederate men came mostly from Nelson and the eastern counties in Kentucky, from Texas, and from

Mississippi.[15] The 2/3 Union men came from states above the Ohio River and parts of Kentucky, including Breckinridge County and nearby Nelson and Meade Counties. Kentucky was a border state and never seceded from the United States. It was divided in its opinions about the war and the question of slavery, often even within counties, but it was considered a valuable prize for both the Union and the Confederacy.

Kentucky was a central state in the fight for America's waterways, a necessary means of transporting supplies and troops quickly to the battlefields. Among these waterways, the Ohio and the Mississippi were key rivers, as well as the Chesapeake Bay and its river tributaries in the East. Because of all this, raids into Kentucky were a part of the war strategy for the Confederates throughout the conflict, and the Union strategy lay in defending the state and keeping the Confederate armies in Tennessee and points south.[16] In Kentucky and in the Crume family, the questions of the war and slavery could be answered either way in conversation, depending upon who was talking at the time. For the most part, the Crumes refused to discuss the war, even years later.[17]

As an illustration of the mixed feelings of the Crume family about the war, Jesse Crume in his diary of 1859-1864 never mentioned the Civil War at all and did not include Abraham Lincoln, who was President of the United States at the time, on his list of great Americans. However, he was reported to have laughed upon hearing the rantings of a red hot rebel relative who declared that he would go straight into Louisville and clean up the Yankees, and Jesse continued to taunt him by daring the young man to try.[18] This young man was another Philip Crume, the fifth of six Philip Crumes in six generations, who had been living in Texas prior to enlisting in the Confederate Army. He was in Nelson County, Kentucky, in 1862 as a part of the Confederate force under General Braxton Bragg who was intent on capturing Louisville, a major port city on the Ohio River. Small battles had taken place up to the arrival in Bardstown of Bragg's army, and Bardstown had partially evacuated its citizens. However, the campaign was ended when the Confederates met an overwhelming force of Union soldiers commanded by General

Don Carlos Buell at Perryville, the fighting involving the town and the country around it and resulting in 7500 casualties. The Confederates were forced to retreat to Tennessee due to a lack of provisions and men. Kentucky was still in Union hands and remained so throughout the war.[19]

In 1863 and 1864 confrontations continued in central Kentucky as the Confederate army would make raids and be forced to retreat. In July of 1863, the Confederates made their deepest incursion of the war into Union territory when they crossed the Ohio River at Brandenburg in Meade County and rolled into Indiana. As usual, they were forced to retreat.[20] No huge battles were fought in Kentucky during the war, but the constant raids and violence must have been hard on the civilian population. By the 1860's Bardstown had grown in size from the small settlement of 1800, and it had become a home for well-to-do businessmen as well as a favorite stopover for men of letters such as Stephen Foster who used Federal Hill, a local home, as inspiration for his composition, "My Old Kentucky Home." Bardstown was also the home of the Kentucky long rifle and several large bourbon whiskey distilleries.[21] None of these attributes made it an appealing target for the Confederacy though as they were interested mainly in establishing a safe corridor through Kentucky to the Ohio River. They created much havoc in trying to accomplish their goal but were never successful.

Dr. William Crume, according to an account by one of his descendants, exchanged letters before and during the Civil War with President Lincoln, his first cousin. The Lincoln letters written to Dr. Billy supposedly burned in a fire. There was even one family report of Dr. Billy visiting the White House. Unfortunately, these same types of stories were recounted by many in an attempt to claim a closeness with the President, but they certainly could have been accurate. Even up to the present day, researchers continue to look among Lincoln's papers stored at the National Archives for letters that were written to President Lincoln by relatives. One letter did survive from the President to some of his Crume cousins. Mrs. Susan Weathers of Rossville, Clinton County, Indiana, had sent the President some hand-knit socks for Christmas, and from his reply in a thank you letter, it was obvious that the lady was related in some way to the Crume family. The President assumed it was to his uncle, Ralph Crume Jr., and he was right. Susan Weathers was a daughter of Daniel Crume, son of Philip Crume Sr., by Daniel's first wife Mary Dodson. She would have been Ralph Crume Jr.'s cousin.[22]

> Executive Mansion
> Washington

December 4, 1861
My Dear Madam,
    I take great pleasure in acknowledging the receipt of your letter of November 26 and in thanking you for the present by which it was accompanied. A pair of socks, fine, soft and warm, could only have been manufactured in any other way than Kentucky fashion. Your letter informs me your maiden name was Crume and that you were raised in Washington County, Kentucky, by which I infer that an uncle of mine by marriage was a relative of yours. Nearly, or quite sixty years ago, Ralph Crume married Mary Lincoln, a sister of my father, in Washington County, Kentucky. Accept my thanks and believe me.

> Yours forever,
> A. Lincoln

Daily life during the Civil War in a state under siege was annoying, frustrating, and often dangerous. Even when Kentucky was not being raided, the Union troops stationed there often confiscated private homes and institutions of one kind or another to use as barracks for troops or to provide hospitals for the wounded who were brought to Kentucky, especially after a large battle. One particular instance in Louisville involved an institution for the blind being commandeered, but it was later released to its former occupants. Homes and businesses of rebel sympathizers were particular targets for confiscation, and sometimes schools or courthouses were claimed as well. Local citizens were sometimes accused of being Southern sympathizers, were arrested, and faced trial and possible deportation to prison camps at Vicksburg, Mississippi. At times food was taken by troops from both sides as were farm animals such as mules or horses. People regularly buried their valuables to keep them from being stolen by the armies. Commanding Union generals had to be constantly vigilant that the local citizens were not being abused by the troops stationed in their area. It was not an easy time for anyone, even those who did not want to get involved with the politics of the war.[23]

One particularly gruesome incident occurred in the Crume family in Nelson County. Squire Crume's wife, Sarah Ann "Sally," died on December 27, 1864. All the men of the family and neighborhood were away serving in the war; therefore there was no one to make a coffin for Sally or to bury her. The body was made ready for burial, but it had to remain at the home, Seven Cedars. Even though residents had been cautioned not to have lights at night, a small light was needed to keep the rats from bothering the body, so the women hung heavy quilts over the windows and kept one candle burning. Sally's daughter, Mary Ann, sat up with the body all night, and other family members took turns with the vigil during the day because movement in the room helped to keep the rats at bay. As she sat with her mother through the long, seemingly endless hours, Mary Ann could hear soldiers marching over the cobble stones of the turnpike outside her window and officers issuing commands. The experience must have seemed totally surreal. After a day or two of this impossible situation, some citizen finally notified the local authorities, and men were relieved of duty long enough to bury the civilian dead. Squire Crume had died in December of 1860, just before the war started, and now at the close of the war, Sally was finally laid to rest beside her husband at Poplar Flat Cemetery.[24]

Although there were no longer any Crumes living in Virginia, the ones living in Kentucky followed with great interest the progress of the war being fought on Virginia soil. In 1862, a series of battles were fought in the Shenandoah Valley, all Confederate victories, and this caused some excitement in the Crume family, especially for those who could still remember living there. A grandson of Jesse Crume (son of Philip Jr.) recalled how excited Jesse became when he read an account of the battle of Front Royal in the newspaper. The grandson, also named Jesse, was only nine or ten years old at the time, but he could remember the occasion, although he misinterpreted the name of the battle, perhaps due to his advanced age and poor memory when he wrote the letter years later. There were two places named Manassas in Virginia, connected by a railroad, with the town in Prince William County being named for the Manassas Gap near Front Royal in Shenandoah County. Young Jesse confused the battle of First Manassas or Bull Run fought in Prince William County with the Front Royal battle. The place names he lists in his letter were obviously in the Front Royal area. [25]

> When this battle was fought I was big enough to go after the mail at High Grove, and when I got home with the paper after this battle was fought he [Jesse, his grandfather] was terribly excited, and as soon as he saw the headlines he got a large sheet of paper and drew a map of the battle ground, which on comparison with the map afterwards was correct. His nearest town was Woodstock, Romney, Strassburg, Front Royal, and have heard him talk about Winchester and Harper's Ferry. They used to go seining in the Potomac River.[26]

The battle of Front Royal was partially fought on what was formerly Philip Crume Jr.'s (Philip Withers Crume) land, first owned by his grandfather, Ralph Withers, and where Philip Jr.'s son Jesse grew up. This land was located just across a bend of the Shenandoah River and north of the town of Front Royal on Crooked Run. There was a high hill beside the river at Front Royal that created a bluff, an excellent place for artillery batteries. This hill, known as Guard Hill, was described in the original Crume land records and also in the official records of the battle. The Union troops failed to hold Guard Hill and tried to retreat to the North on the Winchester road that passed by the bluff, got caught by the Confederates, and made their last stand a few miles past Guard Hill on what was probably former Crume/Withers land.[27] In 1862 and again in 1864, there was extensive fighting up and down the Shenandoah Valley, both battles and skirmishes. The beautiful valley was torn asunder, and it is entirely possible that Philip Sr.'s former Virginia land was also ravaged.[28] It must have been hard on the family to know their long-ago home was caught in a terrible whirlwind of destruction, but they had troubles of their own in Kentucky and were probably glad they were not in Virginia. The long and bloody Civil War had become a nightmare, seemingly without end.

In another odd twist of fate, two young members of the Louisiana Jordan family were a part of the Confederate troops who

James Monroe Jordan, buried at Lynchburg, Virginia

Floyd H. Jordan, buried at Winchester, Virginia

fought in the various battles in the Shenandoah Valley in May and June of 1862, quite likely on former Crume land at Front Royal. Their regiment was the 9th Louisiana Infantry, and this was their first real action of the war, having spent most of their enlisted duty fighting disease. They had a sister at home who later in life married in Texas and had a daughter, Lanora, who in turn married a Crume, Dr. William Crume's grandson, Samuel Augustus. One of the young Jordans, after surviving the battle of Antietam, died of disease at the hospital in Winchester, Virginia, and was buried there - only twenty miles from some of the former Crume land.[29] Thus, the Jordan/Crume connection got an early start in 1862.

Dr. William Crume in Breckinridge County weathered the war years, waiting for news of his sons who were fighting in the war and continuing to do the things he had always done - farm and practice medicine occasionally. His daughter, Eliza, came home to live with him and her mother while she waited for her husband to return from the war. As in most parts of Kentucky, Breckinridge County endured its share of harassment by both armies, and it was divided in its sentiments as was the rest of the state. On one occasion, Confederate cavalry troops burned the local courthouse, which was being used as a barracks for Union troops, but the townspeople managed to save most of the records stored there. This was a good example of private citizens being caught between two armies and enduring frustrating, sometimes violent, behavior from both. Another incident in the county was the capture of a noted Confederate guerrilla, Sue Monday, near Irvington.[30]

Having survived the violence and uncertainty of the war and looking forward to some peace for a change, life was to take a sudden, cruel twist for Dr. Billy. Sometime in the mid to late 1860's, Dr. William went blind. As it was described by him and the description passed down to his descendants, "he was driving home a herd of cattle that he had bought. At first he could see the horns of the foremost cattle, but by the time he got home, he could barely distinguish those of the hindmost." It was a sudden onset, possibly caused by a burst blood vessel. His descendants remembered, "he was a jovial and witty man until this happened, but afterwards he was contrary and hard to handle."[31] Small wonder! After this and probably before September of 1875, his wife, Mary Ann, suffered a stroke and was paralyzed. Dr. Billy's choices for how to go on with his life and see that his wife was cared for were fast diminishing. He finally decided he had only one option.

On September 27, 1875, he sold his land to his son, Ralph Mark, in exchange for care from his son for the remaining years of his life.[32] This arrangement lasted only three years before Ralph Mark in 1878 sold the land and the care of his parents to the Hartwell Bashams. Mary Catherine "Katie" Basham, the daughter of John Daniel Crume, was a granddaughter of Dr. William and Mary Ann Crume and a cousin of Ralph Mark. It is not known whether the Bashams ever provided the care because they moved to Edmonson County, Kentucky, before 1880 where they spent the rest of their lives. They did not make payments on the land in Breckinridge County, so it eventually reverted to Ralph Mark.[33] In 1883, a notice in the Breckinridge County newspaper reported the following:

> Dan Smith was allowed $7.55, the amount advanced by him to Wm. Coomes, a blind man 81 years old, and a cousin to the late President Abraham Lincoln. Coomes' wife is paralyzed, and they were both adjudged objects of charity and their cases referred to the poor house commissioner.[34]

It is not known whether the Crumes actually went to the poor house, but they almost certainly died within a few years of the notice in the newspaper. In 1886, Ralph Mark sold the land out of the family for the final time and spent the last years of his life with his wife at Harned, Kentucky.[35] This sale probably meant that the William Crumes were dead. Dr. Billy and his wife were more than likely buried in the Crume Cemetery next to their little boy that died back in 1852 and Dr. Billy's father and grandfather. It is not known why William and Mary Ann's children did not take care of them in their last years, but perhaps the burden of their care was too much for the children, at least those with large families of their own to support. It was a sad ending for this Crume generation. However, Dr. Billy's children lived on in Breckinridge County, Kentucky, in Texas, and in other places in the West. After the Crume land was sold out of the family, the cemetery went to sleep and the knowledge of its whereabouts eventually disappeared except in the minds of a few family members and their descendants who still lived in the immediate area. The only grave markers were fieldstones, at least one of which had scratched-on initials of the two Ralph Crumes who had created the vast Crume Valley settlement and made it their home.

Slavery and the Crume Family

"So much history, and the Crumes were right in the middle of it, from the beginnings of colonial America up to the current time." My mother was speculating out loud about her family research in preparation for putting it into final form and getting it printed for distribution. She was determined to leave some information about her family lines for future generations. Why do all that work and then let it disappear when she was gone?

"Yeah, I am getting that idea loud and clear," I agreed. I was in junior high and not always interested in or willing to discuss what my mother was doing. "However, if the Crume story is history, there is one part that I have not heard you talk about very much, and I am wondering if you know anything about it. What about slavery? That was a pretty important issue in American history."

"Well, actually we do know some things," Mom replied. "The growth of the involvement in slavery in the Crume family parallels the growth of slavery in America. The Crumes were not known slave holders when they lived on the frontier of Virginia, probably because of where they lived and the size of their family. With that huge family, they did not really need an outside labor source, and they did not live in the Tidewater (Atlantic coast) area of Virginia where the large slave-holding plantations were located. At this juncture in American history, the use of slavery was growing but not as prevalent, even in the southern states, as it would be later. After the Crume family's move to Kentucky, things were different, although it was a virtual wilderness as well."

"What do you suppose drove some of our family members to get involved with slavery when we know today that it was a horrible mistake?" I was trying to puzzle out the thought processes of my ancestors when there was really no way to know for sure what they thought.

In answer to my question, Mom began to describe the Crume involvement with slavery. "Philip Crume, Sr. may have been the first Crume to purchase slaves although Eleazar Birkhead, his son-in-law, was already experimenting with it as early as the Revolutionary War period.[1] Philip had a young family in Kentucky, and his other children were too busy with their own families to be a reliable, steady source of labor for him. This may have pushed him to try slave labor. He had several slaves when he died, and his will gave most of them to his various children, keeping them in the family at large. This did not mean that slavery automatically then became prevalent in the family. Some family members never accepted slavery. Slavery in the family lasted only one or two generations at most except in the instances in Nelson County, Kentucky, and Cherokee County, Texas. Several of the Crume families that stayed in Nelson County and some of those that moved to Texas kept their slaves and added to the number of them as the years went by leading up to the Civil War.[2] John and Squire Crume owned moderate numbers of slaves (fifteen- twenty), and their farm holdings were referred to as plantations. These plantations apparently were similar to the ones described in historical accounts and novels, but there are no mentions of physical cruelty towards slaves in the Crume experience."

"So that meant that the family was divided in its acceptance of slavery, just as they were divided in which side they chose in the Civil War." I concluded from this that tension in the family grew over the years because of this issue.

"Exactly," Mom agreed. "By the time of the Civil War, many Crume families were living in Northern states, and those that lived in Kentucky were divided between North and South. In our family line, Dr. William Crume was not a slave holder and his son Ralph Mark fought for the Union. Dr. Billy's eldest son, Silas Moses, who had moved to Texas, fought in a limited way for the Confederacy, and he was a slave holder. Several of Squire's sons fought on opposite sides. This was not an easy time for the family or for anyone in America. Of course, the President of the United States was related to our family as well."

"Well, do you know anything about the slaves who were in the Crume family?" I was imagining trying to trace the slaves through history and getting the hiccups thinking about it.

"We know a little," Mom began. "For one thing, it seems that whenever slaves had to be sold, most of the Crumes who owned them tried to sell them as families and find good homes for them when possible. Jesse Crume writes about this in his diary of 1859. 'Sold Alfred to go with his wife and children for $900 to George Sloan' and 'Sold Abraham to be with his wife and children for $900 to live with the Murry's'. This was in 1860.[3] When slaves had to be sold in a hurry to settle an estate, such as in the case of Ralph Sr. in Breckinridge County, then it was harder to keep families together and try to find good homes for them. In some cases in the Crume family, without considering the family situation of the slaves, they were sold and the proceeds divided to settle an estate or simply to obtain cash, and in the same manner families were split up when some individual slaves were given to other family members. The most notorious case of this was when 'Little Phil' Crume returned to Kentucky from Texas to claim his inheritance. Tales of his thoughtless actions in selling his slaves were passed down by the slaves' families and eventually written down at a later date.[4] Incidentally, only two of Ralph Sr.'s children owned slaves for any length of time, and they were Rachel Lucas and John Crume. Apparently Ralph Crume, Jr. was active in the Abolition Society in Breckinridge County because he sent out an invitation about a meeting of the society in 1824 to David C. Hoskinson.[5] There is a family story which has been passed down about Squire Crume freeing his slaves right before the Civil War began,[6] but there are no public records to support the story. Squire died in December of 1860 with his will providing for his slaves, and the census of 1860 lists his slaves."[7]

"It seems that each Crume family member had a mind of his own, and that those who did have slaves tried to treat them decently, at least in most cases," I concluded.

"That's what I think also," my mom agreed. "And there was one incidence of slave ownership which is really interesting. We know enough about it to be able to form some opinions."

"What was that?" I was getting a little tired, as I usually did with family history discussions.

My mom began the story, "Anna Barret Crume, Philip Crume, Sr.'s second wife, had a slave named Charlotte who was probably purchased in Kentucky after the big family emigration in 1795, but we don't know for sure about that. It is possible that she could have belonged to the family in Virginia and made the trip with them to Kentucky. About five years later in 1801 when Philip died, he left Charlotte to his wife in his will. Charlotte and her son, Will, together were appraised at $266.75 at that time. According to Philip's will, Charlotte's children were given to other family members when the estate was settled. One of Philip's slaves was sold, but not Charlotte or her children.[8] Anna remained in Nelson County and married Jacob Marks, but this did not change Charlotte's status in the family. It is not known what her specific job was in the household, but she seemed to be attached to Anna. When Jacob died unexpectedly at a fairly young age, there was no will, but when the estate was settled, Charlotte continued on with Anna."[9]

"When Anna married for the third time, her husband Rev. William Morris must have been an abolitionist because he went through the courts to try to get Charlotte emancipated. He began the struggle in 1821, shortly after he married Anna and was still trying to get Charlotte free in 1837 when he died. We don't know what Anna and Charlotte thought of all this, but by this time Charlotte had been with Anna for so long that she might have stayed with her even if Charlotte had been given her freedom and could choose. When Rev. Morris died, he stipulated in his will that $100 should be used to try to emancipate Charlotte, and in failing to accomplish that, then the money should be used to supply any needs or wants that Charlotte had.[10] This effort must have failed also, however, because Charlotte stayed with Anna. In 1844 when Anna sold her land in Breckinridge County and moved back to Nelson County to live with her sons there, we don't know if Charlotte went with her or was already deceased. Anna was old and in poor health, and Charlotte, if she was still alive, would have been the same. There are no records of slaves for Anna's sons in Nelson County who would fit Charlotte, although there was another slave with the same name.[11] Anna died on December 27, 1848, in Nelson County, Kentucky, most likely at her son Squire's home.[12] Charlotte probably did not live to see her own freedom or even witness the brutal Civil War which brought it about. Her life had been her owner's life, but perhaps she felt her years with Anna and her part in all the great endeavors of Anna's life with her husbands was not a bad way to have spent her time on this earth. Who knows?"

"That is really neat that we know so much about this one slave in the family," I enthused. "I wish we could know how Charlotte really felt about it all. It wouldn't have mattered what she thought or felt in the times in which she lived, but I hope it was a situation where two women cared about each other and had found peace with their relationship. Perhaps occasionally the horror of slavery was overshadowed by simple friendship and loyalty. But, like you said, who knows?"

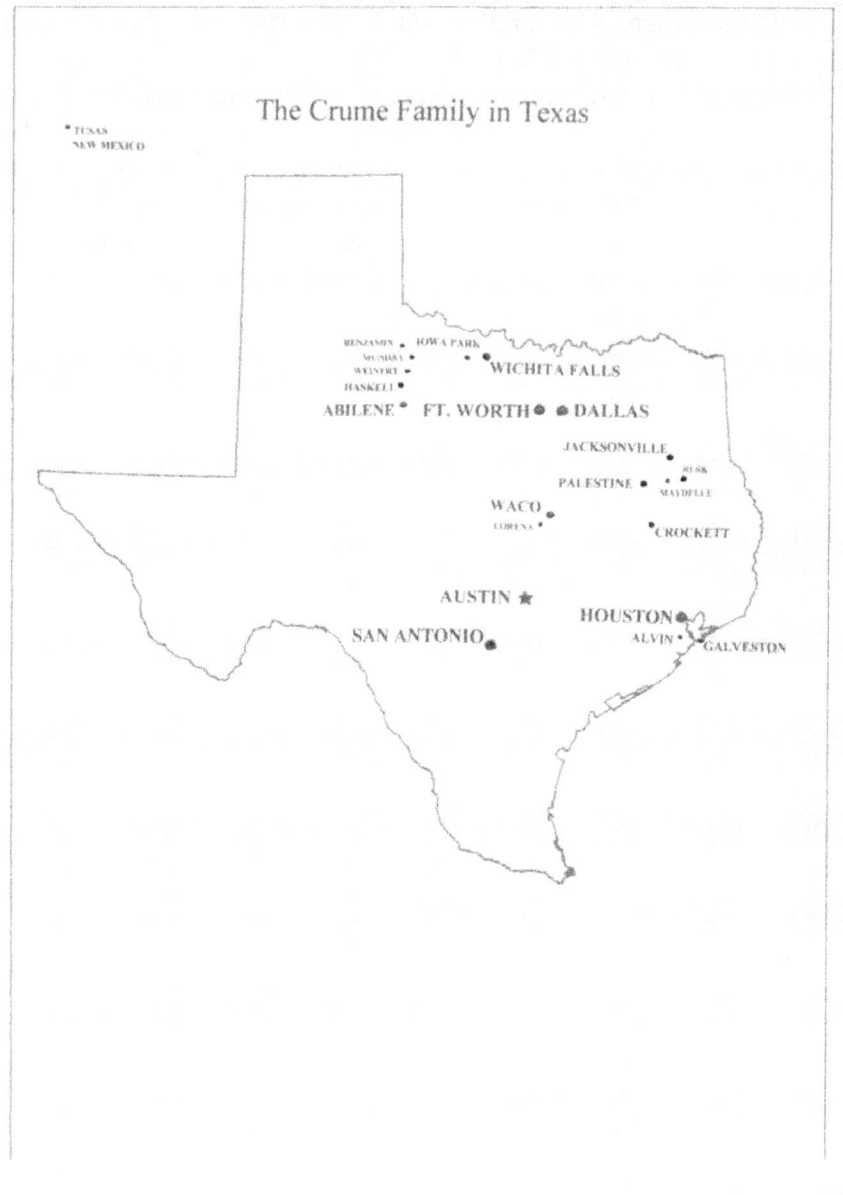

Going to Texas

Once it was the Cherokee Indians land, lying east of the Neches River in central Cherokee County, where Indian and Republic of Texas militiamen vied for ownership. Low hills, timbered with a variety of hardwoods and shortleaf pine, are drained on the east by One-Arm Creek and on the west by Tail's Creek. Both streams bear titles of former Indian residents. ---Bernard Mayfield[1]

In the late 1840's, Silas Moses Crume, Dr. William Cox Crume's first born son, was living in Meade County, Kentucky with a relative, William Marks, and his family. He was working as an overseer for the John Finley Williams, Sr. family who lived in the beautiful farm valley country outside of Brandenburg, a river port town that was situated on the Ohio River. The Williams family was large and prosperous, John having owned good land and sired eleven children, who would later ally themselves through marriage with other families in the neighborhood such as the Shackletts, Stiths, and Kendalls. One of the eleven children, Richard, had died as a baby, and two of the children, Samuel and Elizabeth, were married and on their own by 1850. This left eight children at home, James age 24, Anthony age 22, Fanny age 20, Nancy age 18, Thomas age 16, Mary Jane age 12, John Jr. age 9, and Sally age 5. Only three of those were under age 16, so there were plenty of helping hands to keep the farm running smoothly.[2]

It is not known if Silas ever met and subsequently was hired by John Williams because John died on May 24, 1848, at the somewhat early age of 51, three years after his last child was born. Silas may even have been hired because of the death because John's oldest son was away from home managing his own farm by that time.[3] In any case, perhaps Silas saw in the

Williams another family like his own who possessed good land sense and stewardship and who was living on land in a beautiful location. As he had done for the past few years, he had placed himself in an excellent position to learn more about successful farming methods and uses of the land and to exercise his inherited abilities and already acquired experience in farming. He was young in years, age 23, but he was steadily moving towards complete independence and his own land holdings. With his salary from the Williams family and the value of his land in Breckinridge County which he intended to sell eventually, he was amassing the capital he would need to fulfill his long-held dreams and ambitions.

Silas was also a religious man, following an inclination that was prominent in his family. It was his nature to believe that building a successful life on the land was God's plan as well as his own for his future. He had great, great uncles who had become ministers in their later years, and he was not adverse to the idea for himself. He had much to think about and plan for at this time in his young life. He had friends and relatives in Meade County whom he could count on

Silas Moses Crume

for support and social interaction, William Marks and his family with whom he lived and Adin Crume and his family. William was the son of Anna Crume Marks Morris, and Adin was the son of Charles Crume, Silas's great uncle. William had a young family with four small children,[4] and Silas apparently fit in well with them, perhaps picking up some skills in dealing with little people. His old life in Breckinridge County was slowly fading away. It is not known how often he went home to visit his family or what his independence meant to them.

Nancy Catherine Williams

By 1850 when the new decade arrived, Silas was well established in Meade County. In the course of his duties as overseer for the John Williams farm, he must have interacted with the Williams family on a daily basis, and one member of the family made a real impact upon him. He began to take a serious interest in Nancy Catherine Williams, John Williams' daughter. She was seventeen when her father died in 1848, but by the year 1853, she was twenty-one and fully of an age to be married. Silas was twenty-six years old by this time, he had spent several years in Meade County adding to his experience and getting to know Nancy, and he was ready to make some important decisions. He obviously felt it was an advantage to be married and have a partner in building his land holdings, but he was also thinking about his future children, part of the legacy he would leave the future. Nancy was a pretty girl, but she was also strong, knowledgeable about life on a farm, and not so young as to be frivolous and useless. She would be able to weather the challenges of life in a pioneer area. Nancy Catherine suited him on all counts, and he was ready to ask her to marry him, irrevocably changing the direction of her life.

Silas was a strong man by this time, committed to building a bright future, as he had been for years – all qualities that would appeal to a young woman making a life-changing decision. She must have loved him a lot because she agreed to marry him and go wherever he chose. They were married on February 6, 1853. The wedding was held at the Williams' home with the Marks family in attendance as Catherine Marks served as a witness along with Ellen Holman.[5] It is not known where the new couple lived for the next month or so, but by the time March had arrived, Silas had made the decision to move to a bold new location to start his new life with Nancy. They were going to Texas.

It was a long ways to East Texas by wagon, horseback and on foot; therefore the journey would take several weeks, if not months. The terrain contained hills, mountains, and wide rivers to cross, so it was necessary to find established roads and river crossings to make the trip easier. Even established roads would be dusty on dry days and muddy if not impassable on wet ones, especially if the wagon train included farm animals as well as the horses, mules, or oxen pulling the wagons and people walking. As well, there were always dangers along the trail from outlaws or Indians. The wagon train which left Meade County was sizable, and the people involved in the trip were slaves as well as free. Silas wanted every advantage he could get in his new enterprise. Part of the party was walking and not riding in the wagons, making the journey slower. Silas was later to tell the story about one elderly slave who walked all the way to Texas, knitting socks as she went.[6] She must have made socks for the entire party!

Nancy was leaving her family behind and her beloved Kentucky, perhaps forever, but she was committed to Silas and his ambitious plans. In the history of the Williams family, she and one sister were the only ones of her brothers and sisters to move away from Kentucky. Her younger sister, Sally Stanfield, moved, along with her family, to Kansas in the 1890's.[7] Nancy didn't make this commitment lightly. However, at this point, she could not know what the future would bring or how much her loyalty to Silas Moses would cost her. Without knowing, she was still strong enough to make the choice. To make the journey more complicated for Nancy, almost from the time it began, she was pregnant with her first child. Thankfully the journey was completed long before the time arrived to deliver the baby.

After an exhaustive journey of several hundred miles, the Crume party arrived in eastern Texas near a small service community called Pine Town in Cherokee County. The country that they found there consisted of pine forests, but also rich underlying land which could be used for farming and raising cattle. Cherokee County was located between two rivers, the Neches and the Angelina, with many small creeks to provide water for agriculture, and for some, the ferries on the large rivers were a good business. In 1853 the area was not unpopulated wilderness. Settlement had begun in1845, a post office had been established in 1847, voting had been taking place at Pine Town since 1850, and a well-established road which ran from Palestine through Pine Town to Rusk was being used by stage coach traffic. Pine Town was not a commercial center, but it had several mills and craft shops.

Corn, rather than wheat, was the grain of choice at that time, and it required grist mills. Cotton was the main money crop and would remain so for many years, and it required gins. Many business transactions were conducted using cotton bales for money. Cattle and hogs had been running loose in the county for several years after the Cherokee Indians left the area and were just beginning to be brought under the control of area stockmen. Although Pine Town was not a commercial center, supplies for all the businesses in the area were hauled from Palestine, Texas, along the Palestine Road.[8] Silas assessed the possibilities and decided to acquire land on Tail's Creek near Pine Town and One-Arm Creek, just north of the Palestine Road which carried the stagecoach and wagon traffic.[9] He could raise his own cotton, but more importantly he could build a grist mill and cotton gin, perhaps even a cane mill and saw mill for the local lumber businesses. The possibilities were almost endless.

In the first few months in the area, Silas quickly put his plans in motion by first doing some planting and drawing up designs for constructing a grist mill and cotton gin. As well, he probably oversaw construction of modest structures for his family, slaves, and farm animals with the view in mind of building a larger home and better outbuildings later. Timber was plentiful, and shelter was needed before the winter weather set in. It was a busy time of

Silas Moses' Pine Town land on Tailes Creek and the Palestine Road

construction and beginning farm life in the pine forests. All was ready by the time winter arrived, and Nancy was ready for her first child to be born. On December 25, 1853, John William Crume made his appearance. [10] What a Christmas present! He carried the name of both of his grandfathers back in Kentucky. It was a great beginning for Silas' new life in Texas, and he must have felt a sense of satisfaction. However, he knew there was much more to be done to fully take advantage of the local opportunities. Following in his ancestors' footsteps, he was an over achiever with a great deal of energy.

Cherokee County, as its name would imply, had a long history of Indian settlement, going back to the earliest Indians on the continent. Many tribes through the years had called this place home before dying out or moving on. The Spanish and French had come and gone, and there was little conflict between the Cherokee and other tribes and the white settlers until the 1830's. In 1839 it became obvious that the two could not live together peacefully when violence broke out. It was settled by the removal of the Indians from the area, and they left behind much of what they had built in farms and livestock. The white settlers quickly moved in and began to establish their own institutions and communities. When the Crume family arrived in 1853, they were among many others, particularly Southerners, who were looking for new land, and they found a peaceful area with the Indians removed.[11]

However, this did not mean that there were not occasional visits by transient Indians. On one occasion in the early days of living on the farm near Pine Town, Nancy was outside with the baby working on some project when a group of Indians approached her. One of the women drew a knife and started swinging it back and forth over the baby's cradle, saying "Brod" over and over. They wanted bread, and they had a very effective way of asking for it. Nancy saw to it that they got what they wanted, and they went on their way.[12] One of the keys to establishing a successful way of life in this new land was learning how to deal with people – all kinds. One can almost imagine what Nancy had to say to Silas Moses after this incident, but she had almost as much determination as Silas did to make a success of their venture. He had married the right woman.

In the years leading up to the turn of the decade and the Civil War in America, Silas Moses and Nancy worked side by side to build a home and a business which was really a conglomerate of businesses. They also added to their family. Thomas Anthony was born on September 18, 1855, twins Susan Cole and Mary Elizabeth were born on November 9, 1857, and James Richard was born on November 5, 1859.[13] Nancy and Moses had five children under seven years old by 1860. The amount of work involved in caring for these children and keeping the household chores in order must have been enormous, but Nancy was up to the task. Just as their family was growing, their slave population was growing also. The 1860 federal census for the county showed that Silas Moses had fifteen slaves, seven of which were children too young to do much work.[14] The other eight helped immensely in his ability to run all his various businesses. He was a farmer, ran a cotton gin, ran a grist mill for processing corn and after 1860 flour, and according to some family records, had a cane mill and saw mill.[15] Running a grist mill could be particularly labor intensive if it had many customers. The grain had to be cleaned and moved upstairs by hand, moved through one end of the grinding process to the other and finally sacked by hand. This process could require several men to keep it going. Grist mills were also social gathering places which tended to slow down the operation.[16]

Silas was a very busy man, and his interests were wide. He and Nancy were interested in church and eventually in a school for their children. They, along with fifteen other people, started a church in 1854 called the Pleasant Grove Missionary Baptist Church. Silas served as the church clerk for many years up until 1879.[17] He probably preached a sermon or two during those years as well. He was also a member of the local Masonic Lodge which had a building on the south side of the stagecoach road.[18]

In 1858 Nancy received bad news from her family in Kentucky. Her older brother Anthony had died on February 20. He was only 30 years old. Apparently he had come out to Cherokee County to live for a time either after the Crumes had arrived there or perhaps before. Perhaps he was the reason the Crumes decided to go to Cherokee County first to see what was available. He never married and was buried next to his father in the Williams Cemetery. This occurred a few months after Nancy's twin girls were born and must have reminded her of the great distance between her and her family.[19]

Pine Town flourished due to the stage line and the many new families, mostly from the South, that moved into the area. Cotton was king in Cherokee County, the slave population was high comprising twenty-six percent of the total population in the county in 1860, roads were good for transporting the cotton to market, and so as the talk of war and secession grew, it was fairly obvious which way Texas and Cherokee County would decide to go. Because cotton was such a valuable commodity for both the South and the North, Cherokee County was not going to lose, no matter which way a war went.

Included in the families who moved to the Pine Town area were children, and where there were children, eventually a school would be needed. The Pine Town School District was created in 1854, just after Silas Moses and Nancy moved to the area. Philip Williams started a semi-private neighborhood school shortly thereafter. It is likely that this was where the Crume children attended school until the A. Jackson Masonic Lodge in Pine

Town started the first public school in 1868.[20] Often the school master boarded with one of the families in the community who had the room and needed the money. In this case Mr. Williams may have run the school out of his own home.

Tailes Creek on the north side of the bridge over the Palestine Road.

It is not known when Silas followed through with his plans to build Nancy a larger home, but at some time during the sixties and seventies, he built the largest home in the area and probably improved his outbuildings as well.[21] He was continuing to buy and sell land to increase his holdings and his income. Nancy was probably in charge of the many other jobs around the farm which arose because the family undoubtedly kept chickens, milk cows, sheep for wool, cattle and hogs for meat, and a large garden for vegetables. It is not known whether the Crumes had an orchard or simply fruit trees, but there was great interest in orchards, especially peach orchards, in Cherokee County. The climate and sandy soil were ideally suited for growing peaches as well as cotton in the county, and apparently peaches had been raised by the Indians for many years before the white settlers adopted the practice. They were grown extensively in the areas where the

Cherokee Indians had lived previously, and this was true in the southeasterrn states as well as Texas.[22] The connection between peaches and the South was hard to miss. Down through the generations of families who lived in the South, there were discussions of peaches being eaten in pies or just as a table dish.

In 1861 when the Southern states seceded from the United States, it didn't take long for Texas to make up its mind. Sentiment had been running high for years in favor of the Southern position of states' rights. Texas was out on the western edge of the Southern states that seceded, and it contained a huge amount of land. Union attempts to "conquer" Texas never progressed any farther than a draw or standstill. However, as the war progressed, Texas was more and more isolated from the rest of the Southern States by the Union blockade, and this was especially true after the capture of Vicksburg and the Union gained control of the Mississippi River. Texas was then not as able to supply the South or to even supply its own state. Due to shortages in everything manufactured, Texans went back to making their necessities themselves and substituting for the goods that were unavailable. They also began to set up manufacturing plants to provide for their needs. Still, Texans were not in a comfortable position for the four years of the war.[23]

They did manage to avoid the major battles on their own soil that the Confederate states in the East had to endure. However, there were many small battles and skirmishes, some won by the Confederates and some by the Unionists, and actually the last battle of the Civil War was fought in Texas near Brownsville. All of these clashes inevitably brought casualties. It was also a dangerous challenge for the cotton producers to try to circumvent the Northern blockades. As their largest contribution to the war effort, Texas supplied troops to fight in the major battles of the war (some 90,000 of them), some brilliant generals, and unfortunately many casualties. The cotton in Texas was very important to the Confederacy as a source of income, especially in the beginning of the war, and eventually the North cut off most of the trade in it. This damaged the economy of Texas for a certain period, but it served as a vital weapon in destroying the Confederacy as a whole.[24] Silas Moses served in the war on the

Southern side as a lieutenant in the Texas State Troops which was basically a home guard[25], so it is not known how much he was away from home, leaving Nancy to take care of things, or if he fought in any battles.

During the years of the war, Nancy received more bad news from home. Her younger brother Thomas died on January 13, 1863. He was twenty-nine years old, not married, and he, like his brother, was buried next to his father in the Williams Cemetery. Thomas and Anthony were almost the same age when they died, and both were unmarried. It must have been hard for Nancy to watch from a distance beloved family members die, and at an early age. However, it was not over. Her older brother, Samuel Best Williams, died at the end of the war on October 15, 1865. He was married and the father of ten children, but only forty-two years old.[26] He had been the oldest child in the family and the one the rest depended upon for support. It seemed fated that the Williams men were doomed to die early.

The Crumes persevered through the war years, undoubtedly worried about the folks in Kentucky, but when the war was finally over, life returned to its normal routines. The Reconstruction period in Texas passed rather quickly in Cherokee County because once more there was a great demand for cotton. Even the destruction of the slavery system did not seriously impact production. Land owners just switched to a tenant sharecropper system and continued to produce with the labor of their former slaves.[27] During the war more children were born to the Texas Crumes, Ada Belle on August 28, 1861, and Samuel Augustus on August 21, 1864.[28] These new children may have helped Nancy and Silas to accept the loss of other family members. However, there was one dark period for the family,

Susan Cole Crume

and it came with the loss of one of their own twins, Susan Cole, on November 9, 1862. She was five years old, and it must have broken their hearts to lose that precious little girl. She was the first family member to be buried in the Pleasant Grove Missionary Baptist Church Cemetery.[29]

The Crumes had taken on another business operation in the sixties. They ran a stage coach stop on the Palestine Road. The four horse stage of the Bradfield Line arrived in Pine Town on Saturday, Tuesday and Thursday, bringing the mail from major stops such as Shreveport, Henderson, and Rusk. Undoubtedly the mail was disrupted and delayed during the war, but it still came. Nancy was put in charge of this operation and she became the postmistress for Pine Town on July 10, 1866. She held this position until the office was discontinued in December of 1874.[30] The stage line probably stopped running as well when the International and Great Northern Railroad arrived and began to draw business away from Pine Town and towards Jacksonville.[31] When little Samuel Augustus got old enough to sit on the fence which ran in front of the stage stop, he would sit for hours and shout "Howdy" to the travelers up and down the Palestine Road, going east and west. If they were going east, he would also add, "If you're goin' to Kentucky and see Grandma, tell her 'Howdy!'"[32] The little boy perched on the fence with a big grin on his face was a picture that lived in the family's memory and was passed down to all the generations to come.

Nancy was also the person in charge of health care and medical emergencies for the farm and other businesses. Whenever someone was hurt, she was called. One story remembered by her son, Samuel Augustus, was when the boys had gone fishing (slave and free alike), and one little boy had gotten a fish hook caught in his ear. The children rushed him to Nancy to get it out. Samuel was later to comment that he would never forget that little boy hopping on one foot as Nancy cut the fish hook out of his ear with a razor and crying, "Cut Miz Nancy, cut!" "Cut Miz Nancy, cut!"[33] She may have been the one to pull bad teeth with the tooth pliers as well (one of the items discovered years later in the old family trunk), but perhaps that job fell to one of the men.

The first public school was begun in 1868, supported and housed by the A. Jackson Masonic Lodge, located on the south side of the Palestine/Rusk Road and bordered on the west by Brigman Branch. The first teacher was Phillip Williams who had been teaching at the semi-private school which he had started in 1854. Dr. J.L. Moore also taught at this school in the late sixties.[34] When Samuel Augustus was old enough to attend school, he collected a few stories which he would tell in later years to his own children. One time at school, he was sitting on a long bench in front of the fireplace with the other boys working sums on their slates on their laps. Every time Samuel started to write, the boy seated next to him would push his elbow. Finally Samuel grew tired of the annoyance, and turning quickly he grabbed one of the boy's ears, giving it a sharp twist. Of course the boy yelled, and the teacher only saw Samuel's act, so he called him up to the desk for an explanation. Samuel would not tell on the boy, so he had to take a whipping. The teacher later told Silas Moses that he hated to do it because he knew there had to be more to the situation, but Samuel wouldn't "tattle." Another time, there was a kid who giggled at everything he saw in the school room until, in desperation, the teacher seated him close to the wall, facing it. After a little time passed, the kid suddenly burst out giggling. The teacher demanded, "Now what are you laughing at?" He said, "I'se laughin' at dese ants goin' up de wall."[35] Why teachers get gray!

In 1869 at the close of the decade, Nancy wrote to her family back home in Kentucky. This was the only surviving letter of the many which she must have written over the years.

                                  Pine Town, Cherokee County Texa
                                          March 21, 1869

Dear Sister and Nephew,

I take my pen in hand to answer your welcome letter which I received a few days ago. We all are well and hope these few lines will find you and your little ones all well and doing well. Sis, I haven't much news to write that would interest you. The health of the country is good at this time for which we have a great reason to be thankful for the spring is backward and cold. We have not had any pretty open weather yet for farming. We have not planted any corn yet though will commence in the morning if it is not raining. My gardening seed has come up and looks very well. Sis, I wish you would send me some strawberry seed if they will come from the seed.

I wish I could see you all. I could tell you a heap and all about the folks out here. We have some strange cases to contend with. I was at a big quilting last week and I suppose they danced all night. I left before sundown. They all laughed at me for running they say but I tell them the Bible tells me to shun the very appearance of evil.

Well John, I would be glad to see you. I would encourage you to come see us if your Mother could spare you, for nothing would give me more pleasure than for some of my relations to come out here. Your little cousins would be so proud to see you or anybody they think is kin to them for it is all their talk – they want to see some of their kin folks. I tell Hannah that her Uncle Moses says he wishes he could see her and her little babe. I know he would soon have it spoilt for he is worse to spoil children now than he was when she was little, for we have two cute little fellows.

Sis, you must write soon and give us all the news of the sacred old country. Give my love to your Mother and all inquiring friends and tell them I would be glad to see them once more. I would be glad to get a letter from any of my old acquaintances that want to write to one in the far West who often thinks of them and wonders if my name is forgotten in that old country which I ever will hold dear to me the longest day I live. All I want in this world is to raise my little children to have plenty to come back there once more to see you all. That is all I crave is to live in old Kentucky once more. Well I will close. Kiss the little children for me and tell them their Aunt would be so glad to see them. Sis, look to the Lord in all your troubles and he will bless you. Give my love to all and accept a large portion to yourself so no more at present. Write soon and often.

Sister, tell Mandy when you see her I think she has forgot me. I never hear from her. Tell her I want her to write to me and let me know where all of her sisters is and everything she knows.

Sister, I send you some of my four boys hair. I will write their names with their hair.

John Willie	age 15	Dec 25, 1868
Thomas Anthony	age 13	Sept 18, 1868
James Richard	age 9	Nov 5, 1868
Samuel Gus	age 4	Aug 21, 1868
he is my baby		

It is obvious that Nancy had a bad case of homesickness in this letter. However, her feeling of loss ran deeper than just an occasional mention of homesickness in a letter. All of her life, she probably felt that Kentucky was home and not Texas. This did not affect her loyalty to her family in Texas and their plans and ambitions, but home would always be Kentucky. She did indeed send her boys' hair in the letter, and the hair remained attached to the letter for all the years into the future, carefully preserved by loving hands. Silas Moses probably did not think about his old home in Kentucky as much as Nancy did. He was too busy building his own small empire, and home was where he and his family were. It is not known whether he kept in contact with his own family in Kentucky in the early years in Texas, but it seems likely that he did, especially his brother John Daniel.

As the decade was drawing to a close in 1869, the people in Texas were not unhappy to see it go. They had endured a lot of misery during the war. On the other hand, Silas Moses had made great strides in the sixties. He had continued to buy and sell land, and along with all of his businesses, he had increased his income. He was no longer a slave owner, but he was able to afford workers. Life was changing, but he was ready to change with it if necessary, continue what he had started, and make it grow. The family's clothes in the portraits that were made of them, the framed portraits themselves, and Silas' ability to buy land at will and build new buildings were all testaments to his success. Perhaps more important to him, he was respected in the community. He was a part of the community, a member of its organizations, and a contributor to its welfare. He had become the very image of his great grandfather, and there was no one else he would rather be – the next great steward of the land.

Silas Moses' Land on Tailes Creek near Pine Town

Pine Town's Crume Family

In 1872, the International and Great Northern Railroad constructed a line through East Texas. Its track lay to the north of Pine Town, and this made a significant impact upon the community. Even in its heyday, the town had never developed into a commercial town with stores, residences and community buildings. It had remained essentially a loosely-knit service area for the surrounding farms and timber businesses. Now that the railroad had gone elsewhere, it was destined to slowly fade out of existence, but this would not happen overnight. However, it did cause Silas Moses to reassess his prospects for the future. He was a man in his late forties, in his prime, but looking at the years of his life that he had left to keep building his land holdings. In what direction did he want to go? It was something to think about. One action he took was to increase his land holdings to the northeast of Pine Town, closer to the new railroad. He had already been doing some of that in the 1860's.[1]

By 1870, Silas and Nancy had a family of growing children. Their oldest son, John William, was seventeen, almost ready to be on his own. Thomas Anthony (known as Tony) was fifteen, Mary Elizabeth was thirteen, James Richard was eleven, Ada Belle was nine, and Samuel Augustus was six. It had been six years since a new baby had been expected, but 1870 changed that. On February 23, 1870, Sarah Jane (Sally) arrived with great joy and excitement.[2] Although prospects for Pine Town had begun to dim somewhat, cotton production and marketing continued at a brisk pace. Cotton was still the best bet for making money, although transporting the cotton to market in Louisiana by ox wagon and then river flatboat was not easy or inexpensive.

Some tried using the rivers in Cherokee County and shipping by barge, but were not very successful. The fortunes of many in the neighborhood varied according to what they attempted to do – for some, the 1870's were a rough ride. Pine Town lost its mail contract in 1874 to Rusk, Texas, and the stagecoach line on the Palestine Road began to falter with the coming of the railroad.[3] Although Nancy lost one of her jobs, the postmistress, the Crumes still seemed to prosper, but Silas was watching the situation carefully.

By 1874, Silas and Nancy's son John, the first born, was twenty-one years old, and he was ready to go out on his own. A local girl had caught his eye, Sarah Sherman, and he married her on November 26, 1874.[4] It is probable that Silas provided some land for his son, and John may have already been working for his father at the cotton gin or grist mill as well. Silas' other sons who were old enough were probably doing the same. Every hand was needed. John's wedding was a happy occasion – hopefully the first wedding of many to come for Silas and Nancy to enjoy. However, in 1875, the family suffered a blow which was unexpected. Silas and Nancy's son Thomas Anthony (Tony) died on November the 9th.[5] He was only twenty years old, really just beginning his life, but he became the second family member to be buried in Pleasant Grove Cemetery, laid to rest beside his little sister. The family was crushed, and Christmas that year was rather bleak, but they had to continue on and they did.

Thomas Anthony "Tony" Crume

A little less than a year later would come the most cruel blow of all. In October of 1876, Nancy Catherine was not feeling well. She was forty-five years old, and although the family thought she was not old enough to be worried about the end of her life, they were wrong. Doctors were available in the area at Gent, but apparently they couldn't save her if they were consulted at all. She died on the 14th of October, 1876.[6] This was catastrophic for Silas Moses. Not only was he personally staggered, but he now had a houseful of children to see after alone. His daughter Mary was eighteen, James was seventeen, Ada Belle was fifteen, Samuel Augustus was twelve, and the baby Sarah was six. He hated to think about going on without Nancy by his side, and his children were just as bereft. Nancy would never see her beloved Kentucky again, but she had been for Silas a rock in a period of new, and by no means certain, ventures. Together they had built a family and a small kingdom all their own. Now she would take her place at Pleasant Grove alongside her beloved children. Although it felt like half of him was gone, Silas would go on with his life because he always had, and he had the children to comfort him.

One of Silas' children, his daughter Mary, was old enough during this period to get married at eighteen, and she had met someone that she favored. She married Alexander Acker, a local boy, on January 7, 1877, three months after her mother died.[7] It is possible that the wedding was already planned when Nancy died, but then again, Mary may have felt a sense of urgency to marry, with her mother gone and Mary not wanting to take her mother's place as a surrogate mother for the family. No matter the circumstances, the wedding took place, perhaps a break from the sadness in the family. Mary probably had to do most of the work for the occasion and it may have been more subdued than would be normal, but she was just as married and ready to start a life of her own.

However, if Silas was counting on Mary to take his wife's place to help with the younger children and take care of the house and other responsibilities, at least for a little while, he now had to rethink the situation. Without a doubt, his role and the rest of the family's part in household duties would have to be expanded to take over Nancy's responsibilities. As a partial solution, it probably fell to Ada Belle who was fifteen to take care of the house and help supervise the younger children. Fifteen-year-olds were expected to help with many of the household and farm chores in the rural families of the 1870's, but not normally to take the role of the mother in the family. This was exceptional, but Ada Belle probably had help from the other children. They were all accustomed to being busy working to keep the family going. Silas Moses was always occupied at many different tasks; his children could not be any different. He had a great interest in children and education, and so he added being a trustee for the local school district to his long list of activities.[8] He may have been a trustee for several years, but he definitely was in 1877 when he was listed as being so in county records.

In 1878, Silas apparently decided that he needed help raising his children and keeping his house in order because he remarried on October 1, 1878, to a widow, Sarah Lucinda Sherman Dendy. She had four children by her first marriage to Sidney A. Dendy, all grown and on their own by the time she married Silas Moses.[9] Silas was trying marriage a second time, probably because it suited him to be married, and to his surprise, he found he was able to care for someone else after losing his beloved Nancy. Silas's daughter, Ada Belle, had been running the household for about two years with the help of her younger brother and sister and caring for them when needed. How did she feel about the change in her position in the household? Was she relieved or resentful? Perhaps it was a little bit of both. She was seventeen and probably liked having more time for her own pursuits, but she had become used to caring for Sally, who was six when her mother died, and she was close to her younger brother as well. In any case, she had little choice but to accept the situation.

About a year later on December 5, 1879, Silas and Sarah produced an addition to the family, a little girl, Ida.[10] Her closest half-sibling was Nancy's last daughter, Sally, who was nine years old. Silas was very fond of children and had been since his years of living with the Marks family back in Meade County, Kentucky, in 1850, so the new little one delighted him. At fifty-four, he was probably proud of the fact that he was not through having children. However, things were not quite right with Sarah Dendy Crume's health after she had the baby, and she died in October of 1880.[11] Silas was a widower again, and this time he had a baby who needed care. He was not devastated this time; he

A Journey of Voices: Stewards of the Land 129

Silas Moses Crume House and Family. Silas is sitting on the porch holding the baby.

was shocked. He could not believe that this second marriage had lasted such a short period of time, had caused more pain, and had left him with another child to care for alone. It is hard to imagine that life was so hard on the Pine Town farm with the amenities that Silas was able to provide for his family that the women in the family could not survive. It probably had more to do with individual health problems and the uncertainty of life without the medicines and medical procedures which would be coming with the turn of the century. Whatever the reason for his losing his wives, Silas never tried marriage again. He did not want to take the risk, even after all of his children were grown. He was done.

The new decade was not starting out very well. It was almost as if the family could not turn things in a better direction, no matter what they tried. However, things were more encouraging for business in the Pine Town area in general. In the 1880's the Texas Penitentiary System built an iron smelter plant at Rusk, and the area for producing charcoal and gathering iron ore to supply the blast furnace was near the railroad about nine miles west of Rusk near Pine Town. A new trade center, Java, was created to service this industry, complete with stores, mills, a cotton gin, and a post office. This seemed to stimulate Pine Town as well for a few years.[12] There was also another small community nearby called Gent which had reached its zenith in the late 1870's. It offered mail service, a school, a cotton gin, two general stores, two churches, and several grist and saw mills. It was located north of the railroad on a high hill nine miles northwest of Rusk, Texas, which was referred to as Gent Mountain.[13]

Silas still had a feeling that the Pine Town area was not as prosperous as he would like it to be, so he continued to hedge his bets and buy land to the north closer to the railroad. He was not ready, however, to give up his current home place and business operations there. He was undoubtedly distracted through these years with his family problems, but his great love for the land wouldn't allow him to be depressed. It is not known how Silas' family situation worked itself out. Ada Bell did not marry until after the turn of the century, so perhaps she went back to taking care of the household duties and raising the younger children until they could fend for themselves, including the new baby, Ida.

The 1880's were a quiet period for the Crume family. The children grew up, and baby Ida grew older. Silas' business affairs seemed to still be profitable. With the bump in activity around Pine Town due to the charcoal and iron ore business nearby, he was doing well but still making plans for the future. He was selling off his land near Pine Town, perhaps in preparation for a move to his land farther north. He was still buying land, but not around Pine Town. More and more, he was feeling the need to relocate. In 1889 he sold the bulk of his land near Pine Town to the local doctor, R.A. McQueen, and Silas' son John sold his land also to the same man.[14] John may have decided to just help his father for a few years and save his money or perhaps he had business interests of his own. Sarah Jane, Silas's daughter, had apparently been given her own land by her father, and she sold it in 1891, also to R.A. McQueen[15]. The other children may have been given land also, but were not ready to sell. Of the children still not married, James was 30, Ada Belle was 28, Samuel "Gus" was 25, Sally was 19, and Ida was 10. Silas kept enough land to support the home place and his cotton gin and grist mill. He was a grandfather by now as well. John had five children, and Mary had six. Silas was 64 and perhaps feeling his years a bit.

In 1890, Samuel Augustus, "Gus" as he was known, decided at the age of twenty-six that he was ready to take a wife. He had been living and working a few miles away from the home place over at Gent where he became familiar with the Crawford family, long time members of the community who were originally from Georgia and Alabama. They had come to the Gent area around 1860, with Aaron Crawford and his son Isaac both being experienced farmers and operators of grist and saw mills. They each had eight children.[16] Gus married Elizabeth Isabel "Lizziebeth" Crawford, daughter of Isaac, on January 16, 1890, at her family's home in Gent. It was a large wedding, and the appropriately-named Rev. Perry Holyman officiated at the ceremony.[17]Gus was a big man like his father and had retained his friendly attitude towards the people he met. He never met a stranger. He was a farmer, knew something about keeping accounts, and may have been working some of his father's land or helping him with his mill and cotton gin. He might also have been working for the Crawfords or perhaps working for both his father and the Crawfords. In a year's time Gus and Lizziebeth had their first child, a son named Ernest Elmer, born on February 2, 1891.[18]

Sally, Ada Belle, and Gus Crume

The next year saw Gus's sister, Sarah Jane "Sally," following in her brother's footsteps because at twenty- two years of age, she was ready to leave home and have a home of her own. She was marrying Seborn Tankersley (whose name incidentally was a real mouthful). Although she did not have a mother to help her plan, a big wedding was in the works. She probably enlisted the help of her sisters, and all was ready on the night of December 6th, 1892, for the wedding the next day. However, Mother Nature had other ideas. A tornado struck the Pine Town area, and demolished several homes and businesses, killing at least one person and injuring many. One of the homes destroyed was that of Silas Moses, the storm destroying his cotton gin building and its contents as well. He was the only family member seriously injured, but the exact nature of his injuries is not known. A Rusk newspaper account a week later did not specify. A house belonging to Gus Crume was also destroyed. This probably meant that Gus had moved back to the Pine Town area after he married.

> Rusk, Texas, December 13, 1892
> The residence and gin house of Moses Crume was in the path of the storm. Both of them are completely wrecked. Mr. Crume was severely injured, the rest of the family are

unhurt, except slight bruises. The gin house contained about six bales of seed cotton which is almost a total loss. The house Gus Crume [was living in] was also carried away. It is strange how any of the people escaped, as the houses were blown level with the ground and the timbers scattered in every direction. No fences are standing in the track of the storm and but very little timber of any kind.[19]

What was Sally to do? Her wedding gown had blown away in the storm as well as all of the flowers and decorations and prepared food! Well, she was determined, and she married Seborn the next day right on schedule, at least according to family lore.[20] There may not have been any fancy trimmings, but she was just as married. This whole tornado event may have been a sign from God to Silas that it was time to move his family to the land he had been accumulating to the north. At least he probably reasoned it out that way because as soon as he was back on his feet, he rebuilt in the new location.[21]

Elizabeth Isabel "Lizziebeth"

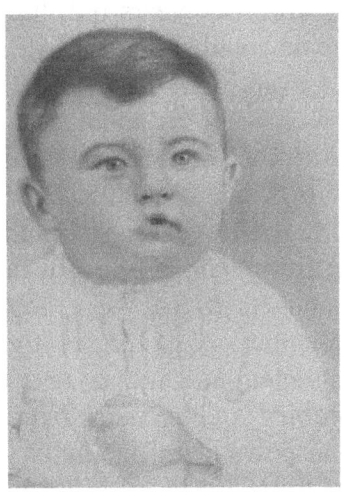
Jewel Luther Crume

The year after the tornado Gus became a father for the second time in 1893 when his son Jewell Luther was born on August 2.[22] He probably let Lizziebeth pick out the name. His sister Sally Tankersley also had a child, her first, in August of that year on the 31rst. The child was a girl, and they named her Velma.[23] In 1894, Silas Moses sold Gus 100 acres of land eight miles west of Rusk, Texas.[24] This land was in a very good location, although Gus and Silas would not be sure about that until a few years later. Silas' instincts had been telling him about the worth of the land for years, and he had bought a lot of it. It was a good two-year time period for Gus, but unfortunately, not for his sister Sally. On July 1, 1894, she died at the age of twenty-four of now unknown cause, another child of Silas Moses and Nancy to die early. She was buried in the Pleasant Grove Baptist Church Cemetery next to her family.[25] The "Crume row" at the cemetery was becoming longer. By this time, Silas had used some of the iron ore which was prevalent in the area to construct a walled structure at the cemetery around Nancy's grave and that of his little girl Susan Cole.

The Crume fortunes in personal matters were on a roller coaster it seemed, and 1895 was to prove to be another year on the ride. It started out on a happy note with the marriage of James Richard Crume to Mollie Elizabeth Stewart on January 30. James was thirty-six years old, had waited to get married, and by this time he could support a wife and family. He more than likely had land from his father and perhaps land of his own. His wife was thirteen years his junior, but she made a good partner for him. He and Mollie had three children by the end of the decade. [26]

In March of 1895, Gus and Lizziebeth's little two-year-old son, Jewell became sick and unexpectedly died, not an unusual occurrence for families of this time period but still very hard to accept. As if that were not enough for the family to bear, on September 26th Lizziebeth gave birth to another son who contracted pneumonia and died the same day. Drained from childbirth and heartsick over the loss of the baby, Lizziebeth also came down with pneumonia and was too weak to fight it. She died four days later.

In lightning quick succession, these events caused Gus's family to form a second row for the Crumes at Pleasant Grove Cemetery.[27] Gus was in shock and devastated. All he could think to do was to take his surviving son, Elmer, who was four years old, to live with his mother-in-law, Elmer's grandmother. He could not take care of his son and farm all day. It was a sad state of affairs from which Gus would need time to recover. He had lost all of his family except for this little boy in one year's time.

Also in 1897, Silas Moses had to hire lawyers to defend him against a suit by the State of Texas over delinquent taxes from a land purchase he had made with the heirs to the Roach estate. The question to be settled was who should have paid the taxes.[28] The outcome of this trying situation is not known, but Silas certainly would not have been happy to have to pay more taxes if that is the way that the case was settled. He was buying and selling land almost continuously during the 1860's through the 1890's. Occasionally things did not turn out as well as he hoped, but overall he was very successful at land speculation. His Crume genes held him in good stead. He sold more of his land in 1898 and 1900, and in 1901 he sold an oil lease to the Texas Western Oil Company[29]

Ida Mae Crume

In 1897, Silas's youngest child, Ida, was eighteen years old, and she had met a man that she wanted to marry. The wedding to William Merrell Stewart on March 11 was probably at home.[30] She was not the last child to marry, however. Ada Bell had remained at home taking care of her father and younger siblings since she was fifteen. She was now thirty-six years old and probably considered to be "on the shelf." But at the turn of the century, her life was in for some changes and the same was true for her younger brother, Gus.

By 1900, Silas Moses was seventy-five years old and not in good health. He had become his father. He was blind, had lost the use of his legs, and he was in a wheelchair. His father's blindness had proven to be hereditary. But he did not have to face his troubles alone as his father had. His children were there to meet his needs as his mighty strength waned. He did not have many years left.

13
The Birth of Maydelle, Texas

They named the new town Maydelle in honor of the daughter of Governor Thomas Mitchell Campbell, who had been instrumental in extending the State Railroad from Camp Wright to Palestine. Maydelle Campbell sang at the opening of the townsite.[1]

The land that Silas Moses had been buying for many years which was north of Pine Town and closer to the International and Great Northern Railroad was in a prime location. As early as the 1840's there had been settlers living in the area, and a prison branch known as Camp Wright was built there to house the convicts who came to cut wood for charcoal for the prison iron foundry at Rusk.[2] Silas owned land around Camp Wright and slowly began selling it off in the years before the turn of the century in 1900.[3] This land would be very important in the founding of a new town called Maydelle. Silas and his family continued to live where they had been, somewhat north of Pine Town, but they were close to the prison camp, Camp Wright, and therefore close to the future town of Maydelle.

In 1899, Gus received a letter from his aunt, Silas Moses's younger half-sister Eliza Jane. She and her husband had moved out West from Kentucky about fifteen years before, living part of the time in Nebraska and part of the time in New Mexico. This letter, although one of the few saved, does indicate that Silas Moses had kept in touch with his Kentucky family. However, in his last years when he was blind, communications with them had to come through his son, Gus.

A Journey of Voices: Stewards of the Land

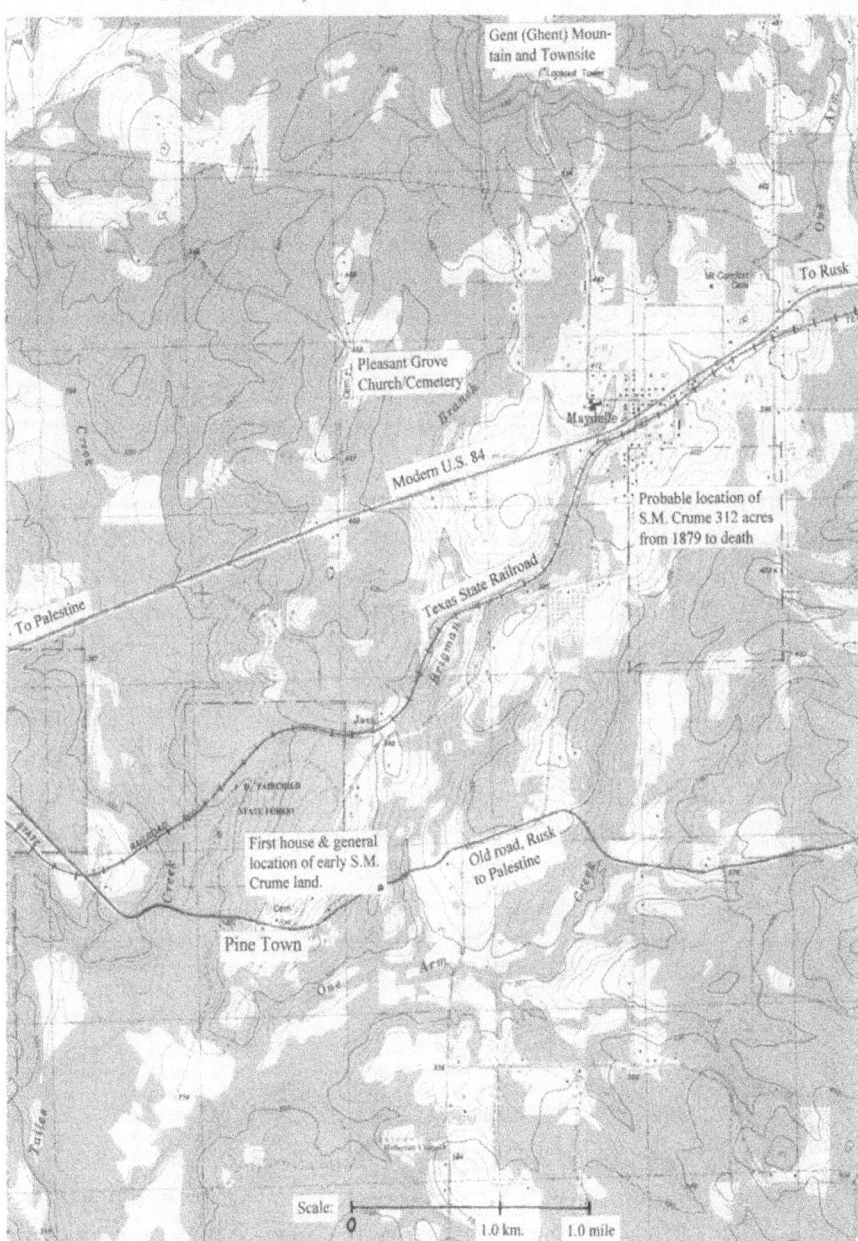

Created by Dean Gladow 2012

Lura made me a visit of one week. She is well. Says you must write her.

May 18, 1899
Tusas, Rio Arriba County, New Mexico

Mr. S.A. Crume
Dear nephew,

    I received your welcome letter some weeks ago. Was glad to hear from you all once more and to hear Brother Mose was improving. This leaves us well as common. Your cousin Katie's health is improving although she is very weak yet. She and her children, your cousin M.E. wife and children, started to Nebraska the 15th and M.E. and Katie's husband started to Idaho. I don't think Katie will stand the trip very well although she only has to be in the cars a part of two days or one night. I expect a letter tomorrow which I await its arrival anxiously. We shall have a lonely time this summer all the children and grandchildren gone but Oscar. I wish I could visit you folks and get some of them good watermelons. I don't get any good ones here. The seasons is too short to grow them but south of here the Mexicans raise muskmellons. They pack them in here on burros but they pull them green and when they get here they are not good. Your cousin Mary C. Basham wants to correspond with all of you folk. She is your Uncle John Crume's youngest child. She corresponds with me and sends her regards to all of you. Says you remember her to her Uncle Mose. Her P.O. address is Huff, Edmonson County, Kentucky. Give my love to all. I answered Fannie's letter. Write soon and often.

From your loving aunt
E.J. Hudson

    Eliza Jane had been the first child born to Dr. William C. Crume's second marriage, and thus she probably had the most interaction with Silas Moses before he moved away from home. Eliza Jane Hudson became the postmistress for Tusas, New Mexico in Rio Arriba County and served in that position for at least seven years. Her husband William Hall Hudson, a farmer in

May. 18, 99
Tusas
Rio arriba Co
New Mexico

Mr S A Crume
Dear Nephew I received your
welcome letter some week
ago was glad to hear from
you all once more & to hear Bro
Mose was improving this leaves
us well as common your cousin
Katie's health is improving
altho she is very weake yet
she & children your cousin
M.E wife & children started
to Nebr the 15 & M E & Katies
Husband started to Idaho I dont
think Katie will stand the trip
very well altho she only has to
be on the cars a part of 2 days &
one Night I expect a letter tomorrow

[margin: Iura made me a visit of one w[ee]ke she is well says you must write her] which I await its arrival anxiously we shall have a lonly time this summer all the children & grand children gone but Oscar I wish I could vis it you folks & get some of them good water melons I dont get any good ones hear the seasons is to shart to grow them but South of hear the Mexicans rais Muskmellon they Pack them in hear on Burrows but they Pull them green & when get hear they are not good — your cousin Mary C Basham wants to correspond with all of you folk she is your Uncle John Crumes youngest child she corresponds with me & sends her regards to all of you sais you remember her to her Uncle Mose her P.O. address Huff, Edmonson Co. Ky give my love to all I answered Fannies letter write soon & often from your loving Aunt E J Hudson

Kentucky and veteran of the Civil War, worked as a gold miner in New Mexico for seven years and eventually died there. The family lists William as being buried at nearby Tres Piedras along with a son, William P. However, Tusas had a cemetery and the men could have been buried there. Eliza moved back to Nebraska with the rest of her family and died there in 1917.[4] The cars that she speaks of in the letter were most likely railroad cars, as the automobile was barely in existence in 1902 and would not have been widely used in the West with its poor roads. The watermelons she mentions were as popular as peaches in the lives of many Southerners, including the Crume family.

Another letter to Gus from his Kentucky relatives arrived in 1902, and this one was from his uncle in Meade County, his mother's younger brother, John Finley Williams Jr.

Ekron, Kentucky
November 24, 1902

Mr. S.A. Crumes
Dear nephew,

I seat myself to drop you a few lines tonight. It has been raining all day today. We have been trying to gather corn, but it rains so much we get along very slow. We have a very good corn crop. It is selling at 35 cents per bushel. We have machines here that shuck our corn and tear the stalks all to pieces and blow it in the barn that are called shredders. It makes fine feed for stock. I did not have any shredded. They charge ten cents per shock, and it takes six wagons and ten men to run it. It shreds about 150 shocks a day. I hauled and put one hundred shocks and 5 tons of straw in the barn that will feed me most all winter. We have had a very warm winter so far and have just commenced feeding stock.

I suppose you saw in the paper a notice of brother Jim's death. I and Kate [John's wife] was there when he died. It was sad to me there was a ton of us children that are all gone but me. One buried in Kansas, four buried here in our family burying ground, and one in Texas, and two at Buck Grove Church. There was a large crowd at Buck Grove. Brother T.J. Duvall preached the funeral. Brother Jim lived in a Catholic neighborhood and all his neighbors were Catholics, but they thought a great deal of him.

There is a heap of sickness here such as typhoid fever and diphtheria among children. Tony [Anthony Vernon Williams, John F. Williams' son] has sold his farm and is going to live with his father-in-law Sam Allen. His children are all married and left him and Tony is going to live with him. He lives about five miles from here. Tony is teaching school this winter at a five months school.

I got a letter from you directed to James Williams in my care. I sent it to Emmett Williams and I have not seen any of them since I sent the letter. Do you raise any turkeys out there? There is a great many raised here. Everybody has a turkey on Thanksgiving Day. Kate [his wife] raised thirty-two. I have been trying to get her to kill one but she says they are too high at ten cents a pound and she has some that weigh seven pounds. So I will have to put up with a chicken.

This leaves us all well but Tommy [his son]. He has been in bad health for several years with nervous trouble. The doctors cannot cure him around here. We are going to send him to Vine Grove that is in Hardin County to a doctor. He is called a homeopath. He don't give medicine but doctors by sweating and bathing. He has cured several of nervous trouble so we thought we would try him.

Where is your sister Mary Acker? Does she live at the same place? I have received all of your receipts but hers. Well, I will close. Give my love to all and share a large portion to yourself. Write soon.

Your uncle, J.F. Williams

This letter revealed new inventions and some changes in farming practices which came with the turn of the century. It also discussed medical practices of the day. And, as John Williams sadly relates in this letter, he was the only Williams left of his generation, Nancy Catherine Crume's generation, in Kentucky. He eventually died in 1925, the last of the lively, industrious people that made up the John Finley Williams family. They were gone, but they left a rich heritage for the generations of family members that followed them. John spoke of the cemetery which was located on the family farm. It remained neglected and in a state of slow disintegration for many years until it was restored in 2009 by a descendant of the family, James Kendall. In a way, Nancy finally came home again in the person of her great granddaughter when the great granddaughter visited the area and the cemetery in 2009.

John Jr. and Katherine Williams

Another letter arrived from Kentucky in 1903 from one of Gus's cousins.

June 7, 1903

Mr. S. Crume
Java, Texas

Suppose you think I have gone off and died sure enough, but Mother has been sick and I have had so awful much work to do. I thought of you most every day last week, but when night came I was so tired, I would fall down to sleep. You must excuse me this time, and I will do better, but you always wait so long to write, you will know now how it feels.

You say the Texas people is lazy. I am anxious to come out and catch the disease for we Kentucky folks have to work and then barely live. Brother was on the train and saw your Mollie the other day. She said she was coming home soon. I haven't saw her for sometime. Well, I almost know you hear from her, and you won't tell me. You had better be good to me, for I may be the cause of you marrying. You will marry I know for you can't stiff me that way. We all will when the right one comes along.

Oh, I have a fat hand tonight. A bee kissed me on the back of my left hand, and it is hurting so. The colored boy was standing close by, and one kissed him on the nose. He will have closed eyes by morning. We all laughed till we cried at him before he went to bed. I am awful busy house cleaning and tending to meals. I taken up two hours house cleaning, and we had company every day. Aunt Catherine and Uncle Jack Williams [John Finley Williams, Jr.] came in the midst. I thought my time had come. I wished for my old rich bachelor. No, I have never met the bachelor I spoke of.

We have a lovely garden and have had some vegetables, but you folks have the soil for gardens. I am a gardener, so if I had the sandy, loamy soil for garden, I would soon get rich. Henry Williams has lost some of his cattle, said they had a terrible spring.

Now cousin, write me soon. I will have some pictures taken soon as I can. Many good wishes to Uncle [Silas Moses] and whole lots to you. Write soon.

Your Kentucky cousin Ree

Gus's light-hearted cousin wrote a teasing letter, referring to one of the ladies interested in Gus as a possible marriage partner. Although a widower with a somewhat tragic past, he was evidently popular with the ladies who perhaps felt badly that such a nice, friendly guy should have had such an unhappy experience early in his life.

Up until 1902, Ada Belle Crume had been living at home and taking care of her father, Silas Moses, and his house. She was forty-one years old and had never been married. However, in 1902 a newly-single man whose wife had died came calling. John Thomas Ferguson was fifty-eight years old, had been married for thirty-seven years to the same woman, Margaret Jane Jordan Ferguson, and all of his children by her were grown, if not yet gone from home. His wife had died in April of 1902, and he began to see Ada

John T. Ferguson

Belle sometime after that and before October of 1902.[5] He lived in nearby Anderson County near Alder Branch, the ancestral home of the Ferguson family. John was a farmer, an itinerant minister, and he was a congenial sort. Ada Belle must have seen in him a chance for a different life, and she was more than ready to make a change. In October of 1902 she married John Ferguson and moved to Anderson County.[6] This left Gus, Ida and Merrill Stewart and their baby, plus a boarder still living on the farm with Silas. Gus's young son, Ernest Elmer, continued to live with his Crawford grandparents.[7]

Although neither John nor Ada was young, they did produce a child about a year after they married on September 15, 1903.[8] Harold Augustus Ferguson would be their only child together, but Ada Belle was very happy and grateful to have him. After waiting as long as she did to have a family of her own, she wanted to make the most of the years that she would have to enjoy that family. She felt blessed.

Ada Belle and her brother Gus had become close over the years probably because they had lived at home longer than the rest of Silas's children. Gus, being a sociable fellow, didn't hesitate to go visit his sister in Anderson County. It was through these visits to his sister that he became acquainted with John Ferguson's older children who were still living at home. John's only daughter Lanora Belle (known as Nora) was a twenty-five-year-old school teacher, teaching at Crockett, Texas, but she came home to Alder Branch on the weekends when possible. She had a younger brother, William Hugh (known as Willie) who was nineteen and still living at home.[9] Gus began to take an interest in Nora and wrote her letters when he wasn't visiting. Just five days after John and Ada Belle had their baby, Gus wrote the following letter to Nora.

Java, Texas
September 20, 1903
Miss Nora Ferguson
Palestine, Texas

Little Niece,
   Your letter to hand. I received one Thursday also. It had been all over the world except this place, and it came here Thursday. I

had begun to think you had forgotten me already, you see, but I guess it was about so anyway. Well, the widow was here all day with all them sweet little children, and we sure did have a time. Just left, and I thought I would tell you about it. Well I did not attend the carnival. I was over there the week before and could not go twice – two times you see – ha ha!

Well, I have picked out one bale of cotton and did not pick as much as you did either in one day. Say, I tell you, you come over and pick for me and I'll board you and do the cooking. You see, that [is] a big thing. Then I'll let you stay here during the associations – ha ha! You see I know how to fix it, don't I.

Well, we had roasting ears for dinner today. Oh, it was a sight to see me and that widow eat corn and smile at each other across the table – ha ha. Well, I am sorry I can't get to come to see my new kinfolks, but I guess I'll see him when he comes to see me. This is a busy time with me now gathering my crops and cooking.

I am sorry Tom says I must quit writing to you. You tell him I said he had a widow and for him to stick to her like a leach. Oh say, tell me who that batchelor was that wrote you from Cherokee. I'll quit – I won't run against a batchelor. They are a tough set, and I don't think it would be any use for me to swim against him. Do tell me in your next, "well, that was a good letter you wrote. Write another one like it." I think I have done well this time, don't you?

Well, give my love to all and also the young nephew, John Thomas, Ward, and teacher Talmage. Write soon and a long letter. As ever your loving uncle.

S.A. Crume
(drew flowers around Nora's name)

Obviously, this letter revealed that Gus liked to tease. He did refer to his new nephew and the fact that he was busy farming and cooking for the small group left at home – his father and sister and her family. The associations he referred to were district meetings of the Baptist church. It sounded like he was trying to make Nora jealous, and she was doing the same thing to him, but in a teasing way. He addressed her as his niece because she was

Nora Ferguson Crume

the stepchild of his sister, making for a somewhat complicated relationship. It was soon to be obvious that there was more involved between Nora and Gus than teasing, however, because when the fall weather set in that year, Gus asked Nora to be his wife, and she accepted. The corn-eating widow with the sweet little children had lost out. Gus knew that at long last he had found the person to complete his life and be a mother to his young son. On November 19, 1903, the wedding took place, perhaps where Gus had been living near Gent, Texas, or where Nora had been living at her father's house.[10] At least two accounts were written for the local papers.

Mr. S.A. Crume and Miss Nora Ferguson were married Nov. 19, 1903 by Rev. P.C. Shilling in the home of the bride near Gent, Cherokee County, Texas. The two thus made one are to be congratulated in their choice of each other. I heartily extend wishes. The groom is a fine specimen of young manhood. An Apollo and a Hercules almost combined. The bride, daughter of a loved minister, will prove to be a wife such as Paul and Soloman say should be. The groom's father is a saint over 80 years old and blind. It was good to talk with them both – strong friends and true of Brother Hayden.[11]

Dear Echo:
Yesterday evening, the 19th, it was the writer's happy privilege to unite in the holy bonds of matrimony Brother S.A. Crume and Sister Nora Ferguson. Bro. Crume resides in Cherokee County near Gent. He is a member of Pleasant Grove Baptist Church, and a well-to-do and all-around good citizen, having an enviable reputation for honesty in his business dealings and steadfastness to Baptist ideals and standards in his religious life. This I consider is saying a good deal for a fellow,

especially in a time of general financial depression like this. But there are two things the boll weevil will never do, viz: Dam up the matrimonial stream or bankrupt the undertaker. Thank God Cupid has still got a monopoly of power in East Texas. Bro. Crume remembered us liberally and it was gratefully received.

Sister Nora is the accomplished daughter of Rev. J.T. Ferguson, and the only thing that I regret about this marriage is that Walston Springs church will lose the help and influence of Sister Nora, as she will remove her membership to Pleasant Grove. She was also a member of ladies' society, and certainly she has ever been an aid and helper to her church and pastor.

After the wedding ceremony, the assembled guests (with your scribe several feet in the lead) repaired to the spacious dining room where we proceeded to do ample justice to the old-time wedding repast that was set before us.

After the supper was over and the guests were making preparations to leave, Sister Nora presented me with six volumes of Ridpath's Universal History. I could not express my thanks then or now. May God's blessings be upon them, for Jesus' sake, Amen!

P.C. Shilling[12]

These news clippings were effusive to the point of gushing in their praise of the bride and groom, probably to the embarrassment and chagrin of the groom. Being rather humble, especially about his appearance, he would never have considered himself an Apollo or Hercules. However, he was a good looking man, and he did have a good reputation in the community. The articles revealed the depressed economy of the times and the minister's ecstatic joy at being paid well. They also demonstrated that the Crumes and Fergusons were still doing reasonably well in spite of the times. They were able to afford a nice wedding and a gift of books for the minister. That gift may have been costly because books were not all that common in rural areas. The gift also demonstrated Nora's teaching background and her interest in learning. The two articles seemed to confuse the place of the wedding. Nora should have still been living with her father in

Anderson County and not at Gent in Cherokee County where the groom was living. Also, Shilling was obviously the minister of Nora's home church, Walston Springs, in Anderson County, although he could have performed the ceremony at Gent.

At long last Gus was able to retrieve his son from the grandparents and provide a home for him. However, it was not to be an easy transition for Elmer who was twelve years old by that time and had been indulged by his grandparents, partly because they felt sorry for him in the loss of his mother and partly because he was their only grandchild from their daughter who had died.[13] Nora, however, was a school teacher used to dealing with all types of children, and she was up to the task of making a home for Elmer and bringing him into the warmth of her family.

Nora also took on the task of caring for Gus's father, Silas Moses. Silas was in a wheel chair by this time and blind. He still had all of his mental capabilities, however, and he didn't want anyone feeling sorry for him. For most of his life, he had been a powerful force in the community, a tremendous energy source for his family. According to family accounts, whenever he sensed that someone was feeling sorry for him, he would shout, "I think I'm gonna get married." This would usually tone down the pity party that some well-meaning person was trying to get started.[14] Nora was patient and kind in her dealings with Silas Moses, and she had the help of Gus. With the marriages of John T. Ferguson and Ada Belle Crume and Nora and Gus, a link was formed between two great family lines, the Crumes and the Fergusons, and also the lines which had converged with the Crumes and Fergusons in the past – the Jordans, the Williams, the Lincolns, and the Withers as well as others. The children of Gus and Nora would have a rich heritage on which to stand and launch themselves into the future.

In 1906 a new resurgence of energy came to Cherokee County in the form of the Texas State Railroad which was being constructed through Cherokee county from Rusk to Palestine in Anderson County. Construction had actually begun in 1896 to support the iron foundry at Rusk, but by 1906, passenger service was being considered, so depots and communities would be needed along its route. In 1910 the new town of Maydelle was constructed near the site of Camp Wright. The land upon which Maydelle sat was purchased by three investors, indirectly and in part from Silas Moses Crume who had sold land in the area years before in 1891 to one of them, J.R.(S?) Sherman.[15] Although the other small towns in the area received a slight boost from all this activity and actually did construct some new businesses, it soon became apparent that Maydelle was going to take people and businesses from them in order to grow. There was no stopping the growth of the town in the next few years, until finally by 1914 Pine Town, Gent, and Java had essentially become deserted ghost towns.[16] Silas' uneasy feelings through the 1890's had been justified, but he had planned for the future, so his family was in a good position.

In 1908, Silas Moses decided to transfer his remaining land parcels to his children. This was reminiscent of his great, great grandfather, Philip Crume Sr. Silas felt this would be cleaner than waiting until his eminent death and trying to use a will. He gave each of his remaining children fifty acres. John William, his first born son, got the home place except for the house, outbuildings and ten acres which would remain with Silas Moses until he died. They would then be transferred to Gus. Perhaps Silas was remembering what happened to his also-blind father, Dr. William Crume, and so he kept something for himself. He also provided a small sum of money for his granddaughter Velma Tankersley, daughter of Sally who had died at a young age.[17] John William then sold his portion of the land to Gus, and in 1908, John and his family moved to Grady, in eastern New Mexico. He was looking for a new area to try to build something on his own and perhaps also had health problems which prompted the move to a drier climate. Ada Belle Ferguson did the same thing – sold her land to Gus.[18]

On March 23, 1912, Silas Moses Crume's successful life in Texas ended. He died peacefully and took his place beside Nancy in the Pleasant Grove Cemetery in the long Crume row.[19] He was eighty-six years old and had lived a long, full life, although his last years were not ones he would have chosen. He would prove to be the last of the great stewards of the land in his particular Crume family line. Circumstances would prevent the emergence of another of his stature although there would continue to be farmers among his descendants. Agriculture was changing all across America. Silas had profited from cheap and plentiful land, just as his ancestors had, but those conditions were beginning to disappear for the vast number of farmers, even in as land-rich a place as Texas. Nevertheless, Silas had achieved the dreams of his childhood. He had inherited the skills to manage and develop land, and he had built through a powerful energy and strength a very successful life, an endeavor he felt was his God-given purpose. It had not always been easy, especially in his personal life, but overcoming the challenges had given him much satisfaction. He had known what he wanted to do, and he had accomplished it. He had left for his children a legacy of hard work and purpose, a reliance upon divine Providence, and a willingness to contribute to the community in which he lived. At the end he was ready to go, to be with his loved ones.

Ironically, his first born son, John William died a month before Silas did, almost to the day, on February 26 in Grady, New Mexico. His opportunity to build something of his own was cut short. His widow returned to the Maydelle area along with their one remaining unmarried child. Of their ten children, all had been born in Cherokee County, but when the family moved, John and Sarah took the children to new places where the children stayed to build lives in New Mexico and Oklahoma. John's sister

James Richard "Jim" Crume

Mary Elizabeth Crume Acker

Mary also had ten children and lived in the Waco, Texas area. She died on September 8, 1928. James Richard had eight children and moved back and forth between Cherokee County and Anderson County, Texas several times. He died on August 27, 1925. Ada Bell had only the one child and lived in Anderson and Houston Counties. She died on January 22, 1931. Ida had twelve children and lived at Maydelle until 1917 when she and her family moved to Palestine, Anderson County, Texas. She died on August 21, 1926, four years after her last child was born.[20]

None of Silas Moses' children lived to be as old as he did. Samuel Augustus came the closest at eighty years of age. It is not known how many of Silas's children inherited heart and blood vessel disease, but Gus and James did, several of the children died in their sixties and seventies of now unknown causes, and several died young. Ida, his last child, also went blind before her death and died early at the age of forty-seven.[21] In spite of these early deaths, Silas left behind a very large group of Crumes when all of his grandchildren were counted, the better to insure that his name and his genes would live on in Texas and be carried to other locales as well.

Enduring Inheritance
14

"Do you think Great Grandpa knew when he divided his land among his children that it would be hard for any of them to repeat his success?" I was talking with Mom on a lazy summer afternoon about the family. We always liked to sit outside on lawn chairs in the shade. In earlier years Mom had read to my brother and me at these times, but now we just talked.

"I think his thoughts were that he wanted to be fair in dividing what he had left with all of his children. He wanted, in giving them a piece of his land, to give them a piece of himself, which was all the same thing to him," my mother replied. "His thinking was no different from his ancestors."

"But, he lost a chance to help his children, especially the boys, to become the success that he had been," I protested, unable to see the pattern that had developed in the Crume family over the years.

"I don't think the Crume men, or the women, ever expected to receive a large inheritance from their parents which would make their own endeavors easier. They all loved a challenge, and making their own fortune was half the fun of having one if they were successful." Mom thought a minute. "They didn't seem to worry about having more than enough. They were too busy building and creating by any means available. Some were successful, and some were not. It seemed to depend upon the individual skills, energy, and drive that each Crume family member possessed. It also depended upon what they wanted to do with their lives. Some were content to have less and give more."

"Yes, I can see that in looking at the various Crume men and women. A point could be made here that behind every strong, successful Crume man stood an equally strong woman. Philip had his Sarah and Anna, Ralph Sr. had his Mary, Ralph Jr. had Mary Lincoln, Dr. William had Susannah and Mary Ann, and Silas had Nancy Catherine and Sarah. Those women were courageous and sturdy, the rocks on which the families grew and became successful. When I think about Nancy Catherine dealing with that Indian woman with the knife and Anna Crume riding a flatboat down the Ohio River in December with all those young kids, I just get chills." I was glad I would never have to cope with such things.

"By all means, let's give the Crume women their due. There were many like them in American history although they don't get much play in the history books," Mom agreed wholeheartedly.

I could sense a history lesson coming on, so I quickly changed the subject back to Silas Moses. "I guess Silas knew what he was doing after all, and he hoped his children would make their own way just fine."

"They did, but it wasn't easy." Mom was thinking of the next generation, and it was a generation she knew very well. "They lived in a different and very difficult time period. It took a strong will, a stiff spine, and the ability to laugh through hardship to survive. Even if they survived, they were not the same in prosperity as they had been before. Silas was the last real steward of the land in our family line because the ability to own land underwent a vast transition with hard times."

"Well, let's discuss hard times in our own kitchen. Can we bring in hamburgers for supper tonight?" It was time to get back to the present.

A Family on the Move

After Samuel Augustus "Gus" Crume married Nora Ferguson in 1903, the succeeding years up until 1912 when Silas Moses died were spent in continuing the farming operation that Silas Moses had started, perhaps including the cotton gin. Gus had purchased some of his brothers' and sisters' land which they had received from Silas Moses, adding to his own acreage, but it is not clear whether he and his family were living with Silas or Silas was living with them. By 1910, the census records were listing Gus as the head of household and not Silas, so perhaps when Gus married, he became the head of the household because Silas was becoming frail. The house and the small acreage around it probably remained in Silas's name until his death according to his wishes.[1]

The land which had formerly belonged to Silas Moses, and was now mostly Gus's property, was located very near to Maydelle which was continuing to grow and put stress on the neighboring towns. Nora had retired from teaching school when she married and was content to help her husband build a home and a family. On the national level, there had been a small war fought in 1898, the Spanish American War, which lasted about five months and made a hero of Teddy Roosevelt who later became President of the United States. This conflict would have been written about in the newspapers and of interest to the Crumes, but otherwise probably did not affect them much.

Gus's family was continuing to grow in the same way as the town of Maydelle, beginning with James Arthur, born on September 2, 1905, on the Silas Moses farm.[2] Elmer, Gus's first born son, was fourteen when Art, as he came to be known, was born. It is not known what Elmer thought about this new family member, but he accepted the fact that new children would be entering the family. Nora and Gus were determined that the family would meld together even though the older boy would perhaps never be as close to his half-brothers and sisters as they would have liked. There was too much age difference. In 1912 when Silas Moses died, Art was seven years old, but Elmer was twenty-one and would soon be married and gone from home. Art was followed in two years by Samuel Morris on November 11, 1907.[3] He was usually known as Morris, but he used the name Sam in his last years. Lura Gladys was born on December 28, 1910, the first girl in the family.[4] She always used the name Gladys because she just did not like her first name.

As was normal for brothers and sisters, the two older boys were given the job of keeping track of their little sister, and she tagged after them wherever they went. They soon learned how to get her into difficulties which would require their mother, so that they could go on about the business of being boys. Nora and Gus were happy, and these years were still fairly prosperous for the family. The first three children of their marriage were all born on the Silas Moses farm, giving Silas Moses a chance to be around some new grandchildren. Portraits were done of the children and the family as a group - complete with no smiles - and the clothes they wore were formal and very well made. Nora was a very good seamstress and made most of the family's clothes for

The S.A. Crume Family of Maydelle, Texas

much of her marriage, but in these first years the family may have been able to afford some ready-made clothing on occasion.[5]

After Silas Moses died in 1912, a way of life seemed to die with him. Changes were coming in the community and outlying areas. Pine Town and other small towns in the county disintegrated into ghost towns, and the center of activity was Maydelle. The economy of the county still centered in lumber and cotton, but other crops and livestock production were gaining in popularity. The boll weevil infestation had made an impact on the cotton business although cotton continued to be raised. When Gus married Nora in 1903, the minister remarked upon the havoc wrought by the boll weevil, and the years that followed had seen no end to the continuing scourge. The ideas were becoming more accepted that growing cotton was hard on the soil and current farming methods were also harmful. To stay in farming meant learning new ways of doing things and finding new crops. However, no one seemed really interested in attacking these problems seriously until the Great Depression occurred in the 1930's.

Gone were the old days of plentiful land at a cheap price. Land speculation was still possible, but it was riskier, especially on credit. The successful farmers had increased their land holdings to very large amounts, and they utilized tenant farmers or sharecroppers to make the land pay.[6] Gus's holdings were not that large. Even owning a cotton gin was not a simple proposition any more. Technology had provided more efficient equipment to gin the cotton, and the machines were placed in buildings along the railroad rights-of-way to provide for easier shipping of the cotton to Eastern textile mills by rail.[7] All of these problems and new challenges were facing Gus, and although he loved farming the land, the rules were changing from what he had always known.

If cotton was not king anymore, then a new king had arrived to take its place. In 1901 oil had been discovered near Beaumont, Texas at Spindletop, and in 1902 the well at Spindletop produced more than seventeen million barrels. This discovery opened the first of the series of new oilfields that made Texas and Oklahoma the top producers in the nation. Even in Cherokee County, there was oil activity, but unfortunately, not on any of the Crume land.

It made men millionaires overnight. It also diversified the region's economy and fueled, literally, the automobile industry which was to come.[8] Taking advantage of this opportunity required owning land with oil underneath it, and the Crumes were not that lucky. Silas Moses had been fortunate in his land choices, but it didn't extend to this, at least not in his lifetime or that of his children.

After 1912 and perhaps even before, Gus could no longer make a living just farming, and he no longer had a cotton gin business or grist mill because of his location close to Maydelle. He decided to build a nice house on the edge of Maydelle for the family, and it included some acreage for him to use for a farming operation. Gus continued to make improvements on the house in the first years that the family lived there because he knew the carpentry trade, also adding orchards, gardens, trees, barns, and play houses for the children.[9] Because he needed to supplement his income with town jobs in Maydelle, he was in an ideal location. He became the depot agent for the Texas State Railroad and also worked as a deputy sheriff for the county. His cheerful, outgoing personality served him well in both jobs, and he was liked and respected in the community. He also continued to work with the church in various capacities as his father had done. It was very important to him, a part of what defined him as a man.

Nora, along with Gus, was a credit to her community. As well as being a busy mother, she was also a willing worker in church activities and was known as the "go to" person at Maydelle when someone was ill or in need of help. Her home was always open to visits from relatives and people she didn't always know personally who were traveling through the neighborhood. All this increased her work load considerably, but she was a happy person, similar to her husband, and never complained. Because of her years as a teacher and her upbringing in the church, she was a strict disciplinarian as was her husband, but her children always knew they were loved and important to their parents.[10]

Gus's little family continued to grow with the birth of another girl in 1915 on January 21st, Floyce Mae.[11] He also lost a member, at least from the family circle at home, when his oldest son Elmer married in 1913 on August 11 in Maydelle to Bertha

The Gus Crume Family in Front of Their New Home at Maydelle

The railroad train and depot at Maydelle, Texas on the 4th of July

Lee Stidham Moore. Elmer probably never lived with his father's family in Maydelle - only for several years on Silas Moses' farm. Elmer made Gus a grandfather with the birth of his son Brackston on August 9, 1914, and the birth of a daughter Pauline on December 11, 1915.

Elmer and his family, which eventually grew to five children, moved from Maydelle before 1918 and after stays of several years at other towns, arrived in Houston, Texas, where they lived for the rest of their lives. Elmer worked for the railroad as a conductor for a while and then as a city fireman for many years. Their other children were Lucille born on September 11, 1918, Ernest Elmer Jr. born on July 6, 1924, and Joan born on August 1, 1928.[12]

Elmer, Bertha, and Lucille Crume

Pauline and Brackston Crume

Through these years, the Gus Crume family never ceased to find a way to have a good time, and the Christmas season was the zenith of good times. Gladys recorded her memories of the Christmas holidays of her childhood.

One of my earliest recollections of Christmas was going to Grandpa Ferguson's (John T. Ferguson and Ada Belle Crume Ferguson). The trip over in our shiny black surrey pulled by two sparkling grey horses, Ruby and Prince, was exciting in itself. There was a place we stopped to get a drink at a well with a roof over it. Then there was the little sawmill store where we bought sardines, cheese, and crackers. We had to get out and walk up a steep hill, while Dad led the horses, and, of course we walked across the river bridge! We loved Grandpa so, as he romped with us, playing hide-and-seek, roaring like a bear down on his all fours, and playfully popping his black snake whip at us. I remember all of the fresh fruits, nuts, and candy we nibbled on all day.

Then one childhood Christmas was spent with Uncle Floyd (Ferguson, Nora's brother) and his family on his farm. I remember the huge Christmas tree. My aunt and mother made large ragdolls for my little girl cousin and me. Then my oldest cousin, Julius, took my cousin and me to the Christmas service at the church in his pretty little buggy drawn by his black horse. Best of all were the evenings before we retired when we had music – spinet, guitar, and harmonica – and we all sang and danced.

Christmas celebrated 'our way' was best of all, though. The week before we would decorate the house – artificial wreaths were hung at the windows and a huge red paper bell with streamers hung over the dining table. Then there would follow a lot of baking – nut and fruit cookies, cakes, and pies. Dad usually would butcher a hog so that we would have all of that nice fresh meat at that time. Dad and the boys would go to the river brakes for a fresh cedar tree, which we all shared in decorating. Christmas Eve, Dad would wake us calling, 'Christmas

Julius Ferguson and his Black Horse

Eve Gift'! There was such an air of excitement and anticipation throughout the day. Before we went to bed we hung our stockings to be filled the next day with fruit, nuts, candies, and some fireworks. Dad always believed in having firecrackers, sparklers, and roman candles at Christmas. Then Christmas morning, Dad got up early and built a roaring fire in the round iron stove, and began to call, 'Christmas Gift! You better get up! Looks like old Santa's been here!' Feet began to hit the floor running, as each of us stormed in to see what we had. There were always gifts under the tree, as well as the filled stockings which we hurriedly emptied into cardboard boxes. Then Dad got out his pocket knife and peeled an orange for each of us to eat prior to our breakfast. By noon, our dining table was loaded with every delicious yuletide food, and we ate as we wished, after having the first thanks and seated meal, for the rest of the day. Different friends or relatives dropped in throughout the day.[13]

By 1918, in spite of a good family life, Gus had begun to wonder if he could do better financially somewhere else. He may have been under more financial stress by this time than he felt he could manage, but perhaps not. He had been on a trip to the south down on the Gulf Coast of Texas which was a large farming area with plentiful fruit orchards, and he liked what he saw there. He knew the carpenter trade which he could use to supplement any farming that he did and, of course, the railroad business and law enforcement. To sell out and move was not an easy decision – Cherokee County was the only home he had ever known. However, his

Taken just before the move to Alvin, Texas - Still no smiles except for little Floyce

siblings had tried living other places (and some returned to the Maydelle area), so perhaps he felt like trying something different.

In 1918 the decision was made, and Gus, Nora and the children made the move to Alvin, Texas, bringing their livestock with them and buying a farm on the edge of the city limits. This farm did not have large fields, but it did have enough land to have a small pasture, some fields, gardens, and a fig orchard. Besides the house, they had several outbuildings and a barn. The Crumes were not too far from the Gulf of Mexico, and it was a new world of experiences for them. The climate, the land topography, and the close proximity of large cities were all different living conditions from what they had known.

After only a year or two of living in the new place, Gus realized he couldn't make a living just farming and found work in Galveston as a carpenter where he could board and work during the week. Even Arthur, though only fifteen or sixteen years old, also found work in Galveston, as an electrician no less. They could handle the farm work on the weekends. [14]

Arthur "Art" Crume at Galveston

The children were in school, and Nora was keeping the house running, and sometimes the farm, while Gus was away from home working during the week. The children helped with chores on the farm, and as they grew, they generally enjoyed the life in Alvin. However, the move turned out to be a life-changing decision for Gus and his family because in making this decision, Gus forever ended his chance to build an estate such as his forebears had done before him. He would never again own his own land. He, like many others, would become a tenant farmer, a renter, or sharecropper, and this would not enable him to build up enough capital to buy his own land. Perhaps originally he felt the move to Alvin was worth the gamble, and apparently he didn't regret his decision after the move.

Although the move had not worked out as well as he had hoped, he was not going to let this keep him from moving forward. No matter where he was, he had the ability to make something out of nothing and find satisfaction in doing so. And wherever he went, he always organized a church if one was not readily available. He needed the support of a church, and in like manner, he needed to support one. His cheerful, giving nature seemed to carry him through, and his wife was the same sort of person. He carried some of his father's genes, but not all of them. He could provide a life for himself and his family, but not the life his father had built. The family fortunes were slowly heading downhill, but the family members were loyal to Gus and his decisions. It was the way families were supposed to operate in those days.

The years 1917- 1918 were also turbulent for the nation as a whole. The United States had become embroiled in the world war which was currently raging in Europe and around the globe. The President of the United States had declared that this was the war to end all wars, but in this he was overly optimistic. This war utilized nasty trench fighting with weapons such as poison gas, and for the most part it was still fought on land and sea. The airplane was just coming into being and played a small role, but would not really come into its own until later. Young men all over the country were called upon to go and fight across the ocean, and this would be an eye-opening experience for those who survived it and returned. Most had never traveled any farther away from home than their own neighborhoods and farms. This circumstance was to prove pivotal to life in America after the war. For many young farm boys, life would be forever different after what they had experienced in the war, not just from the fighting, and a great number would not return to rural living. The drop in cotton prices after WWI aided the exodus from agriculture. In the words of a popular song of the day, "How you gonna keep'em down on the farm after they've seen Paree?"[15]

In the Silas Moses Crume family, only one fought in WWI, mostly because the majority of the male children and grandchildren were not the right age. James Richard "Jim" Crume's son, William W. "Billy" or "Willy", served in the 90th Division, 359th United States Infantry, Company M with the American Expeditionary Forces in France.[16] Before going overseas, he wrote this postcard to his Uncle Gus.

Hello Uncle,

How are you by this time? Fine, I hope, as I am all OK. Well, say Uncle Gus, I got the box you and Aunt Nora sent and was real glad to get it. ha! ha! The boys don't get such boxes as that often down here. Answer soon. From your nephew WWC Company M, 359th Infantry, Camp Travis, San Antonio, Texas

On the front of the card was a picture of his commanding general and his staff in their WWI uniforms. Billy had taken time to thank his uncle and aunt for a "care package" they sent him at his training camp. He was a big kid, supposedly six feet six inches tall. One story that was passed down by his family told of an incident concerning his height which happened before he went into the army. He was often teased about his height, and one time a rather short individual asked him, "How's the weather up there?" Being more than tired of hearing that question, he spit in the man's face and said, "It's raining like hell!" That ended the discussion. Unfortunately once he entered the fighting overseas in France, he was one of the many who did not survive the war. His height was not a good fit for trench warfare because every time he stood to his full height, he made an excellent target. His body was shipped home to be buried in the Pleasant Grove Cemetery in the Crume row. The family was proud of him but heartbroken to lose him so soon.[16] It is not known what the Crume family felt about the war other than relief when it was over. Sadly, to the bitterly disappointed President Wilson, the end of the war did not turn out to be the beginning of a peaceful world which utilized diplomacy under a League of Nations organization.[17]

In 1919, Gus and Nora's last son, Clyde Martin Crume,.was born on September 9 in Alvin, Texas.[18] Not only was he their last son but he was their last child. Nora was sick for some time after the birth which put a real strain on the family. Everyone had to do more. It was just as well Clyde was the last child because they could not afford any more children, in more ways than one. They welcomed him with joy, however. The whole family did. Everyone in the family considered Clyde his or her baby, and they tried to spoil him at every opportunity. It was a good thing that Clyde was fairly level-headed. He was named for a neighbor's husband who was returning from service in WWI the day Clyde was born. One story of Clyde as a baby was recorded by his sister, Gladys, and it also revealed some of the family's life in Alvin, Texas.

We lived on the coast of Texas then, and a severe Gulf storm occurred. During those storms, we had to nail bars on the doors and shutters on the windows to keep them from blowing out, leaving only one door open away from the wind. The yard had filled with water up to the porch. Then suddenly we missed Clyde, the baby. We searched frantically. The back door was open. I remember rushing out madly into the water, feeling and groping everywhere trying to find him, crying all the while. Then suddenly Mother called, "We found him." Oh, the vast relief of those words! He had got behind some mattresses in the big boys' room, where they had been laid to get bed slats to bar the doors, and he had fallen asleep so he hadn't heard our anxious cries.[19]

As part of moving to Alvin, Gus was dealing with a different county, Brazoria. Farming and ranching animal brands had to be registered by each county in Texas for the ranchers living in that county, so Gus had to go through the County Treasurer to register a brand for his animals. The following letter was the result.

July 26th, 1920
Mr. S.A. Crume
Alvin, Texas
Dear Sir:
I have searched the records fully and find S C taken most anyway that you can think of it with bars under it and above it, half circles above and under it, but no bars after or in front of it, so I have had this recorded for you, -- S C -- to be placed on the left hip on cattle and right shoulder on horses. Hope this will suit you. This is what we call S C bar in front and right both. You can use a small dash on both sides of the S C and you have it, Bar S C Bar. Did not put the ear mark on at all as very few use them, but if you wish an ear mark let me know what it is and I will add it and it won't cost you another cent. You paid me the 25 cents and that is all there is to this. Any time that I can be of any further service to you down this way, whether in my line or not, let me know and I will gladly do it for you.

Very respectfully,
D.F. Remley

1920 began a new decade and was to signal a tumultuous change for cotton growers. Up until this time, even with some down periods, the price of cotton had held up, encouraging farmers to plant more and more of it. Record crops were planted in 1920, but about half way through the summer of that year, prices began to fall disastrously from forty-two cents a pound to less than ten cents a pound. After this huge drop which drove many out of farming, the industry rallied by going to reduced planting, but this did not address the basic problems with cotton production. Because producers failed to address the serious problems of unscientific farming, the crop-lien system, an unsatisfactory marketing system, and overproduction, the industry was doomed to another downturn in 1926 and again in 1931. The tenant farmer was at the bottom of the production chain, and thus was hurt the most when these low prices occurred.[20] Even a small farmer like Gus who owned his land had a difficult time with downturns. In 1920, Gus was in Galveston working and wrote a letter to Nora.

Sunday night
1920

Dearest wife and kids,

Well, I have been busy all day, but I stayed down to the beach all this evening hoping to see Arthur but was disappointed, so if he comes tonight, I won't be there. I am feeling better since I came home and ate supper. I had a terrible headache, but it is about easy now, so I hope you are all well. Well, the cotton brought us $37.50 so I didn't do a thing but go and spend $16 of it to send home to you all in something to eat. I got one package sugar, 50 lbs. lard, some lamb, corn, salmon, and pork and beans. So I will send Mrs. Van $10.00 and when we settle with Otto for rent, the cotton crop of 1920 will be gone. Ha! ha! That beats Krupner though. Ha! ha! This has been a long day.

Say – ring up Mr. George B. and tell him to tell the truck man to call at the ABC Store for those things for S.A.C. and find out from George if you all will have to meet the truck in Alvin or will he bring them out to you. Call him in time for he said he would see him when he carried his milk to him.

I don't know whether Mr. Merchant will come back tonight or not, so I guess I won't get any shirts to wear. So, you all keep well and get up with the work, and if there is any berries, we will pick some Monday while I am with you. So long. I will write again.

Love,
S.A. Crume

On a more pleasant note, Gus's little daughter, Gladys, who was in elementary school at Alvin, was having a wonderful time. She was to recount in later years that she loved school and learning things. She also loved reading – always had her head stuck in a book. She and her older brothers had started school in Maydelle, where they had to walk through town and up a big hill to the old red brick schoolhouse. Gladys loved her teacher there, Mrs. Retilla Ball, and she loved her new one at Alvin. "Miss Ruby had magnolia white skin and gorgeous red hair. I thought she was so understanding and did everything just right. I resolved to be a teacher just like her. It was at this school that I first learned to interact with children of other races which was good experience for me."[21] Nora, being a school teacher herself, was determined that her children would get as much education as possible, and Gus agreed. This was typical of parents in Texas in the early part of the new century. Education became vitally important, the number of public schools grew, and colleges, universities, and trade schools became more common in the West. During this period, there was a feeling brewing that times were changing and children would not necessarily be following in their parents' footsteps as farmers.

In some ways, the 1920's decade was a time of excess. People were in the mood to celebrate after the end of WWI and the victory it brought. Patriotic fervor was prevalent and people felt there was no limit to what they could buy on credit or speculate with in the stock market. America was on a roll which was not supported by sound financial practices. New inventions such as the automobile, the radio, and moving pictures led citizens to believe that anything was possible. The age of the flapper and the speakeasy brought about a new laxness in moral standards, especially in the cities, and this was a great concern among people who still favored rural, church-going values. However, the people of America were throwing off the old restraints in favor of modernism. America was never going to be quite the same again.[22] This decade was the time period when the Gus Crume children were growing up, but beyond trying to keep up with the latest fashions, the children were not going to depart from the way they had been raised, and they remained close to the church and their parents. The girls did raise their hemlines though, although not as quickly or as much as some of the city girls had.

Around 1922, Gus had begun to have doubts about ever making a satisfactory living in Alvin, Texas, and he had another problem. He was diagnosed with a heart condition which meant hard work in high humidity was not a good idea. Although he had possessed high hopes for the Alvin area, he was now ready to think about a new place for his family. The new place was in western Texas at the foot of the panhandle in Knox County. The air there was dry, and the land was at a higher altitude, so the climate would be much kinder to Gus. Nora contacted her brother, Walter, who was living in that area, and he offered to help them get started and made the arrangements to rent a farm for them. So the family packed their possessions and moved to Knox County, Texas, living between the small towns of Munday and Weinert. Munday was very close to the Haskell County line and Weinert was located in Haskell County, so the family would deal with two counties in business matters.[23] The land was flat with red brown dirt and was dotted with cedar, sagebrush, and cactus. This was not lush green country. The large ranches in the area still utilized the native grass of the Great Plains, and tributaries of the Brazos River ran through both counties. Unfortunately, the area soil was sandy and when the wind blew, the sandstorms were something to behold.[24] However, the family was game for new adventures in a new place.

16
The Challenge of West Texas

The Crumes were moving all the way across Texas in 1922, a long trip. After selling the farm at Alvin (for a loss), the family, minus Gus, traveled by passenger train to Munday, Texas. Nora had quite a time keeping track of her five children because the railcar was crowded and the family could not sit together. Upon arriving at Munday, they were met by Nora's brother, Walter, who took them home with him. Gus traveled out to Munday separately on a freight train with the family's belongings and farm animals. Upon arriving in Knox County, the family rented a house on the edge of town briefly before moving to the rented cotton farm that Walter had found for them. Over the years, they would live on several of these rented farms at different times in the Munday area. Each house on the land that they rented required a world of cleaning and repair to make it livable, but all of the family worked on it together and made for themselves a decent place to live. Nora set to work with her scrub bucket and thoroughly cleaned each place, and then freshly papered the walls with clean white builder's paper. Gus took his tools and repaired the windows, doors, fences, etc. [1] The family, no matter what their circumstances, had the great capacity to make things work and to be happy. It was a good thing because they were a long ways from the days of Silas Moses and his small kingdom at Pine Town!

From the beginning the children attended school in country schools close to Weinert and Munday. They were excited to be living "out West" where the cowboys lived whom they had read

The Cowboys - Art and Clyde

about in books. When they first arrived in Munday and saw the dirt streets, hitching rails, and horses, they were thrilled. However, they found the schools in their new area to be different from what they had known to this point. The students seemed to be rougher, and they did not dress up for class, but the Crume children quickly adapted. They were interested in learning and wanted to make good grades, and they all participated in the extra activities at the schools they attended. They first attended a two teacher school, one teacher for the older kids and one for the younger. When it was time for them to move on to the eighth grade, they attended Gillespie High School through grade eleven. If they wanted the last year, grade twelve, they had to attend the high school at Munday, Texas. In this system, the Crume children actually finished high school with two diplomas, one from Gillespie and one from Munday.[2]

One family story which came out of these years concerned the year the kids went to school in an old Ford roadster which their parents had purchased. It was an open-air car with one seat for all four children. In the winter time, the kids were wrapped in pre-heated quilts, and warm water was put in the radiator while the car was kept running until the children were ready to take off. Art was the driver, Morris sat next to him, then Gladys and then Floyce. Art always drove like "a bat out of hell," and on one occasion, the accelerator stuck to the floor board. The car swept past the school house and on up the road with Morris frantically trying to pull up the accelerator pedal. He finally succeeded, and Art drove the car in a slow circle back to the school house, unloaded, and the kids were in time to march in with the rest of the students.[3] It was never mentioned what the other students thought of all this, but the Crume kids were probably a little unnerved when they started their school day.

Not only were the children learning and adjusting, but the parents were also. Farming in West Texas was very different from any place the Crumes had known up to then. For the first year they tried it, Nora's brother proved to be an invaluable help. He had been there for a while and "knew the ropes." The farming

The Farmers: Walter Ferguson, Morris, a cousin, Art, Clyde, and Gus Crume

was dry land farming, involving the tricky business of dodging the sand storms, so the crops wouldn't be covered over with deep drifts of sand or blown away in the wind when newly planted. The family had always been self-sufficient and had plenty to eat from raising their own hogs, beef and chickens. Any excess that they didn't eat provided extra income for the family, and so this familiar routine was continued at Munday.

The biggest adjustment they had to make was in the weather. At Alvin, they had worried about hurricanes and Gulf storms. In West Texas they worried about tornadoes and sand storms. The whole family hated having to get in the storm cellar because it was like being buried alive with insects crawling everywhere in the small space, but they did it when the weather turned nasty. The sand storms were so bad that the sand penetrated the house through every tiny crack, and this necessitated sweeping out sand by the bucketful when the storms were over. The food on the table had to be covered with cloths until everyone was ready to eat. These sand storms would become much worse in the years to come because of the drought and condition of the soil in West Texas. As was a usual activity for them, the Crumes made every effort to fit into the community. There was no Baptist church at Munday, so Gus organized one which met at the little schoolhouse. It eventually grew large enough to have its own minister.[4]

One organization in Texas which was prevalent in the early years of the 1920's decade was the Ku Klux Klan. The Klan had been in existence since the end of the Civil War, but from 1922 to 1924 this secret order was the main influence in Texas politics. It elected sheriffs, attorneys, judges, and legislators, and perhaps as many as 400,000 men belonged to the organization at one time or another. How did the Klan's growth occur when basically they were a racist group which preached hate for blacks and other minorities? The answer may lie in the fact that they broadened their activities in Texas to include punishing wrongdoers such as bootleggers, gamblers, wayward husbands and wives, wife beaters and other supposed morally corrupt people who in many cases could not be touched by the law. The Klan still conducted racist activities, but it was easier to cover this up with other moral issues being touted. However, their activities were still vigilantism and terrorism, no matter if they were in defense of Victorian morality and/or upholding what was right.

The membership of the Klan was often reflective of a lack of education which hardly qualified these men to make judgments on the actions of others, but the Klan gave them a feeling of importance with the bonus of anonymity. As for the respected members of the community, the churchmen, and the educated, often it was a business, political, or religious decision to support the Klan or accept support from them, whether they were members or not. However, explaining the growth of the Klan in no way could explain or condone the actions of the organization which were reprehensible.[5]

In 1924, many citizens of Texas had become angry with the continued power of the Klan, and matters came to a head with the gubernatorial race in Texas. Miriam (Ma) Ferguson, running because her husband had been banned from public office for corruption, defeated the Klan's candidate, Judge Robertson, in the primary and the Republican candidate, Butte, in the general election. Some of the "clever" slogans which came out of the campaign were, "Me for Ma, and I aint got a durn thing against Pa" and "a bonnet and not a hood" and "two governors for the price of one." The opposition's slogan was "Not Ma for me. Too much Pa." It was a vicious election including much stronger language than the above, but it spelled the end of the Klan's political power in Texas. They were never the same.[6] Interestingly enough, Gus recorded in his account book a letter to the editor of the Cherokee County newspaper about this campaign. The letter was unsigned so it is not known if Gus wrote the letter or simply copied it from the paper because he agreed with it, but the writer was obviously from Cherokee County and had been a deputy sheriff.

Dear Sir:
Being an old Cherokeean, I would just like to say a few things before the subscription runs out which will be in a short while and I may not have the price to renew, you see. Mr. Editor, I don't guess I know you or at least I don't remember your initials, but I guess you are all right for I knew a lot of Martins that were all right and besides I see Walter Long is with you and that is proof that you must be on the square for Walter is like myself, so straight he is _____. Yes sir, I know every cross road and pig trail leading in and out of Rusk. As I write I see a picture of the old square and courthouse and jail across the northeast corner of the square. I have been in your jail a many time, Mr. Editor, but not as a prisoner. I was deputy sheriff for four years under one among the best sheriffs Cherokee County ever had - John B. Reagan - long since passed on to his reward.

The Hon. W.E. Donnelly was district attorney right about the time I was sworn in as deputy, and he would hold the list of witnesses in his hand and read off in a low tone and have me to call the name in a loud tone out of the window. And he had a friend he would insist on me calling his name at the bottom of the list. I forget his name, but W.E. knows it. His initials were J.P. Mr. Editor, if the Hon. W.E. is still living ask him if his physician will allow him to eat supper these times. If he has passed on, no harm meant.

I see by your paper a lot of the old land marks has passed out and gone on to their reward. Others will take their place and time goes on, but some of them will be hard to fill for they were the salt of the earth.

I notice in your paper some time ago, in fact, before the last primary, Judge F. B. Guinn and one Mr. Bagley had a little spat over for and against the Klan. I read that with interest and was surprised at the stand the Judge taken in claiming the Klan to be undemocratic, knowing him to be the broad-minded man I always taken him to be. I am wondering if the Judge is not about ready to join this new Good Government Democratic Party that I see they are organizing in Dallas and are going to make a state-wide campaign for Dr. Butt. I wonder what Ma thinks now since they kicked the Klan out at Austin and these same people that helped nominate her are now organizing a Pure Party, as some of them claim. Dr. Butt, the new party and Fergusonism all opposed the Klan. Poor Klan, he is like the Irishman turtle with his head cut off - he is dead but don't know it.

Don't you never believe, my brother, that the Klan is dead. No sir. He got his head cut off it's true in this last primary, but look who did it. The papers state that fully 100,000 Republicans went into this primary. Shall I name the balance - a lot of good uninformed men and women voted for Ma. Now hold still. Don't get mad. I don't mean to say I have got more sense than you have, but I do know what the Klan stands for and you don't. Therefore I say uninformed. I believe if the good people knew the principles of the Klan and what they stood for, Robertson would have been nominated. They voted against the Klan not knowing why. To prove I am right, why the new party, they see their folly.

That is why, and are coming out of it.

Now shall I name the rest that have cut off the Klan's head. All right, let's take your own community. Look around you. Everyone that has nothing to do with your church, that has a knock for your town, bootleggers, gamblers, lawlessness of all kinds - these voted for Ma. Take a look at them. There they stand in your community. Did not a one of this last class vote for Robertson. Which side are you on, brother? A man is known by the company he keeps. It has been a long time since Texas had one, but this is one time the Republicans are going to land a governor - mark my prediction.

Unsigned.[7]

If Gus wrote the letter, it is not known if he actually submitted it to the paper. Perhaps he did write it and submit it. He was not adverse to speaking his mind. However, this letter does illustrate how one individual, perhaps Gus, felt he knew what the Klan stood for when he didn't, or if he knew, he ignored the racist, terrorist side of the Klan's activities. Along with this letter, Gus's record book contained notes of what he owed people, what they owed him, his profits and debts, current events of interest, the work he did for others as well as the land owner who he owed shares of his crop, and writings that he liked. It seemed that many men of this time period, if they were literate, liked to keep record books, account books, or notebooks of their various activities. Gus may have gotten into the habit when he worked for Silas Moses and others in Cherokee County.[8]

The farming on shares or renting land worked fairly well for Gus during the twenties; some years were better than others. Sometimes he had trouble getting loans from the banks to buy seed and other necessary items in order to put in a crop, but he managed. When the Crumes sold their farm at Alvin, after they paid for the move to Munday on the train, they had a small cushion of money that if they were careful with spending, helped with their expenses through the decade of the 1920's. Economic conditions were good nationally, or at least they seemed so on the surface, and this made credit easier to get, and a reasonable life possible as a tenant or sharecrop farmer. However, there was no money for extras such as a college education for their eldest son or store-bought things that could be made by hand.

By 1926 changes were happening in the family. Gus's third son Morris had gotten married on May 27, 1925, at Benjamin, Knox County, Texas, at the age of eighteen to Onah Day, a girl from a farm near Benjamin, also eighteen, who he may have met at school. Their son, Samuel Elvis Crume was born on December 13, 1925.[9] Apparently they lived close to the Day family, or with them, in order to set up housekeeping. They were hardly more than children themselves, and they now had the responsibility of a child. This was not exactly a happy occurrence in the Crume family, but it was accepted. Samuel Elvis was always called Buster by the family, and he was to be an only child. Morris tried farming as a beginning career, perhaps working for his father-in-law.

In the spring of 1926, Gus's second son, Arthur or Art graduated from Munday High School when he was twenty-one years old. Transferring schools and working part time had probably cost him some school time. He had been on the debate team at Gillespie High and Munday High along with his brother, and they had competed all over the state of Texas, winning many honors for the school. They were also athletes, playing basketball

The Toughest Basketball Team in Texas
Art holding the ball and Morris standing behind him

There were no indoor gyms for playing basketball in those days in West Texas, so it was played outside on hard-packed dirt most likely. Art was a big kid and used to fending for himself (He had been working to support the family for years already.), so he didn't take well to being heckled by an opposing team's fan during one of their games. He solved the problem by grabbing the guy and scouring his head in a patch of grass burrs beside the basketball court. Of course he got thrown out of the game for his solution. Basketball in Texas changed considerably over the years which followed.

Art was the salutatorian and president of his class, and some thought that Art had the speaking ability and argument skill to become an attorney, but it was not to be. As soon as he graduated, he went to work for an electric company.[10] He needed to have an occupation which would provide for his financial needs immediately so he could decrease the number of mouths to feed at home and also perhaps help the family monetarily. He started in Phoenix, Arizona, and had trips into Mexico as well. Art, Morris, and their stepbrother Elmer were the first men in many generations of Crumes who would not become farmers, although Morris tried it for a short time after he married. That way of life was coming to an end for the family.

Gus was to be the last of a long line of farmers, and he was a natural. He loved farming. He especially liked to plow, breaking his furrows straight and neat. Nothing smelled quite as good as that freshly plowed soil in the spring of the year. Probably his preference would have been to own his farm and not have to answer to anyone else, but renting land did not take away from his joy in the act of farming itself. His daughter, Gladys, recorded her memories of life on the farm, especially the farm which the family loved the best among the ones in West Texas.

It was the old home place of an old couple who lived in the neighboring town. There was a large, rambling two-story house, and a huge barn and other outbuildings, cowpen and sheds, pig pen and sheds, and chicken and turkey pens and houses. There was a beautiful grove of Paradise trees on the north side of the house and a nice vegetable garden. There was quite a large acreage of tillable soil on which we raised cotton, maize, corn, and cane for bundling; and there was a good-sized pasture in which the stock could graze. Our stock consisted of eight head of horses and mules, several milk cows with calves, a large flock of white Leghorn hens, flocks of Bronze turkeys, and several fattening hogs.

The West Texas Farm the Crumes Loved the Best

My two older brothers had left home, so there was only my younger brother and sister and myself at home. Dad would get up first, start fires when necessary, and put the coffee pot on and a large tea kettle of water. Then as soon as Mother was dressed, they would wake us to get dressed and go to milk the cows and feed the other stock. My sister and I would make the beds, set the table, and get the breakfast started. In winter, we would get ready for school, and in the summer get ready for working in the fields. We worked in the fields like men. I rather enjoyed hoeing and "go-deviling" (riding small plows with wide knives on them to cut the weeds in the middles between the rows of crops). However, I fairly despised picking cotton; it was just a back-breaking job to me! I enjoyed cutting the large golden heads of maise and throwing them in the wagon, but I would get hay fever from the chaff, so I couldn't do much of that. Lots of times our entire family would go to the field together and work all day, taking a large dishpan full of food and eating lunch in the shade of the wagon. Then we would take off

Saturdays to wash, iron, clean house, bake, etc. Dad would fill the big black wash boiler in the yard with water and build a fire under it; then fill the wash tubs on a bench in the shade of a tree, and all hands would pitch in and soon have the week's wash on the line. Our family always worked together to make the farm life work.

Then there was the mid-summer canning season in which we all worked storing foods in cans by pressure cooker for the winter use. Then came harvest time in the fall, golden days of gathering and storing the crops – we would sell the cotton as the bales were ginned. Finally came long winter evenings spent reading or studying, popping corn, eating apples, playing Checkers or Dominoes.[11]

In 1927 and 1928, Gladys was ready for her senior year in high school at Munday. Because she needed to attend Munday High School and it was a good distance from the family farm, the family decided that she should board in town until she could finish. She boarded for a small amount of money and helped with the landlord's children. The family's name was Haymes, and it was through their understanding and help as well as that of other members of the community that Gladys finally finished high school. She could not come home on the weekends unless the weather was good and she could find someone to take her. There wasn't money for her family to come get her, even if they had a vehicle which they may not have owned at this time. For the months of January through May 1928 Gladys wrote a series of letters home which her mother faithfully saved. The letters gave a picture of what it was like being a young person away from home and trying to finish school with no money to speak of, and the letters also gave a glimpse of what rural life in 1928 entailed.

Wednesday

My dearest Mother,

I thought I'd write you a few lines while I have time. A bunch of we senior girls are going hiking this afternoon out to Odell Freeman's. It is still pretty here, don't guess we're going to have any cold weather. I wrote Mrs. P'Poole and Arthur and did my best in both letters. Well, I'm just studying my head off, have something to do all of the time. I guess I'll go down town tomorrow afternoon and see about getting a little dress and pair of hose. I hope I can come home again next weekend. Maybe I'll have an answer from Mrs. P'Poole by then. I went to church last Sunday night. Tell Sport Ring and the rest hello. Some of the kids here at school are talking about Arthur being such a great speaker. Now they're wanting a great debater. Boy, I wish he could enter the World's Oratorical Contest that's going on. Well, I gotta go.

Love
Gladys

I didn't get to mail your letter so thought I'd write another scratch. I got back from the hike about sundown. We sure had a lot of fun. There was about a dozen girls. We hiked out there (4 miles), cooked us the best supper down in the pasture. I ate more than I ever did in my life, I think. Mr. Martin brought us all home. Well, I can't think of anything else except I'm tired as can be. Mrs. Haymes has gone to a party – don't be shocked – and I had to fix supper and wash all the dishes. I'm going to bed in a little bit. I'm hoping it's pretty Saturday and Morris comes to go home.

Gladys

In this letter Gladys talks about her transportation situation. Her brother Morris evidently had access to a vehicle, perhaps through his father-in-law, but no one had the money to waste on constant trips home. Gladys was like her parents, outgoing and fun-loving. She always had a circle of friends with whom to do things, and she liked to pull pranks as long as they didn't hurt anything. She was a faithful church attendee, and she got much support from the church when she needed it. In everything that Gladys did, she did her best, whether it was having fun or studying or working. She was busy, and she liked it that way.

Munday, Texas
February 14, 1928

My dearest Mother,

    I'll write you a little while I have time. It seems that I am kept busy all the time, but I'm glad of it. Have you heard from Arthur yet? Surely he has not forgotten us. I'm still doing all my school work fine. Poor Ruby, everything she does is wrong. She wants me to go out home with her to the dinner-on-the-ground next Sunday, but I'm not going to do it. I feel pretty sure that Mr. Haymes will move next week, and I'll stay here Sunday. How is your throat by now? I hope you all are feeling just as fine as I am, for I'm well as ever. I don't know just when I'll get to come home again. I want to go to see Morris and Onah the first pretty Friday or Saturday. Mama, I don't say it bragging but I don't see how on earth Mrs. Haymes gets along without me. I do so many little things. She is gone to see a little sick girl now, leaving me to tend to the kids. They're not a bit of trouble to me as they do just what I tell them to. If papa can't find a Negro, he can let me know, and Mr. Haymes may be able to find one. He said Negroes come in the store every once in awhile hunting a place on the farm. Mrs. Haymes said Brother O'Brien's old Negro's son was a mighty good farmhand, but he has been working at the Compress. She didn't know whether you could get him or not. I'm going to try to keep my dresses clean until I can come home so I can wash them in that soft water. Gee, but I'm getting tired of school. I'll be glad when it's out and I can come home. Mrs. Haymes said today she didn't think you could get old Brook's son as they are going to have an increase in the family pretty soon.

    Try to get everything you need for the house. When I come home again, I guess everything will be bright and shining with new curtains. Oh say, I wish we could get some checkers and dominoes. I know we have to be saving but they don't cost much. The tournament ended last night, so I didn't get to go to any more ball games. I didn't care much. Say, Gillespie beat Munday one point last night, never was so shocked. You know I told you that Miss Compton was going with the new chiropracter, well, they married and she is so happy she can hardly stay still. I'm glad I didn't try light housekeeping with her now. It's beginning to get

Wednesday

My dearest Mother:

I thought I'd write you a few lines while I have time. A bunch of us Senior girls are going hiking this afternoon out to Odell Freeman's. It is still hot up here, don't guess we're going to have any cold weather. I wrote Mrs. P'Poole and Arthur, did my best in both letters. Well, I'm just studying my head off, have something to do all of the time. I guess I'll go down town tomorrow afternoon and see about getting a little dress and pair of hose. I hope I can come home again next weekend, maybe I'll have an answer from Mrs. P'Poole by then. I went to church last Sunday night. A little queer Simmons preacher took Bro. O'Brien's place. Tell Sport Kirsey and the rest Hello. [some of the kids kept at last] They're talking about Arthur being such a great speaker now, they're wanting a great debator, boy I wish he could enter the world's oratorical contest that's going on. Well I gotta go — Love,
Helyn.

I didn't get to mail your letter so thought I'd write another scratch. I got back from the hike about sundown. We sure had a lot of fun. There was a-bout a dozen girls. We hiked out there (4 mi) cooked us the best supper down in the pasture. I ate more than I ever did in my life I think. Mr. Martin brought us all home. Well I can't think of any-thing else except I'm tired as can be. Mrs. Haynes has gone to a party (don't be shocked) and I had to fix supper and wash all the dishes. I'm going to bed in a little bit. I'm hoping it pretty bad and Marie comes to go home.

      Gladys

colder – looks like we're going to have a norther in the morning. Well, I gotta go. Write and tell me everything.

With love,
Gladys

At school
Monday

My dearest Mother and all,

I'll write early this week as I know you are anxious to hear from me, as I didn't come home. It turned off right pretty, and I went to Morris's Friday afternoon. They sure were glad to see me, as they get so lonesome staying there at home by themselves. Their little old house sure is pretty on the inside, especially their bedroom and kitchen. The breakfast set was awfully pretty. They sure do want you all to come and see it, but you never know what this weather is going to do. It looks like it had just soon be bad again as not. I'm not going to see anyone else for a long time, but I did want to go see them before I came home so I could tell you all how everything looks. Buster is the biggest monkey you ever saw. He cuts up all the time. When they brought me home to Munday, and as we passed the old place, he says, "we're going to see Clyde." He thought I belonged there. I wish I did. Maybe I could come home every weekend. I haven't got any money from Arthur yet. I guess he will send some pretty soon. And I haven't heard from Mrs. P'Poole. I can't understand her. I have just got to come home Friday. Mrs. Haymes and them will be moving along about then, but it can't be helped. I'm not supposed to help them move. I'll get some way to come home. My, I have got more work to do. I have got to make a poster this afternoon, and I don't know what else. Monday night I didn't get to finish my letter this morning so will write some more. I talked to Mrs. Whittimore a little bit ago. I told Mr. Haymes to look out for you all a hand. He said he knew of a white man and his wife, but he didn't talk like they were very favorable. I tended to the kids this afternoon while Mrs. Haymes went to a party. Well I'm spending my last penny when I mail this letter, and it's almost the first of March. Oh say, I heard today that Callie Faye and Earl were married. Several told me so I guess it's true. Floyce, you'll have to write them congratulations. I can't think of anything else, so I guess I'll see you Friday. I sure do hope we get a good hand. Well bye bye till then.

Your daughter and sis,
Gladys

Gladys Crume - High School in the 1920's

Gladys was not shy about asking the people she knew in Munday about rides out to her parents' farm, and often they helped her. Gladys's financial situation bordered on perilous most of the time, but once again she was not shy about asking for help, and once again the community members she knew came through for her. When she borrowed money, she always paid it back, and she was a good student and a hard worker. The townspeople knew this and tried to support her. They also knew what kind of family she came from, and this enhanced her reputation as well. Her parents were not going to put her in a place where she had no friends and no support, even if they didn't have money for her expenses at times.

March 14, 1928
Wednesday night

My dearest Mother and all,

Well I got here safe even if I didn't feel so good. That man carried me right up to Maples Hotel. He made 35 and 40 mph all the way and never said a word, but once slowed down to ask me if he was driving too rough, and I told him no and to keep it up.

When I got out, I was so stiff I could hardly walk. Brother O'Brien happened along, picked me up and carried me home. Then he went on to town, got his mail, came back by and carried me all the way to school. Boy, I sure was glad because I never could have walked it. I was so sick at my stomach I could hardly stand up. I was just twenty minutes late at school. I have been sick ever since until today. I went to school but had the stomachache. Mrs. Haymes gave me "Baby Percy" – all she has is baby medicine – and I'm all right now.

Have Arthur and Mosie left yet? I never got to tell Mosie goodbye – left in such a hurry. I'm sending those pictures and a lot of negatives that they didn't develop. I'm getting along all right at school. I don't know for sure yet, but I don't think I'm going to be in the senior play. I don't have much to do here at Mrs. Haymes now. The house is so full of closets, it's no trouble to keep it clean. She has more company than she used to. I kept the baby this afternoon while she and the other kids went to see Mrs. Hardin. I wrote Mrs. P'Pool the card. My dress hasn't come yet. I read on the piece of paper and it said to wait a week to see if it came before writing them. I guess it will be here this week sometime. Well that's about all I can think of this time so bye bye.

Lovingly,
Sis Gladys

Just imagine being a high school student without transportation, sick, and needing to get back to school which was miles away. Gladys never ceased to be grateful for the kindness of the people she knew in Munday. She did not have the money to see a doctor unless it was an emergency, so she doctored with her employer's baby medicine. Where did the Crume courage and drive come from? Perhaps these qualities came from generations of very strong, very committed people. This could also be said for Nora Crume's family, the Fergusons. Gladys continued to hope that Arthur would come through with some money. He was the hope for the family on many occasions, a burden he willingly carried on his broad shoulders. He did his best when he could, when he wasn't scrambling to make a go of his own life. Gladys was hanging on, but the expenses kept coming as graduation approached.

Achievement Through Struggle

In April of 1928 life was still good for most Americans. They were living a dream built on credit which often had no sound basis to prop it up. Citizens had been "keeping cool" with President Coolidge and now switched their allegiance to Herbert Hoover of Iowa who had promised continued prosperity. The problems with the farm situation across the Great Plains were still being ignored. New inventions continued to come on the market, and more people were driving automobiles, using cameras, and listening to the radio. Modernism was the way to go, collecting material things was what mattered, and people had no patience with prohibition or any restrictions on their behavior. Texans shared the optimism of the rest of the country if not the loss of moral values. The storm clouds were gathering, but no one could see that. They were too busy enjoying life in America.[1] It was at this time that Gladys Crume was getting ready to graduate from high school in Munday, Texas, and then hopefully go on to higher education. Her thinking was that anything was possible if you just believed hard enough, worked hard, and had faith in God to provide. This was a little different take on the then national philosophy, but in the long run, it would prove to be healthier and bring more success.

Slightly over one month remained of Gladys' high school career, and she was definitely ready for it to be over. She was tired of the stress of studying, getting ready for graduation, worrying about money, and trying to make plans for a future. She wrote her mother a letter on April 2.

Munday, Texas
April 2, 1928

My dearest Mother,

Well, how's everybody by now? I'm still kicking – doing fine. I've been having a pretty good time. I went to the tacky party last Friday night. Sure did have a lot of fun. My but I was the tackiest thing. I got some films and Mrs. Haymes took my picture in my rig. Well, I went home with Ruby and Elizabeth Saturday evening. I wanted to go to Gillespie to church. Mrs. Myers and them seemed mighty glad to have me come. She said she sure did want to come see you and that she was coming before long. I went mainly to see Mrs. Shannon. She said they couldn't come next Sunday because it was Easter, but that they would try to come the next. She sure was tickled to see me and is crazy to see you all. So I may not come home next Sunday, unless Morris comes by.

I got my books, and believe me this old gal is going to study. I think I'll see Mrs. P'Poole tomorrow and she is going to bring those school annuals over. That will just about take my last penny. I'll declare I think I need an oil well I need so much. Try to have all of my old dresses fixed when I come home because I'll need them, especially my old batiste. I wish you could get me a little old blue checked gingham dress to wear to school, you know with organdy cuffs and collar. But we're going to do the best we can until this dreadful school is out. Just six more weeks after this one, but they seem like years. I'm not in the senior play – good! Mama, I guess I'm crankier than most girls, but I'm still as homesick as ever. I try to be brave but I sure do get blue. Bertha McNeil was telling me about seeing Floyce, and I saw Callie Faye at church. Everybody seemed mighty glad to see me. Well, I can't think of anything else. So Bye. Be good.

Gladys

Miss Hodge asked me about Clyde. She sure was tickled when I told her he was in the third grade. She said he ought to be – said he could do anything because he was so smart.

In spite of going to parties and participating in activities with her school friends, Gladys was wearing down under the strain. The expenses were an ever-present worry, and she continued to miss her home and family. The numbers of people that she mentions in her letters to her family indicate that the small towns of Munday, Weinert, and to some extent Benjamin and Knox City and the farms around them made one big neighborhood where everyone knew everyone. It was comforting to have that support system. As the end of her high school days drew closer, Gladys grew more concerned about her future. High school graduation had always meant the beginning of something new, which was a scary thing if you weren't sure what that new thing was going to be or how you were going to make it happen.

Another letter arrived from a different child with bad news for Gus and Nora. They were worried about Arthur and Gladys, and now they could add Morris's family to the list.

Tuesday

Dear Mama and all,

Well, it is still blowing up here. I haven't planted yet. I am afraid it will cover up. Buster is in mighty bad shape. We carried him to the doctor yesterday. The doctor said he has the infantile paralysis. He can't walk but just a little at a time. Every evening he walks a little but every morning he can't walk at all. We have to bathe him in alcohol. The doctor said to watch him and if his feet or legs want to get crooked to bring him in. His legs are like match stems. He is better today. He has been walking all morning. I think he will be all right.

I talked to Mrs. Whittimore the other day. She said Clyde was back in the bed. Mr. Day traded his truck for a car so we may not get to come soon, but if nothing happens, we will come when it gets pretty. You can write us and let us know how you all are. We will close.

With love,
Morris and Onah

This was bad news indeed. Infantile paralysis was a serious viral infectious disease which attacked the central nervous system, and it could paralyze and kill a person or leave them severely disabled. It seemed to affect all ages but was typically more severe in children, and it was a growing concern for people because it was contagious and could break out in epidemics. It had been in existence for centuries, but it became more prevalent in the early 1920's in America, especially in epidemic form. In later decades it would become known as polio, and a preventive vaccination would be found in the 1950's, but until then, people had to use what they had in order to combat it.[2] Apparently Buster had a somewhat light case because he was improving. Although Gus had grandchildren from his first son Elmer, Buster was the only grandchild of Gus and Nora, and he would remain so for some time. Morris, his father, had married very young, and the rest of Gus and Nora's children did not. Morris referred to the wind and sand blowing, and he was afraid to plant his crops because they might get covered up with sand, and he would have to start over. This was a common problem in this part of Texas and becoming worse as the 1920's drew to a close. The Crumes had learned to work around it, at least for the first years in West Texas.

At long last Gladys was nearing graduation, and she was to say later that she received a greater thrill from graduating from high school than she did from completing college. She wrote one final letter to her mother.

Sunday night

My dearest Mother,

I will write to you before I go to bed because I may not have time tomorrow. Mrs. Haymes, her mother, and I went to church tonight. My, Brother O'Brien sure did preach a fine sermon. Well, I had so much to tell you I didn't know where to begin. I visited Mrs. P'Poole Saturday night and sure did learn lots. Oh, she is the sweetest thing. She said I would have to take all of the examinations for my second grade certificate in two days, and then to get my high school certificate, I could take the examinations at different times. She said for me to take the exams and if I passed, go to school this summer and up until Christmas. She said she could get me a school here in the county beginning about then and I could teach until the next summer, go to school then, and by the next August, I would have one year's college work, a first grade certificate, and have taught some too. She said I could then get a school with some real pay and acquire a good place, as I would have had experience in teaching and have gone to college too. She said she would arrange for me to take the examinations whenever I want to. I would like to take the elementary subjects in May and the others in June. If I can I would like to do what she suggested. She said she would get me the school, and she named several girls that she has got schools. She gave me a book explaining the subjects to be taken and how to get certificates. I'll come home next weekend and show it to you, talk everything over so I can let Mrs. P'Poole know what I have decided to do.

 Well, there's lots of work for me, but let 'er rip. The pictures were no good. Were not developed so I still have my money. I won't need any money unless it's to get Floyce and I some slippers. If I had the cash to get them, I believe I could get them at a pretty reasonable price. I hate to get anything on credit. Well, I'm worried about Arthur and Mosie. I sure do hope they hear from that fellow. I can't think of anything else. Oh yes, my dress hasn't come. If it doesn't come tomorrow, I'm going to write them. Well, it's getting pretty late and in the morning is Monday morning. So goodnight

With Love
Gladys

Say, how do you want me to come home? Mr. Mitchell came Saturday but I had to keep my date with Mrs. P'Poole. I guess I can come on the bus and get Mrs. Haymes to come after me Sunday. Write me and let me know. Tell Clyde to not let the mumps get him down. Does Floyce have them?

With this letter, Gladys was trying to develop a plan for her life for the next few years. It would not be easy, but she was thinking of alternating working and going to school in order to pay for her schooling. She was her mother's daughter, and she desperately wanted to become a teacher. It would take her longer to finish, but at least she would get to go to college. She just needed to get her parents approval of her plans.

Finally the big day arrived, and Gladys went through the graduation ceremony with her family proudly in attendance, even some extended family from East Texas. Gladys was the valedictorian and had carefully composed her speech. In somewhat of a youthful turn of mood, she expressed, on behalf of her graduating class, sadness at leaving her high school years behind, but perhaps more importantly, her great hopes for the future. In 1928, everyone was optimistic about the future. Gladys loved to write and had a genuine feel for the drama of the moment. Her concluding words on that day were, "Teachers and school companions one and all, with a last lingering look at the setting sun of our high school days shining with a tender radiance, clothing all the scene with glorious beauty, we turn and fix our gaze upon the day just dawning."[3] This somewhat flowery speech showed Gladys's basic optimism in the face of what looked like nothing but obstacles in making her future plans become a reality. She also had numb toes from a lovely pair of high heel shoes which were one size too small.[4]

As it turned out, Gladys was to get some help with her higher education. She applied for a scholarship and needed some recommendations. One of the people she asked was a former teacher and Munday high school principal, H.V.Standley.

Abilene, Texas
July 3, 1928

Miss Gladys Crume
Weinert, Texas
Dear Gladys:
To hear from you renewed fond memories of the past. I hope you are enjoying the summer as much as I am. Tomorrow is our "big day" in Abilene, auto races, etc.

I can sign the scholarship with a clear conscience. I suppose you have heard me say often that I was always ready to assist my students in any way. I am glad to assist you in any way possible to make a success in college. If there are other things that you need my assistance in, be sure to call upon me. I hope you have a successful year in school, and I know you will have it. I would be glad to hear from you in the midst of your year's work, telling me how you are making your work.

Don't forget that you are one of my ex-students that I have great faith in.

Your past teacher,
H.V. Standley

Gus and Nora were not as excited about Gladys's education plan as she was because they knew she was very young, and they would like for her to be in a protective environment for a little longer. Therefore they decided to send her to a Baptist Junior College in Sheridan, Arkansas, where Gus's old friend was President of the Board of Directors. It would be a two-year stay and some of the happiest years of Gladys's life. She lived in the dormitory, participated in all the student activities, and made some life-long friendships.[5] The financial burden still existed, but it could be handled with scholarships, loans, and part time jobs. The small country schools back home in Texas could wait a little longer for Gladys to be their teacher. Her family wanted her to be in a safe place and were willing to sacrifice so she could have her education. The family always, always hung together to support each other. Art even came home at the request of his mother to accompany Gladys on the train to Dallas the first time she went to Arkansas. He made sure she made her connection from Dallas to Sheridan, Arkansas,[6] where she was met by school officials. However, being in school at Sheridan meant coming home only once or twice a year. It was a long trip to Arkansas from West Texas.

While Gladys was in school, her family continued to do what they could to maintain their farm and to raise the youngest two children, Floyce and Clyde. However, the year 1929 was to bring some drastic changes in the national outlook. All the optimism and excess of the 1920's came to an end, like the popping of a giant balloon, in the fall of 1929 when the New York stock exchange crashed. At first the farmers of Texas, and the Crumes included, could divorce themselves from the trouble and conclude that it only affected the eastern cities of the United States. As the years which comprised the 1930's decade rolled forward, they were to learn that this was sadly not the case. There were disquieting hints at trouble to come with the ups and downs of crop and stock prices and the lack of credit, but after the excess of the 1920's years, people had a hard time believing that the trouble was serious.[7] In 1929, Gladys received a letter from her brother Art.

382 N. 1rst Ave.
Phoenix, Arizona
Sunday Afternoon

My dear sis,

How are you this nice fall afternoon? I'm fairly well excepting that I have a stiff head ache. So Morris and Onah are in a huff are they. I'm sorry but never mind, dear, for you know your old bro loves you, believes in you, and is proud of you more than you will ever know. I know I may seem, and rightfully so I'm afraid, to neglect you all and never write, but, dear, it has been so awfully hot here up till a few days ago that when my day's work was over I was all in, given out, no energy or life to me.

I sent Mother a box of fresh fruit late grown here in Phoenix. I'm sure she will send you some of them. The country here still seems to be booming, but development is slow because of shortage of money for the big development projects. The Salt River Valley may in time be a great thing, but I'm afraid the summers are too severe and too long. Everyone says the winters are ideal here, and I really think they must be.

Was sorry to hear that the school had to cut you to $35.00, but, honey, I'm glad you have that each month anyway. I'm going to do my best to send you ten dollars this weekend that will help you some. Also, dear, what size bloomers and underthings do you wear? I can get them here real cheap, you see. There is a Sears Roebuck, Montgomery Ward, and several other large chain stores here that I can find some real bargains in several places.

Dear, I must write Mother a little. Then I'll be ready for supper. So, I'm going to close with this excuse of a letter. When you see Brother Bogard, tell him hello for me. I was sure glad to get your picture. You know it is the only one I have of you. Be good dear and write me once in a while. You know your old bro loves you still.

Your loving but neglectful brother, Arthur

This letter was perhaps written shortly after the stock market crash or perhaps a little before in the fall of 1929. It mentions shortages already and lack of credit. For the Crumes, who were always living on the edge of disaster financially, the changing conditions probably did not make much of an impression. They kept doing what they had always done – work hard and make do. Arthur's circumstances were about to change, however. He married in 1929 to Beatrice Moore Bayley, a widow with two children, Doris and "Chub."[8] His financial responsibilities were about to double.

Gladys spent two years at Missionary Baptist College in Sheridan, Arkansas, and was able to come home in the summers to Munday. There was never a time during these years that she did not have to worry about money and not find work where she could, but she was happy. Her friends were high spirited, fun-loving people who, in some cases, would remain her friends for the rest of her life. One of the things the group loved to do was go "kodaking." They would go on a picnic or just a drive and take pictures with their Kodak cameras.[9] This is an example of how photography had changed since the turn of the century. When Gladys was little, families were dependent upon traveling photographers or sometimes photography studios in mid-size towns for pictures of their family. These were always formal portraits where no one dared smile. When inexpensive cameras were invented, anyone and everyone could have one and make their own pictures whenever they pleased. Film and the development of it were fairly inexpensive also. Even in the worst years of the Depression, people continued to use cameras as a form of entertainment.

"Kodaking"
Gladys in the Middle of the Front Row

During her summers at home, Gladys received letters from her school chums, both male and female. The following letter was written when she was at Sheridan, so she may have still been at school and getting ready to leave for a visit home. Harlan Walker was at the College of the Ozarks at Clarksville, Arkansas, so he may have already graduated from Missionary Baptist which was a junior college and been attending a different college for his last two years.

Saturday night

Dear Gladys,

You don't know how sorry I am that I had to miss that reunion. There were three reasons why I could not come. In the first place, I had a final exam in Economics on Saturday morning. I had to take it. I had a tooth pulled Friday a.m. and my jaw swelled up like a balloon. Next, I could not get transportation home in time as I had to work and the highway is torn up so traffic is slow and scarce. I won't mention any other reasons.

How many were there? Who was there? Was Ruby? Gib? and the rest? You don't know how sorry I am cause I missed it, but you understand.

Did you have a big time? Write me and tell me all you did. How long are you going to be in Sheridan? Will you be there when my school is out the third of June? I want to see you and as many of the gang as possible.

I have three of my final tests off with, I think good grades on them.

Say, I'm courting the sweetest girl in school. She was voted that in Who's Who and she is too. I have eliminated some pretty stiff competition, and I think I'm sitting pretty. She says so too. She's got plenty of brains. I'll show you her picture when I come home. She's plenty hot looking and "stacked" like a brick outhouse. Write me and tell me all the news.

Love to all,
Slim (Harlan) Walker

P.S. I was toastmaster at our Junior-Senior Banquet. I have been elected into the Chesterfieldian Collegiate Club, a club of twelve high-rating juniors and seniors. It's an honor to be one. Tell all hello and I'm sorry I missed it. Slim

The Walker boys, Harlan and his brother Dalton, were involved with various newspapers during their college years, both at school and for the local communities where the school was located. Harlan was the more outgoing of the two. They were a part of the group of friends that Gladys ran around with at school. Gladys' feelings for Dalton ran a little deeper than friendship, but the relationship never progressed, perhaps because Dalton's feelings were not the same. In January of Gladys' last year at Missionary Baptist College, 1930, Nora wrote her a letter.

Monday Night, January 6, 1930

Dear little Lura Gladys,

I have been thinking of nineteen years ago when you was a tiny baby and with me. I enjoyed your sweet letter. Glad you had a nice time and your turkey helped you so much. I hadn't dreamed of you pulling off such a big one that you would have Mildred and Normer and a few others.

Well, I have planned to write you a big letter and I can't get my mind to work right some how. I have just wrote Velma Acker. She is in bad condition. Baby Flotsome [Floyce, Gladys' sister] went back to Munday yesterday. I miss her so much. We talked about you so much. I ordered the goods and made her a new coat, took the fur collar of your old red coat and put it on and those fur pieces on the sleeves. My she was so surprised and tickled crazy over it. I made her a new school dress, got her a pair of oxfords, some bloomers and hose. She is so hard on clothes she was most naked. She likes to stay with Mrs. Haymes all right. She went to a class party at Atkinsons Thursday night before Christmas, said she had a fine time. Everyone was nice to her. She said she felt as free and welcome as anyone. Some of the girls carried her home, but she longs for you all the time. She would laugh at me last year about wishing to see you but she is all different now.

I want to talk to you so bad at times. You know I have all confidence in the world in you, but little dear it is just motherly instinct that speaks out to beg and warn and plead for you to be very careful and don't make any mistakes, do wrong, get in a mess. You are so dear to me. If any boy ever hints of ugly things to you, quit him cold for he don't care or respect you. If he is a gentleman, he will apologize and act right. I don't care how much you care for a boy, Gladys, remember your honor and know when he humbles you to him, he will cease to care, if he did before. Don't think I am not trusting you, praying for you all the time for God to lead, guide, direct and keep you from all harm. I know you liked Dalton, I won't say loved him, don't know how you are now, but if I knew him well, I might feel different. You are young yet and don't love any one too much.

I hope and pray that you get a good school this winter. Dad laughed about you inviting the County Superintendent. He said you were trying to stay on his warm side. Well, I'm still hoping and praying that the college will get enough help to hold all it has gained. Sister, the women in the churches could sell almost a thousand dollars worth of hens. Anyone can give one to four hens and never miss them, then get them all together and sell them. Each church can canvass their women, get their names and the number of hens. You know Gillespie did that. All the women do out here.

Well, a blizzard has struck from the north, cold too. I will write Arthur tomorrow to help you all that he can spare. Floyce has plenty and we can all get by somehow. If we get some good rains, we will get help. If not, we don't know the future. Pray for us, pray for us to have rain if it's God's will. I hope and pray you make good on midterm study and do your best. I love, love, love you always.

Mama

Nora was concerned for her daughter as mothers have been concerned about their children, particularly daughters, from time immemorial. Gladys was on her own and making decisions critical to her future, including her emotional commitments. Other than through letters, she was separated from her family and could only depend upon her friends and her school. This applied to illness as well. At one point during her school career, she was desperately ill with tonsillitis. She had the tonsils removed, but they continued to bleed, and she almost bled to death before she could get help. Another time she had a serious case of pneumonia for which there were no antibiotics, and she just had to tough it out. It caused her to miss six weeks of school. Perhaps most serious of all, while she was in college, she was diagnosed with a heart condition which could have been hereditary or could have been the result of having rheumatic fever as a child. She had a hole in the mitral valve of her heart which was leaking. At this point, she was not ill from the condition itself, so she was advised to pursue normal, healthy activity and diet but avoid extremes.[10] Out of necessity, Gladys learned to survive at an early age without the help of her family, but there were times when it was a close call.

This letter from Nora also discussed Gladys' sister, Floyce, and how she was progressing through her education. She was following in her sister's footsteps and finishing high school in Munday. The family, though apart, never ceased to miss one another and send their love across the miles in letters.

Gladys and her friends did graduate from Missionary Baptist College in 1930 at the beginning of the Great Depression years. Gladys immediately got an Arkansas teaching certificate and a job teaching math at Central Junior High School at England, Arkansas, for a year. By the end of the school year in 1931, Gladys knew that she did not want to teach junior high. If she wanted to teach senior high, she was going to have to complete a four-year degree, so she went back to school at Arkansas State College at Conway in 1931-32 for her junior year. Here she renewed her friendships with the people she had known at Missionary Baptist and spent all her holidays that year with their families.[11] It was a good year. However, her family in Texas was not doing any better as the Great Depression lengthened out and hard times settled in for the duration of the decade. Much worse conditions lay ahead for all of them.

Gladys and her Buddies

18

The Great Depression and the Dust Bowl Years

In 1931 Texans had finally begun to accept the fact that the Depression was for real and was not going to be over in a hurry. Fundraising efforts began to help the poor and displaced, but the number of these people was growing faster than ordinary efforts could address. The price for crops dropped to unheard-of lows and banks began to close. Tenant or sharecroppers were used to living on the edge, but debt was rising and farms were being foreclosed. The mood of Texans had turned against Herbert Hoover, blaming him for their troubles. It was this attitude that swept Democrat Franklin Delano Roosevelt into office as the next President of the United States in 1932. With his administration, many Texans became influential in the federal government, serving in Congress, in the cabinet, and in government agencies. This did result in money and support coming into the state from the national level, but this was not as effective as it might have been in helping Texas farmers and businessmen for two reasons. The first was corrupt politics in Texas during the 1930's, and the second was a drought of monumental proportions which turned West Texas into a dust bowl.[1]

The Crumes, living in Knox County, were not quite in the defined area of the country termed the Dust Bowl, but they were very close and did have to bear increased problems with dust storms and getting their crops to grow. The Brazos River was probably running very low if not dried up in places, and water was at a premium with the drought. The disastrous farming practices of many years of tilling the soil into a fine powder were finally coming home to roost. In many areas the soil would not grow anything, and when the winds came, the soil blew up into the air causing dust storms that lowered visibility, caused fine dirt to seep into dwelling places, and choked the life out of animals and people alike. The drought grew to affect seventy-five percent of the United States, including twenty-seven states severely, and the decade of the thirties became known as "the dirty thirties." Many tenant farmers moved away from the middle of the country to California, hoping to get work as migrant farm workers. It was the end of farming for a great number as they fled to the cities looking for work of any kind. However, the ranches and farms that survived got some help from the many government programs created by the New Deal administration. Agriculture in America was being forced to change the way it operated or go under. [2]

The impossible conditions caused the Crumes to become creative in order to survive, something for which they had been uniquely trained by years of barely surviving with subsistence living. Gus and Nora continued to farm, garden, and raise animals for sale. Everything they could do counted. They had three children still in school, including Gladys in college. In her 1930 letter, Nora expressed some of her concern to her daughter in Arkansas, but she didn't know the half of what was coming. Art was still working for electric companies, which was fairly steady work during the Depression. He made a trip home in 1932 from Phoenix and brought his stepdaughter Doris with him. Even with a family of his own to support, he continued to help the Crumes when he could. Morris and his family were trying something new. They had gotten into the restaurant business in Munday and would eventually move to Seymour, Texas, and then to Altus, Oklahoma. They also helped with money for the family occasionally. Buster, their son, spent summers and other time periods with his grandparents while his parents were busy working or having marital problems, and he truly loved staying with them. In the early years of the decade Gladys was alternately teaching school and going to college in Arkansas. At Arkansas State, she chose a major of English which would become her teaching subject in later years, and she occasionally was able to come home to Texas for visits. [3]

In somewhat of a contrast, Gus received the following letter from Kentucky in 1932. A cousin on his mother's side, Tony Williams, wrote about life in Kentucky.

R. 1
Ekron, Kentucky
April 10, 1932
Mr. S.A. Crume
Munday, Texas
Dear Cousin Sam:

It has been some time since I wrote you. We are all well. We all escaped the flu. We had a very mild winter until the 4th of March. We had a blizzard and had zero weather. We filled our ice house and had snow. The only snow of the winter.

Have had a good deal of rain this winter everything is looking nice. Grass, wheat are growing fine. Nothing wrong except the depression, and that is as bad as ever if not worse. Have not seen farm products so cheap since 1896.

We have enough to eat, a few rags to wear, in fact enough of everything except money and that is as scarce as hen teeth. My stock wintered well. Have nice lambs -31- and a few of them will do to market the last of April. Nice fat lambs weighing from 65 to 85 lbs. are nine to ten cents a lb. in Louisville now. The hogs are $4.20 per one hundred lbs. Veal calves are 5 ½ cents per lb. We have ten calves, hogs counting pigs -40 head. We are about half done our spring breaking. It has been so wet we have not sown our oats yet.

I don't think we had sold all of our tobacco when I last wrote you. We done very well with our first that we sold in December but the last we sold did not bring much. All the crop my individual crop and tenants averaged only six cents a lb. after paying expenses of trucking it to Louisville and the expense of selling it over the floor. Besides we have about seven hundred lbs. of tips on hand that would not have paid expenses had we sold it.

People had a time of paying taxes in fact a good deal of property was sold for taxes but I understand that they have five years to redeem it. But the penalty and interest runs high. I fill out government crop reports ever month and send it to the department of agriculture. They in return send me government bulletins. I got a pamphlet a few days ago called the Outlook for Farmers in 1932. I got no encouragement at all from reading the future prospects in crops. No kind of livestock. I see the government is going to spend ten million dollars on Camp Knox which comes within eleven miles of us. They are going to make it one of the main camps of the United States. Nine thousand soldiers will be trained there this summer.

Several banks failed in our state last year and this winter but none in our county. Three banks failed in Breckinridge County, the county west of us, but two of them have opened up for business. But what hurt so many several large banks failed in Louisville. Works up there are awful dull.

I and our Vernon visited Cousin Emmet Williams who lives in Hardin County, twenty miles from us. We went last Sunday. We went by Cousin Amelia Jenkins, Cousin Ree Husley was visiting her so we taken both of them and went to Emmets. He is very poorly. He cannot live long. He has asthma and high blood pressure. Cousin Ree looks well. She makes her home in Vine Grove. I don't think she will have any time left when her husband's estate is settled up. Emmet is unable to work. Has rented his land to his neighbors. His wife tends the garden, milks his cows and do what they can. He only has one son at home and two sons who work in Louisville. The son at home goes to Rineyville High School but goes from home.

Well, I am glad things are no worse. Things is not as bad as the drought year of 1930. Although times are hard and farm products not worth much but I reckon that it could be worse. Well, Cousin Sam, at last I am going to send you that long promised tobacco. It is in case now this damp weather. I expect it is sorry tobacco but hope you enjoy it. If you will come over sometime, will give you all you can carry home.

With love and best wishes to all. As ever your cousin,
A.V. Williams

Cousin Tony liked to ramble on in his letters about anything and everything, but he also discussed the effects of the Depression. Kentucky was still getting rain and was able to grow crops, but the prices were poor, the banks were in trouble, and the outlook was not optimistic for better. He mentions the creation of Ft. Knox in Kentucky. This was more than a camp in the woods. It was a huge reservation which was comprised of land appropriated by the federal government from what had always been privately held property. Part of this property was formerly owned by members of the Crume and Lincoln families. It included several cemeteries which became inaccessible to the families of the people buried there except for one day a year, and this included the cemetery where Bersheba Lincoln, grandmother of the President, was buried.[4] People may not have liked many of the things that the federal government was doing, but they were desperate to try anything to improve the economy.

Clyde Crume was fourteen years old in 1933 and wrote the following letter to his sister in Arkansas. He was a big tease and a typical ornery little brother.

Munday, Texas
March 24, 1933
At Home
At Night
At Friday
At 7:45
With pen and ink
On paper
Dear Sister:

How are you? I hope you are fine. I am not any good. What are you and Eliz doing for yourself? Tomorrow is the indoor baseball and volleyball tournament. I am going. Say big shorty, what's your name? Ha! ha! Say, what do you and Liz do? We just don't do here, fourteen miles behind the depot at Wienert. I passed all of my books. Did you? Say, how do you like my writing? I think it is good. If you do not like it, you can lump it on down the track. I am answering your letter without reading it, but shoot, why do you want to read a letter for when you know what's in it. All your letters ever have in them is, "everybody likes me." Say, I am going to the shindig and then catch a ride to town, go home with Bus and not come home till Sunday night.

All of them are reading Western stories. I would be but I have already read them all.

Bye bye
Honorable Clyde M Crume

In 1933, it was Floyce's turn to graduate from high school. She repeated the accomplishments of her older sister and was valedictorian of her class. She graduated at sixteen and received a scholarship to attend college. Once again, her parents were reluctant to let their daughter go away from home to school because of her young age. However, she did attend school for a short period to study languages and while there she acquired some bookkeeping and secretarial skills as well.[5] Gladys was finishing up her junior year of college at Arkansas State and was looking to come home to teach in the small country schools around Munday, and she was also applying to schools in Arkansas, trying everything she could. Gladys was finally going to try teaching in the winter and going to school in the summer to finish her senior year and get her degree. Although she had advanced education, it was still not easy to find work in either Texas or Arkansas, even in the least desirable places. Her family was trying to help her in Texas and her friends in Arkansas were also looking for jobs for her. Nora wrote to Gladys about the family's efforts to help her and also their divided opinion concerning where she should teach. These letters also revealed the desperate living conditions in the Dust Bowl and the land close to it.

Friday Morning

Dearest Little Girl,

I was so glad to read your letter. I'm glad that you are pleased with your clothes. I went to Mrs. Meyers yesterday to see if I could find out anything. The old board elected principal a Mr. Kimbrough, also elected Mrs. Davenport back as primary. The new board elected all teachers back except Miss Osborn and put Mamie Crouch in. Mrs. Myers said Roscoe was using his influence through Mr. Peevy as same as if he was trustee only he can't vote. She said Mr. Myers couldn't do a thing only vote. There is two places to be filled Tuesday night – high school English and grammar school English. Louis Floyd is still working for Arnie Freeman, and the new principal brought over an English teacher – has a degree, good volleyball coach and so on, so Mrs. Myers said she was afraid she would get in through that man's pull. She said she hoped you could yet get a place. Mr. Myers said he would do all he could.

Another sand storm Monday finished us up. Dad is planting cotton; will have maize Sunday to plant over. He is at last ready to go to Arkansas. So tell Willie Dad is ready to come to you. If you can find anything, take it. You will be at Sheridan [Arkansas] soon. See Dr. Kelly again – he might hear of an opening. Tell him you have perfect health over there and how bad this country serves you. Dad and Morris may talk or try to see some of the trustees Saturday. You haven't wanted to teach here, nor do I want it either. Clyde said tell you to try hard for a place over there.

I have been so sick. None of them know how sick I was. I am a lot better but I'm not well yet. My right lung in the back part is so sore. My head roars till I can't half hear. Dad has a bad cough, but he is better. He hasn't had such a siege as I have. He will soon be 70, and it is too hard on us here. We could grow so much more in Arkansas. Floyce says hunt a place anywhere we all can move. Mr. Mitchell is planning to take a trip above Dequeen all up the western part, a place called Coolidge. They all seem anxious to move.

May God's richest blessings be yours,
Mama

People in Texas were getting so tired of the dirt and poor farming conditions that they were contemplating moving to a different part of Texas or even a different state. The Crumes were no exception. They wanted Gladys to get a job, but they hated to see her come back to Texas where the family was having breathing problems. They were torn, which brings certain questions to mind. Could the Crumes have survived the Thirties better in East Texas? What if they had not moved to Alvin,

Texas, so many years before? Would they have been able to continue to own their own land? So many questions for which they would never know the answers. Regrets were useless at this point and most of the time they didn't dwell on them. The following letter revealed one of the few times that Nora complained about her life and expressed any regrets for past decisions. She had loved the house that she and Gus had built in Maydelle in East Texas and wished she could still live there.

First Sunday of May
May 8, 1933

Dearest Girlie,

 I got your card but said, "Oh shoot, is this all?" But I was sure tickled to hear from you and know that you had made the fraternity [national honorary education fraternity]. I had a long letter from Arthur. Arthur was leaving for the mountains for six or eight weeks, steady work. He was glad of the work. His wife gets forty dollars per month. Her son has a job, three dollars per week and his lunch each day. That helps. It will be the middle of June before Art gets back. The sand still blows and will til after full moon or some good rains.

 Oh yes, I had a long letter from Aunt Ella [Nora's sister-in-law]. Ella said our old home [in Maydelle], the trees we set out shaded the street and all of the house in the afternoon. Mr. Acker had built a sleeping porch on the back porch and extended it clear around the well. It was so cool and nice. Oh dear, it most killed me. I loved that place so much. Clyde wouldn't write last week because he was afraid he had flunked Algebra, but he didn't. He made a C. Mr. D is now having them bring up their daily lesson on paper and reviewing on the board each day. Eggs were 10 cents [a dozen] yesterday. I got 8 cents for some leghorn hens. Cotton is 8 cents here at Munday. I see it's still going up. I do hope times pick up some. Say, did you pass on everything? You never did say. We will know about these places here before you go to Sheridan. I am going to try to make my dress next week. It is time; I'll need it.

Well, it's hot, sandy wind. It is so bad. I'm all worn out. You people over there should be shouting happy that you can breathe. Everything good.

Same old Moms

Gladys' sister Floyce wrote a different kind of letter. Somehow being young always inspired more optimism in the midst of hard times, perhaps because young people understood less the dire nature of their circumstances and could still believe anything was possible. Floyce's letter was full of neighborhood gossip and light-hearted issues. She wasn't wasting her paper to discuss the dire conditions of life in the thirties.

Munday, Texas
May 8, 1933

Dearest Glad,

This is Monday morning and the sand is blowing again. The wind! The wind! The wind! Remember that story? Ha Ha I don't know "nawthing" to write, but I'm a writing anyway.

J.B. wrote me that he surely did hope you came by there on your way home. He said Bill told him you might. I would like to be hid and hear them talking, wouldn't you? I hear that Irene and William are suing for a divorce. Hasn't Bertha ever said anything to you about them? Someone said Mr. and Mrs. Gaither separated them. I don't know anything about it. I'm

Floyce Mae Crume

sorry it happened. I thought they made a cute couple.

Onah [sister-in-law] said Gladys (Smith) was "that way" again. Ha. I'll tell you all of the gossip. Mama always tells you everything else. I went to see Mrs. Harrison one day last week. Charles always wants to know where you are and when you're coming home. He is a wart. Cle is still in California.

Gladys and Carrie are going to school this summer at Edmond. Thomas surely is tickled they are coming.

Well, I'll be "scramming."

Love,
Floyce

Gladys did eventually find a teaching position in West Texas at a small country school where she could teach during the winter and attend college classes during the summer. She chose North Texas State Teacher's College at Denton, Texas, to finish up her Bachelor's Degree. It took three years and teaching at multiple country schools where she worked hard during the winter, walking to school, lighting the fire in the stove before the students arrived, and supervising the filling of the water barrel for drinking water. Some of her students were as big as she was, and she had a few hair-raising experiences with some of the meaner ones who threatened to beat up their teacher. However, she stuck to it, always trying to do her best to educate her students, no matter the age. She even had special activities for her students such as plays and programs to encourage the parents as well as her students.[6]

Her family continued to endure the dust storms of West Texas while trying to scrape out a living on the land. Not everyone in the family, however, lived in perpetual dust. Nora and Gus's family in East Texas, back home in the Maydelle area, received rain on a regular basis and the extended family in Kentucky did as well. However, most of the family suffered in some way during the Depression years. Nora received the following letter from her sister-in-law in the Maydelle area.

Tuesday night
April 18, 1934

Dear Sister and family,

We received your letter today. Willie [Nora's brother and Ella's husband] aims to write tomorrow but he will just write about the place and the oil business, so I am writing the news around here. We are all well, but I sure am sore. I pruned tomatoes yesterday and today in the afternoon, so you know how I feel. They look fairly well. Olan [her son] has the best ones on the place. He has lots of blooms and a good many second clusters. Most of the tomatoes will be late. It stayed cold and wet so long they couldn't grow much. We have our corn planted and it looks pretty good. Will have to plow a little of it over where it was so wet. They have most of the cotton land bedded but will have to rebed before they plant.

My garden looks very well. The lice nearly ruined my cabbage and greens, but they have begun to grow since the weather is warmer. I don't have but nine little chicks. My hens just won't set seems like. Well, we are having a siege of measles here now. Over half the school children had to quit the last two weeks of school, and they are still having them around yet. Pink Britton died the third of this month. He had been down with T.B. since last fall. Syl Moore died about three weeks ago. He had paralysis. Mrs. Watson is getting along very well now. She was able to come to church last meeting day. We have our church covered, and it looks nice. We plan to paper and paint it if we get any tomato money. Pleasant Grove church has built them a tabernacle to have their revival meetings under. I haven't seen it, but they say it looks good.

I am so sorry you have high blood pressure. Papa and mama suffered so with it. I dread to think about having it myself or know anyone else has it. Harold [Nora's stepbrother] came to see Willie Sunday about the land again. He can hardly give up the idea that half of it don't belong to him, but I think Willie convinced him that it didn't. I guess he will get his eyes open sure enough when he gets your letter. Willie told him a lot too. He says he is not going to set down and give him half for it isn't right. He said your mother and you children worked and paid for

your home in Houston County. Of course your Pa helped, but he was away preaching lots of the time. I could tell you and Harold too a lot of things, but his mother is dead and at rest and we all make mistakes. I think Maude [Harold's wife] keeps him stirred up too. Well, it's 10 o'clock. I had better quit. Willie will write in the morning. Ella
Hope Gladys is feeling fine by now.

William "Willie" and Ella Ferguson

Willie and Ella Ferguson remained close relatives of Nora and Gus all of their lives. Willie was Nora's younger brother, and they were the children of John T. Ferguson by his first marriage. The references made to Harold in the letter revealed the strained situation between John T. Ferguson's two families. Harold was John's son by his second wife, Ada Belle Crume, Gus's sister. After John died, and especially after Ada Belle's death, disputes over John's land arose, particularly because an oil company was interested in drilling on it. Ella made the point that John's first wife and his children by her had maintained the land and helped to pay for it with their labor, long before John married a second time and had a final child. The community property laws of Texas eventually settled the matter, and for years after that, the heirs of John Ferguson were periodically called upon to sign leases for drilling purposes, but nothing ever came of it. [7]

Another letter of the period in 1935 revealed what life was like in a different part of the country, Kentucky. Gus's cousin, A.V. "Tony" Williams wrote about his area and the relatives that belonged to Gus's mother's side of the family.

Ekron, Kentucky
March 31, 1935

Dear Cousin Nora,

Well, this rainy Sunday I am putting in my time writing to my two daughters and other relatives. We are having so much rain now. Did you folks have a dust storm? I read in the papers where it was so bad in some parts of the west You and cousin Sam [Gus] said your daughter Gladys was thinking of coming to Kentucky to visit her kinfolks. Tell her we would be awful glad to see her. I never saw any of our Crume kinfolks. Tell Gladys to come to Ekron on the train and we will meet her and take her to see her kinfolks.

A.V. "Tony" Williams

When my wife and son went to Oklahoma to visit wife's sister a few years ago, they traveled mostly by bus, but railroads have reduced passenger rates now. It is nicer and more safe traveling by railroad anyway.

Wife and daughter have 529 young chickens in two brooder houses. We have stoves built of brick and burn wood. In about a week they will set about 200 turkey eggs. They will buy 100 eggs from a man about 25 miles away. He is the largest turkey raiser in the state. He raises about two hundred a year. Wife just told me he raised 5500 last year.

We have beautiful scenery here on the highway from here to Louisville. The road runs through Muldroughs Hills; they are low mountains with deep gorges between. Then the road runs a piece along by the Ohio River. I wonder sometimes that if the man who composed "Beautiful Ohio" perhaps traveled this road. Then there is the Abe Lincoln farm near Hodgenville and the log cabin where Lincoln was born. Lincoln was born in abject poverty. The cabin has a stick chimney and dirt floor. This is enclosed in a large concrete building. It is about forty minutes from where we live in LaRue County. In those days doctors were very scarce. There was a lady whose maiden name was Mary Brooks. She first married John Lather, he died, and then she married Isham Inlow. She had some knowledge of medicine and she was the doctor when Lincoln was born. I am a descendant of this woman on my mother's side from the Enlows.

Some people think that all Kentuckians are bad. But the mountain counties in the eastern part of the state are where there are so many killings and fights. They do awful bad up there. The people are not so bad here, of course. We have like everywhere else some bad people. Some man living out of Kentucky said that Boston was noted for boots and shoes and Kentucky was noted for shoots and booze. There is so much crime and lawbreaking everywhere.

Well, this is the time of year where we get tired of our own eating. I was up town the other day and got some sweet potatoes, cabbage, greens and apples. I buy such stuff at the A and P store for 4 ½ cents, but they were old cabbage on the market. New cabbage from the South I sometimes buy at wholesale houses, but I have to buy fifty pounds at a time there. In Louisville we have what is called the market about one acre of ground filled with stands where all kinds of fruits and vegetables are sold. I suppose they have this in all large cities.

Well my letter is getting long. Hoping that this finds you and yours well and happy. With love and best wishes to all.

Your cousin,
A.V. Williams

The Crumes must have read this letter rather wistfully. They could hardly remember what rain was, did not have access to any beautiful rivers, and even if they could have visited a farmer's market, they wouldn't have thought to purchase what they could grow themselves. It might have been nice to sell some of their produce at a market like that, though. Gladys did not make the trip to Kentucky until many years later when she went with her own family and fulfilled a lifelong dream.

In 1936, Gladys finally achieved her goal and finished her Bachelor's Degree at North Texas State Teacher's College. It had only taken her eight years, and it had been bought with her and her family's hard work, persistence, and constant belief that it would happen. It was a family victory as well as a personal one. Gladys was later to sum up her school years, "All of my college training was obtained under the cloud of a great financial struggle. What teaching I did was very poorly paid, some of it being script that had to be discounted to be cashed. But having barely enough money to get by did not mar the happy times I experienced. Indeed, it merely taught me greater self-reliance and how to value what I had. I will always recall my school days with pleasure."[8] She had discovered the secret of turning negatives into positives, and it was a lesson she would remember the rest of her life.

After graduation, Gladys began teaching high school English at Mattson Rural High School, a new consolidated school at Haskell, Texas. Her little brother Clyde happened to be attending this same school in his senior year and had her for a teacher. One time in class she was mad at the whole class for performing poorly on an assignment. She mistakenly asked the students what they expected to get out of the class with such behavior. Her brother piped up, his eyes sparkling, and said, "a half credit." She tended to be harder on him than the rest of her students, much to his discomfort,

but he still made an A. His father had warned him when Gladys became his teacher, "Now you behave yourself and help sister make a good reputation as a teacher."[9] Most of the time he did.

Gladys turned out to be a very popular teacher because she involved herself in student activities and took a genuine interest in her students. She even coached some of the athletic teams and drill squads. She was always upbeat and cheerful, and she knew how to teach the young students of the Depression years. From personal experience she knew what hard work and persistence could produce, and thus she could encourage her students to go after whatever they wanted their lives to be. These years of teaching were a real joy for her.

Gus and Nora had no more children to raise and were approaching the last years of their lives. Their last child was a senior in high school and ready to graduate. The Crumes were more than tired of struggling to make ends meet in West Texas, although in their opinion, the time they had spent there had not been all bad. Gus and Nora had raised their children, lived on farms they enjoyed for the most part, and found plenty to laugh about as well as gripe about. The children were self-reliant enough to enjoy life no matter where they lived and to move forward towards a better future. As the decade was drawing to a close, Gus and Nora were facing the decision of where to spend their last years. They decided to go home to Maydelle. Gus was seventy-four years old by this time and could no longer manage the large planter farms, and he wanted to spend his last years in the place where he began his life. Nora felt the same way, even though it meant living apart from her children. So in early 1938, the elder Crumes went home. In doing so, they left their children behind in West Texas.[10]

19
Living Apart

The year 1938 was a pivotal year in the life of the Crume family, but the national problems continued. The "dirty thirties" decade was drawing to a close, but the drought in the Dust Bowl area continued. Over the course of the decade many changes had been made in agriculture – re-plowing the land into contour furrows, planting trees in shelterbelts, strip cropping, terracing, crop rotation and cover crops – all soil conservation methods which were enforced by the farmers themselves through district divisions. On the national level, work had been done on the banks and putting people back to work through the WPA, the NYA, and the CCC. Unfortunately, Texas spent the decade embroiled in one political corruption scandal after another which resulted in high crime and misuse of federal funds. However, by the end of the decade the political situation had moderated somewhat, the crime rate had been brought under a degree of control, education was being funded better, and Texas and the country as a whole were poised to take advantage, at least economically, of the coming world conflict.[1]

In 1938 Art was working all over the world as a driller and supervisor for an oil company, Morris was working in the restaurant business, Gladys was teaching at Mattson Rural High School at Haskell, Texas, Floyce was working as a bookkeeper for Brown and Root in Houston, Texas, and Clyde was finishing high school. In May of 1938 Clyde graduated, and immediately after the ceremony he and Gladys drove to Maydelle in Gladys' new Plymouth automobile on which she was scrambling to make the payments. Clyde had decided to go to junior college at Jacksonville, not too far from where his parents were living at Maydelle, and his sister had borrowed some money to get him started. She never enjoyed buying anything on credit, but at times she did it in order to secure either her education or that of one of her family members or to make a big purchase such as a car. One of Gus and Nora's children would be living close to them after all. [2]

One incident which impacted the family before the elder Crumes' move, perhaps earlier than 1938 but after 1936, was a serious automobile accident involving Floyce. Floyce was home from Houston for a visit at Munday. Gladys received a phone call where she was teaching telling her that her sister had been in a very serious car accident, and the family should come immediately to the hospital. Gladys had managed to acquire an old used car at that time, a Ford, so she drove to her parents' home, and all of them went to the hospital together.

Gladys and the Plymouth

On the way she was driving so fast that Gus had to exclaim, "Well, sister, be careful; don't kill us all." He probably wasn't very comfortable in those aggravating automobiles anyway. When they got to the hospital, Floyce was hovering between life and death, and she stayed that way for days. As Gladys was later to say, "When I saw her in that condition, I felt that the lump in my throat would choke me." Floyce finally pulled through, but her most serious injury, a broken arm, would plague her for all the years to come. It required several surgeries before it would heal, and she was left without the full use of it. Periodically she had to have further surgeries for the remainder of her life. Her family stayed with her and, as usual, prayed fervently for her recovery.[3]

Sometime during the year 1938 Floyce met a young man named Charles Leaverton, known as "Charlie", who was working as a cowboy/farm worker for his father who had a farm in the area of Benjamin, Texas, only about twenty miles from Munday. Floyce may have met him at some of the get-togethers for young people in the area when she was home from Houston. They began to date when possible. [4] Gus and Nora were living in a rented house in Maydelle with a small amount of land attached to it, and Gus continued to farm on a very small scale.[5] He still had the heart condition and had to be careful. They were happy to be "home." For the most part, they could live off of their small pension from one of the places Gus had worked and farm a little on the side. Their son Clyde wrote the following letter to his sister, Gladys, from Jacksonville after he got settled in school.

Wednesday 12:45
In my room 310
on east side of dorm
on third floor

Dear Gladys,

    I suppose you will wonder why I am writing now instead of during the weekend, but when I go home I am always doing something, if not working or company I am fooling around, that I just sit down and scribble the line or two and you don't know anything. So it is quiet and all the boys gone to eat and I just ate since I bring a sack lunch from the café every morning so I won't have to go back til night, and I was kinda in the mood to scribble you a few lines and can mail it as usual when I go home this weekend. [Clyde was working in a café.]

    First, Morris came and then Floyce. But you didn't arrive. I was surely glad to see him. He gave me $2.00 on my tuition. I paid $5.00 yesterday and will pay the other $2.50 the middle of the month. We surely had a good time when we went pecan hunting, got a lot of pecans too. Dad and Mother and him came up Tuesday night just as I was putting on my apron so I was home and did not come back til Wednesday about 4:00. Floyce came in Saturday about 12:00. We were not expecting her at all. Surely enjoyed being with her. Of course we talked and talked and wished you were there. She said she thought she could get me a job easily enough down there next summer. My school is out May 6. I stayed 'til Monday morning before I came back up. Got up at five 'til 5:00. Boy, was I sleepy. Ennis and I carried her to Palestine about 6:45 Sunday night; her bus left at 8:33. She seemed to really enjoy the stay.

The carnival at Maydelle was a bunch of hooey. They made $40.00 though. We had some boxing and I framed up with another kid. He hit me the first lick and I fell and was counted out. Everyone surely laughed, so I guess it went over – ha ha.

I think our home will be rather nice. Of course, it is not fixed up yet, but Lester said he would fix it up. I like it there fine. All the folks down there really seem to like me, but it seems most people do or seem to. ha ha

For Thanksgiving we are going to get a pretty good rest. We get out Tuesday at 12:30 and come back the next Monday. Pretty good holidays, eh? I guess I ought to get some wood cut. I cut the other Saturday and got a nice pile cut. I had a pretty good time Halloween. Me and my roomie really tore up the rooms. The headmaster caught us stacking one. We then went to town and got some oil cans (quart) and stacked them on the stairs. Boy, when the boys came in, there was the 'awfullest' racket you ever heard.

School is O.K. I have a pretty fair time. Of course that blooming work messes up everything. I could have been in the Glee Club and some others, but I have no time or money. I guess I have a pretty hard time – get up in the morning and walk about ¾ mile to eat, then come back and then back at night and then come back after work. But it is enabling me to go to school for $7.50 and I can't gripe. But I surely worked hard to get in school and now I am surely working hard to get to go. Ha Ha But I am doing fine in my school work. I can't complain. Of course, sometimes I get the blues and don't give a "sheet" if I wasn't going to school, but then I get over the blues and wouldn't quit for anything. I keep remembering the fun we used to have in West Texas, and when I think that they'll never be no more, it kinda gets me. But I'm O.K. Don't you think this is a pretty nice letter. I'll mail it this weekend or give it to Mama. I love you lots.

Your bud,
Clyde (picture on next page)

This was a pretty typical "younger brother in college" letter. Clyde, like his brothers and sisters, was a hard worker, but he wasn't above enlisting a little sympathy for his "hard life." He does mention Gus and Nora's new home at Maydelle, and the work they were doing on it.

On Christmas Day, 1938, at Rusk, Texas (about ten to fifteen miles east of Maydelle), Floyce married Charles Leaverton.[6] Her family, except for brother Art, was assuredly in attendance and because of the winter holiday, Charles's family may have been able to attend as well. All of his life, Charles, or Charlie as he was known, was a tough man who worked hard and played hard as well. He enjoyed hunting and fishing and kept hunting dogs. Floyce knew how to handle him, though, at least most of the time, and she was a somewhat calming influence in his life.

He went from one strenuous, even dangerous at times, career to another one. He and Floyce moved to Bakersfield, California, sometime between 1939 and 1940 , and he went to work first as a member of a track laying gang for five years and then as a brakeman for the railroad, the Santa Fe. His two brothers had gotten jobs with the railroad as well, but the oldest one, William, returned home to Texas to run the family farm after their father died, went on to be a foreman for the League Estate, a large ranching outfit, and eventually owned his own elevator business.[7] The brakeman job for the railroad required Charlie to run along the top of train cars while they were moving and to apply the brakes on each car – very dangerous work that he managed to do successfully for many years. Another part of his job was coupling and uncoupling train cars in the railroad yards. His usual "run" was from Bakersfield, California, out into the desert to Barstow,

California. There was no such thing as overtime, and men were expected to work twelve hour shifts on any day of the week in all kinds of weather.

In later years he became a conductor which was a step up, but he stayed with the railroad because of the wages he could make which were good and the benefits the railroad offered through the union. The railroad was dependable work during economic hard times, but it was hard physically. He only had one bad accident in his career. He slipped and fell in between the moving train cars and onto the track when he was trying to manipulate the brakes, and the train ran over him. It rolled him into a ball and spit him out the side of the train, having "skinned him from his head to his toes." That was the only damage he incurred, a miracle. It is recounted in the family that he attended church as soon as he was able after the accident, after having refused to go for many years, and joined that Sunday.[8]

Charlie and his dog

In 1940 Clyde finished his years at the junior college at Jacksonville, Texas, and was ready to move on to college at North Texas State Teacher's College at Denton, Texas, the school where his sister had graduated. He would be moving farther away from his parents but closer to his sister Gladys. He wrote his parents the following letter.

1512 Hickory
Talons
Monday night 6:20

Dearest Mom and Dad,

I received your letter today and I surely enjoyed your letter. It surely made me feel better. I am liking school fine. I like all of my subjects and teachers fine. Well, here I am again. It surely is a pretty day outside; I guess fall is here! You can send a quilt anytime in the next two or three weeks. I think one will be O.K. – two will be thousands. Floyce sent my shoes. I have gotten all my mail. The reason I changed from Mrs. Ramsey's is no privacy. She was old and cranky and mainly I can get by $2.00 cheaper. Also this is just across the street from school. Her home was four and ½ blocks. The money was the main thing. I got my laundry done. Thanks for the dime. I am glad you all are about through work. I hope you get some wood cut, Dad. Maybe I'll be there Thanksgiving and cut some. I guess the church really looks different. I guess Art wouldn't care if Dad's idea of a Gulf Storm would happen. Ha I haven't heard from Floyce yet.

School is progressing nicely. See, I get two meals a day for $10.00 a month, and that saves $2.50. I am not very hungry every morning anyway. I would like to see you all. Has it rained there any? I guess school is doing nicely in Maydelle. Have you all got another dog yet or do you want one? I guess we will miss Ole Pal when we come home. Glad said her school was really running smoothly. There are more cars here than any place I have ever seen. Of course some of the students are as broke as I am. But that is no disgrace! I didn't even remember the day when my birthday came. It was the next day before I realized I was twenty years of age. Boy, there surely is a large bunch of boys and girls going here. They are from everywhere. I saw the Ballard kids from Haskell, an Edwards from Wienert, kids from Rochester, Hamlin, Rule, etc.

Dad, don't you worry about the rifle. I don't ever think about the war. We either fight or we don't. There isn't much we can do about it. I hear something about it on the radio every day. I went to the college show the other night in the auditorium. Man, they really have a real orchestra and band here. There is over 1000 freshmen here and about 800 sophomores. You can imagine what this is compared to Jacksonville's twenty-five. Ha Ha! Denton is not as large as I thought it was. I mean the business parts. There are private dwellings miles in any direction. I wouldn't take for my radio. I surely wish that yours was fixed. Is the lights come through yet? My vaccination is taking. I am glad that it is because I won't have to fool with it anymore. It doesn't hurt much. My side is O.K., I think. I can see the doctor any time I want to. He fixed my arm. Please, don't you two work too hard.

Everyone seems to like me. I am not very homesick now, and I hope I don't get that way often. I am going to go out for basketball when the time comes, and I'll probably get cut the first day. They say that freshmen won't have a chance. I don't particularly care. Tell everyone hello. Goobye and Love

Love
Clyde

Hello. This is Wednesday morning, and I am sending your letter today. I got Evelyn's letter yesterday. Surely enjoyed receiving it. I'll write her sometime. Most of my clothes are clean. I think I can make it OK. I have been gone twenty-seven days this morning! That's a pretty good while, isn't it? I have not had to study much, but I will have to start soon now. Everyone is becoming settled. Well, answer soon and tell me everything. I love you.

Your son,
Clyde

Clyde was experiencing bouts of homesickness with his move to the new school, but he was settling in and getting acquainted. He was concerned about his parents working too hard as well. He, like his sister Gladys before him, was depending upon Art to help him with expenses. It seemed that Art would never be free of his responsibility for his family, but he genuinely did not mind. Although he had the ability and did not get to attend college, he wanted his brother and sister to

Art and "Jap" in South America

have that chance. His generosity was a legend in the family, and this included stories of people beyond the family as well. Every person he met with a sob story got a hand out. He never minded giving when he had the money to give. [9]

In 1939, Gladys changed her teaching position. She had begun to feel that she was standing still in her career, and so she began to look into positions at larger city schools. She moved to Iowa Park, Texas, near Wichita Falls, and began teaching English at Iowa Park High School and also serving as the head of the English Department. She was not too far from Munday and also Clyde at Denton, Texas, but it was not a trip she or Clyde wanted to make every week. This move was a step up for Gladys to a somewhat larger town, and it had the advantage of being close to a large city. She had more responsibilities in her job and more challenges which she relished. She became the senior class sponsor, which involved many activities including a school trip to New Mexico and El Paso, Texas. The Iowa Park years would prove to be some of the happiest and most fulfilling of her life. [10]

Clyde was beginning to feel impatient with the length of time it took to obtain a college education. He knew it was important and that his family would sacrifice to help him finish, but he was beginning to dislike being dependent upon them while attending college full time. He wanted to be working and helping his parents, rather than being a financial burden while going to school. They, however, wanted him to finish college. They had gotten one child through college through her own persistence and hard work and the help of the rest of the family. They wanted another child to have that accomplishment. The division in the family concerning what to do is revealed in the following letters.

Maydelle, Texas
October 2, 1939

Gladys dear,

I can't even think when I mailed your last letter. We finished our wood, all we will cut now, and hauled it in Friday. We sawed and cut part of two days. I was so worn out when we got through and cleaned up. It came a rain and a Norther. Harold came Saturday, wanted us to go to Pleasant Grove to 5th Sunday meeting. We went.

We didn't go to Sunday School. I was worn out. We rested and read a lot.

Maggie is home now. They gave her five blood transfusions and took eight teeth. She is still weak but has a good color and eats all she can, laughs and talks, says she is going to get well. But she may if nothing else sets up and they can get the rest of her teeth out. Clyde said Floyce sent him some money. He paid up everything, had his clothes all clean and found a quarter, had his hair cut but never said how or where he found it. We had a letter from Floyce. She thinks maybe he had better quit, come out there and work, go to school later. Dad says no. He had to quit school too much. Now he was making his grade, and there would be some way made for him to get by. Arthur sent us $10.00 and said as soon as he found out how much it would take for his wife to get home on, he would send Clyde some money. Said he knew how hard it was for you and Clyde both to be broke all the time. I think Floyce don't want to pay any more, only a dollar or two now and then. So you get up the money for his board some way and pay that. Dad paid Lester $5.00 on feed he got last year and ordered himself a pair of every day shoes and socks. Insurance is due again. We have meal, flour, sugar, coffee and lard so we can get by for awhile.

Lester got sorry for Dad. His pension was out and looked like Arthur was not going to write and gave Dad $5.00. He tried to not take it but he insisted so hard, he took it. Then he paid him $5.00 out of this on his debt. The Lord will make a way if we trust Him. I wanted to send Clyde a dollar so bad but looked like Dad had to have the shoes – was almost barefoot wearing one shoe of a kind and them full of holes – ha. We laughed and worked on. We have plenty of wood and pine for kindling and can stay by the fire, don't owe anyone for cutting it either. Pierce has his timber cut out and we want to go up there and cut a load or two of pine wood to burn with the oak. Trees are already cut, get the tops that are left. We are not wasting anything. Still have plenty canned goods and dry peas and potatoes. We have Algie's cow now, has a little heifer calf. Her name is Popeye. Dad said that was really her name so I named the calf Sweetpea – ha. I washed the curtains, scrubbed the floor so it looks better. I keep the windows down, doors shut to keep out the sand. I washed the curtains for this room, will clean it up when I iron.

Maydelle is putting on a carnival tomorrow night. My, they have run everybody ragged for things. Now listen, don't let Clyde quit school. He said we would all talk it over Christmas. You write Arthur another letter and see what you can do about getting him to help all he can midterm on the tuition. If he will pay a big part of that, the hens will be laying and we can help some if they get to work on that lake and dam. Morris will get where he can help some. Well, be sweet and don't worry. We will take care of ourselves. I love you.

Mother

A good portion of Nora's life, when she wasn't working her fingers to the bone, was spent in hatching plans to try to keep the family solvent and working towards a better future. Her intelligence and her teaching background would not let her accept that hard work and planning would not gain her family a brighter future. Most of the time, all she could offer was encouragement and inventive ideas because money was nonexistent. This time she was fighting desperately to keep her youngest child in school. However, her son was moving towards a different goal. Gus tacked a short note and drawing on Nora's letter.

Hello my dearest Gladys,
Well you know I don't like to write to nobody. This old lady Crume that is living with me said I had to write you this morning because it's cloudy and cold. She is ironing and I am smoking the pipe of peace while she is quiet. So now she says you are jealous because I sent Floyce a picture and did not send you one, so here goes. Don't you and Clyde go wild while he is out there. Take care of yourself and tell him to try to stay well, that for both of you exposure brings on colds and colds lead to something else. All right now, laugh. I can't draw a picture but here comes Popeye and Sweetpea. Keep this, you may not get another soon. I am done. Be good and take care of yourself. Tell Clyde to stay on the job. Love to you.

Dad

so glad — is up and down. Mittie will stay with us this week I hope by [illegible] they will be ok. Henry has [brought?] us some wood this morning. I haven't slept but little in two wks, was glad to see Lizzie and John. But oh a crowd was here to see them until I thought I would [illegible]. Dad sits up in a chair [illegible] daily, but his legs either won't stand any [illegible] — mail this. Be sweet — will write again this week — [illegible]

Gus had not lost his sense of humor in all those years of hard living. He was still the friendly, outgoing, big-hearted man he had always been. However, he also wanted his son to finish college. He knew that Clyde had the ability, and he hated to see that go to waste.

1512 W. Hickory
Monday Afternoon 5:00

Dearest Mom and Dad,

I thought I would start you all another letter and then I'll finish it when I receive your letter. Man, it is cold up here today. It has been cool the whole weekend. But I have gobs of cover so therefore, don't worry about me. I wrote Art a letter and raked him over the coals –ha. It is clear as a whistle – a real old West Texas fall. Time seems to be passing rather fast. Is it cold down there? School is O.K. I made 90 on a Chemistry test last week. I'll be glad to get another look at the country. This hustle and bustle gets monotonous sometimes. That Spanish is right down my line. I make good in it all the time. Well, I gotta go eat supper.

Well, I got back from supper and I thought as I set here by myself that I would write some more. I got some money from Floyce and paid up everything I owed and had all my clothes

cleaned, and I guess I'll be clean for awhile now. But again I am broke, but I got two or three stamps so I'll be O.K. I am doing fine in school, but I'll be glad when this semester is over. I'll sho' be glad when Christmas comes. I'll have been exactly two months or sixty-one days tomorrow. That seems a good while. My room is a south room and we have a good stove and it really warms the room up. I hope Maggie is doing better. All the kids are getting new hats and sweaters, but I will go on and never let on that I even want anything –ha. Life is like that. What do you all think about the war? Sometimes I think its about over and then I can see us in there. I dreamed that we got in the war, but I don't believe that it will come true. I don't believe in dreams.
Wednesday Afternoon 3:00

I surely enjoyed the letter. I was beginning to think that I wasn't going to hear from you all. It has warmed up and it surely is pretty outside. School is O.K., but Lord knows it gets me sometimes. It sho' gets rough, and I almost walk out, but I guess I got it about stuck out, I hope. I can take it myself, but when I realize that all the pains you all are suffering, it goes all over me. Especially when I realize that I could help things so much. I aim to go to work at the semester. I know you all would suffer and never say a word, but Mom, I aim to help you all before it gets too late. I can always finish school. Gladys said it looked as if that it was the only thing to do – help all of us get straightened out and then I could come on back and finish. It would take so much money for next semester and I can go to work and start helping. It would take aplenty of worry off of me. So I guess it looks to me like the only sensible thing to do.

I am still making good grades. Four weeks until I go see Gladys. Then it won't be but three weeks until we'll be home. That surely sounds good to me. I sure will be glad to wrap my teeth around three square meals a day. I surely will be glad to see you all. I heard from Floyce yesterday. She said that she was pretty sure I could go to work out there. She said that she guessed it would be best to work awhile and help you all out of a jam. Then I could finish and school would mean more to me. I think it is best.

I guess it has been cold there too. It has warmed up today. I am glad that you all have plenty. I was glad that Arthur came across, I guess he has been in a jam. I was glad to hear about the cow. That was the only thing to call the calf! Dad, you just won't write will you? O.K. I know how badly you dislike to write. I am really doing good in Espanol. I am doing fine. I am gaining weight too. I surely liked the dime. I know you all would go through everything and not say a word, but now I am going to help awhile. I know it is best to have education and I'll get some, but I am going to help you all first if God is willing.

I love you.
Clyde Crume

As 1939 drew to a close, Clyde had made up his mind. The restless feelings that were driving him to do something to help his family were reaching a peak. He could no longer sit in class when he knew they were fighting to survive. When 1940 began, for the first time in a long time, Clyde was not in school. Even though he only lacked a year and a half, he quit. He was going to find a well-paying job, and the place he had chosen to look was California, where so many others had sought a way out of the Great Depression. However, it would take several months of looking for a job before he made the final decision to go to California.[11]

Also, with the year 1939 came the rains which finally broke the drought that had plagued the country for so long. At its height, it was estimated that 850 million tons of topsoil had blown off of the Southern Plains in one year, and the dust storms had reached as far as Washington, D.C.[12] Finally, the national nightmare that had been the Dust Bowl was only a bad memory, but the economy was slow to recover and the Great Depression lingered. This was obvious when looking at the Crume family struggle in that year. However, on the horizon was looming the event which would change the situation. Fighting was taking place in Europe, and it was only a matter of time and circumstance until the United States would be drawn into the conflict. A war which would become worldwide and cost many lives would also ultimately be the salvation of the United States economy.

The Effect of Hard Times

"Well, Mom, your family surely went on a roller coaster ride from 1903 to 1940. They were up and then they were down, but they seemed to take on life just the same, whether it was good or bad." I was thinking about all that I had learned about my grandparents and aunts and uncles, as well as my own mother.

"Yes, that pretty well sums up what happened to them and how they reacted to it. What happens to people generally is a combination of the times in which they live and the decisions that they make in trying to live in those times. My family made its share of mistakes, but the decisions that they made were made in good faith with the knowledge that they had at the time and believing that God would take care of them no matter what happened. In a way, it is hard to argue with that. I guess what is important is that they survived and were able to continue finding satisfaction with their lives. If asked, they undoubtedly would have said that their lives were fine."

"The Great Depression and the Dust Bowl years caused a lot of misery. They changed so many lives, some for the worse and some for the better. The people who came out of that generation were savers. They used, and then reused almost everything, and they revered plastic when it came into widespread use because it would last seemingly forever. They would never again take anything that they owned for granted and especially the ability to get a job and make a living. Even after the prosperous years of post WWII came along, people who had lived through the Depression did not want to give up the habits that they had learned in the Depression years. It was so horrible that it made a lasting impression. I can say that just the word 'Depression' gives me an uneasy feeling, and I wasn't even alive then."

"I hope you never have to know what that was like, lovie," Mom was remembering that past misery. "And yet, in the midst of that time period, many people found a strength and an ability that they didn't know they had. Just as many others were completely devastated and succumbed to suicide or hopeless wandering from place to place, never finding a purpose. I believe that my family was in the first category and that they were survivors."

"I remember one of your old letters where your brother Clyde was grateful for a dime someone had sent him. Anyone today who thinks that the phrase, 'Buddy, can you spare a dime?' which came out of the Great Depression, was an exaggeration of the times, should read your old letters. It was just an unbelievable period in American history."

"Yes it was, and my family lived it, survived it, and moved on to better lives in spite of the mark it left on all of us. If it were ever to happen again, and we hope it doesn't, I would bet the American people would find a way to overcome it," Mom was speaking from experience this time and not just patriotic fervor.

"I would take that bet and double it that you are right," I enthused. "Do you think that Gus and Nora ever thought much about how their lives had changed from the time of Silas Moses with his energy and the successful world that he built at Pine Town?" I asked as a final thought on all of this.

"They may have thought about it on occasion, but they weren't the type to worry about it or obsess over it. They were too busy trying to survive. The sheer amount of work that they had to do kept their minds and their hands busy, and they were always centered on living in the present and trusting God to take care of everything else. They were basically happy, family-oriented people who enjoyed helping others."

"Even there, they made a contribution to society, something different from Silas Moses but just as important." I had concluded my grandparents' family, although poor as Job's turkey[1], had still occupied a meaningful place in the family line.

21
New Beginnings

May 8, 1940

Dear Mom and Dad,

I arrived Tuesday afternoon about 1:00. Floyce wrote a card, but it was not sent off yesterday. Maybe you will get this Saturday. I dropped you a card from Santa Rosa.

I believe I'll really like it out here. It surely is a pretty town. I saw some beautiful country all the way out here. I have registered at the unemployment office. They talked pretty nice. It is clear and hot here all the time.

I hope everything there is O.K. Tell all hello. I guess the crop will be pretty by now. I'll write Aunt Minnie and Evelyn soon. I guess you had a time at the dinner Sunday. Dad, did you give them a good pep talk?

Well, I'll write again soon.

Love,
Clyde

Floyce said she would write in a day or two. She sent the card on.

Clyde had arrived in California, specifically Bakersfield, where his sister Floyce and her husband were living, but he did not immediately go to work on the railroad with his brother-in-law Charlie. He tried a few other things first, but evidently he decided that the railroad was his best opportunity. It paid fairly well, had good benefits, and he would be deferred from service in the army because railroad workers were considered vital to the country's economy and the war effort. He started working as a brakeman and had the same "run" as his brother-in-law. He made friends easily in Bakersfield and found a roommate that he liked, the weather was sunny most of the time, and he was able eventually to send some money home to his folks. He was doing as well as he could have expected.[1] His parents must have been disappointed because he did not finish his education after coming so close, but they held out hope that he would finish when times got better.

Clyde's older brother, Art, was becoming a world traveler. In 1940 he was in South America at Petrolea, Colombia. He wrote the following letter home.

Petrolea   August 13, 1940

Dear Mom and Dad,

Hi folks. I've put off writing because I thought I might have a surprise and get to come home, but "sho nuff" I didn't. It seems as though I'll be here one more year. The boys who were sent to Argentina left yesterday. One of them was a special friend of mine, so I feel kinda left today. Dad, if this man did not forget it, he will mail you an old suit of mine that I asked him to send you. It is that gray suit winter weight that I brought down here. It is almost too small for me, but I think Mom can fix it for you. I weigh 227 lbs. now, got the dangdest little pot belly you ever saw. I can't, to save my neck, seem to do anything about it. While on evening tour, I only eat two meals a day and drink a pint thermos of coffee, but I still get fat. This man's name, who will send the suit, is Albert Brown. He lives at Big Springs and all his people were originally from Lufkin and Troup. I won't know till after the first of the month for sure whether he took it or not as it was in town but am sure he did.

What do you hear from Clyde? Is he working and does he like California? Where is Morris now?

The Indians went on the war path about twenty kilometers southeast of here last week. They ambushed a crew of natives, working for an engineer on a survey job out there and killed one, wounded three others. One of them died here in the hospital. Then last Saturday they ambushed a pack train, killed one mule in his tracks, shot another with three arrows, wounded one of the native packers quite seriously. So far the County scouts have not been able to locate their house. They found five over-night shelter camps, one of them had fifteen sleeping mats in it but no Indians. Mr. Shaffer, chief engineer, and Jimmy Hufendick, my boss, asked me if I wanted to take a party up there and hunt them. I told them no as those Indians weren't lost and I darn sure did not need them in my crew. As far as I'm concerned, if those Indians are lost, they can find themselves. I am just as close as I want to be to them. If I get any good pictures of these wounded natives, I'll send you one.

How does your hat fit, Dad, and does it look O.K.? Jap [Art's wife, Jap was her nickname] said the hat shop did a good job but that the brim was just a bit narrow. Holy smokes, these people never saw a head as big as 7 3/8 till we Americans came down here. A foot over an 8 ½ is almost unheard of.

Well, I guess I better bathe and clean up as it is 11:00 a.m. and we have to eat before 12:00 or else we don't eat till midnight. I will try to be more prompt in writing from now on as I waited this time to see if I could come home.

Tell everyone hello and take good care of yourselves.

Your loving son,
Arthur

Art's life as an oil field worker was never dull. During his career he spent time in some of the world's hot spots. Wherever the oil was in the Western Hemisphere, he was sent there, and he became reconciled to being out of the United States for long periods. He was a tough man and had a hard job to do, but he still had a tender heart when it came to his family or anyone who needed him. He was always thinking of his family and their needs when he was away from them. Did he ever wish his life had been different? Probably not. He liked his work and the challenge it offered, he liked

Art in Columbia

traveling and experiencing new places, and he accepted what life brought him. A college education and a different career were lost opportunities of long ago which he didn't have the time to think about except as an occasional reminiscence.

In Art's letter, he asked about his brother Morris. He was still at Altus, Oklahoma, working in the restaurant business. So, part of the family was in California, one was in Oklahoma, and the rest were in Texas. However, with Gus and Nora living at Maydelle, it was easier for Gus's son Elmer who lived at Houston to come for visits, so it was a chance for Gus to reacquaint himself with that part of his family. Whether this actually happened is not known. In January of 1941, a change came about in the Crumes' lives which had nothing to do with where they lived and was announced in the following letter.

Maydelle, Texas
January 5, 1941

Dear Gladiola,

According to promise, I am writing. Was glad you made your trip home O.K. Also glad that you had a pleasant visit at Denton. Well, Dad suffered terrible with his teeth all last week. Wednesday morning he woke up and had no use of either leg. They would fall over like a baby's. We worked, rubbed linament, kept rubbing them till he could stand and he tried to stomp, beat them with his fist. He could walk by my holding him but had no feeling in them. I gave him more purgative, but he sit around, beat and rubbed on his legs most all day. The weather was bad. We worried on till Friday. Floyce sent $3.00 and that night he suffered terrible all night. Saturday morning Evelyn and I carried him to the dentist. He pulled three teeth; all were infected. The dentist didn't much think that caused the leg trouble but said getting those teeth out would help that trouble. I have kept him in pretty close yesterday and today. His legs still have the dead feeling but seem better when he walks. He and I both think it was another stroke.

I was sweeping the hall and he called me, said he wanted to talk to me, I came on. He asked me if I had thought what I would do if he went away. I tried to be brave, I said not very much. I told him I would stay here. The Lord would take care of me some way. He said but you don't have a pension. I told him I would live on the chickens. The kids would pay the rent. He said he didn't want to leave me. He had hoped we would go close together. I told him not to worry. He would get better. He would get over it. He might not be able to work but we would be all right. We had to stay close till winter was over. So we have those teeth out, and we will see how he gets along by the time they cure up. He walks very slow.

Floyce said she would send $3.00 the 10th. I'm trying to keep him from taking any cold. Now don't worry for I will let you know how he gets along. I saw Cullen. I told him about the debts, and I told him that you have qualified and wouldn't let them down on your teaching. He said he knew that or you wouldn't be holding your job in as large a place as you had. So let's pray on and on for all things. Now, you write Dad to stay in and mind me and you are glad his old teeth are out. I'm going to do all that I possibly can to care for him. I wrote the kids today. He didn't want me to tell them. I told him to not have secrets. All of you know this, if any worse comes, the shock wouldn't be so bad. I'll get cards and let you all know how we are often.

Pray for us and don't worry. God is watching over us all. Prepare yourself for what comes. That is what I am trying to do. I must go to bed. Will send you some change to help along this month.

Love always,
Mom and Dad

Help in this family was always a one-for-all, all-for-one proposition. All of the family members, while accepting help from the others, were also extending it at the same time. Most of all, they all depended upon God to take care of them. The worst possible thing had happened, not only because it affected Gus's health but it also affected the family income. He was the sole support of the family, and now he was not able to work. There was still his pension, but only until he died. Then Nora would be without funds. This situation amply illustrated what the changing American family with its new mobility was leaving behind as a gaping hole. Children now lived far apart from their parents and were not around to help when the parents became elderly and needed them. Gus was worried, and he did not relish the idea of he and his wife being dependent upon strangers or even distant relatives. He was becoming his father who had also suffered from strokes and paralysis, and he feared that his last days were upon him. Nora would not give up though and resolved to keep finding solutions.

Gladys was teaching at Iowa Park, Texas, and as usual, wherever she went, she had a circle of friends and an active social life. However, since her early college days, she had never found a person to date steadily and take seriously. Sometime around the end of 1940 when there was a shortage of men teachers due to selective service being instituted, a young man was hired at Iowa Park to teach social studies who had just "washed out" of the army air corps' pilot program. He had wrecked a training plane and suffered a slight hip injury. At first, all Gladys noticed about him was that he dressed well and had a nice car, but after several dates, he seemed to stand out from her circle of other admirers. He had the qualities that she admired most – honesty, kindness, courtesy, and he was a good teacher and capable at most of the things he attempted. He was very popular with his students, was also a senior class sponsor, and played the piano by ear. He could play anything after hearing it once and was often asked to play at school functions. She felt comfortable just being with him, even though neither one of them had any extra money for dates and gifts. [2]

A few months into 1941, Harry McAdams asked her to marry him, and she said yes. It was to be a long engagement – almost a year. It gave them time to meet each other's families, however, and see if the relationship was going to last. When it was time for school to begin again in 1941, Harry received orders from the Army Air Corps to report to bombardier training. He had never left the service but was just waiting to see where they would station him next. As a bombardier, Harry hoped he had at last found his niche in the Air Corps. He loved flying and was hopeful that it might lead to a career after his service time was completed. He left for training at Maxwell Field, Montgomery,

Gladys Crume at Iowa Park   *Harry McAdams at Iowa Park*

Alabama, the same day he received his orders, while Gladys continued to teach at Iowa Park.³

The training at Maxwell was basic training to get new recruits in shape physically and accustomed to military discipline, and also some beginning courses needed by bombardiers but not the actual bombardier flight instruction. It was a long, grueling three months of work under crowded conditions and hot weather. After it was over, bombardier school would be next, and Harry was hoping that would be closer to home. Harry wrote to Gladys every day and received letters back from her just as often. He said it probably kept him from going crazy. He sent this letter at the beginning of his training in September of 1941.

Tuesday night

Dearest Baby,

I'm almost too tired to pick up a pencil tonight, but I've been thinking of you quite a bit all day and thought I'd better write. We have had two days of real honest to goodness, rough, tough army life this week. It will continue for about two weeks, I guess.

They have reorganized us and placed all the men over six feet in one platoon. It looks like an army of giants. I happened to get in on it and have been placed in a room with five others. They are all big fellows – two from Texas, one from Wisonsin, one from Iowa and one from Massachusetts. One of the boys from Texas was a friend of Berryhill's in California.

Our daily routine now consists of the following: rise at 5:00 each day for police inspection, breakfast call at 6:00. After breakfast we drill until 8:00 and then have classes until 10:00. At 10:00 we begin physical training in shorts and continue until twelve. At 12:00 we eat dinner and soon after begin drilling and drill until 15:00. At that time, we begin two more hours of physical training and continue until 17:00. At that time we go to evening mess and about 6:30 are through for the day but have to stay in the barracks. If I live over all this, I'll be plenty tough when I get through.

I suppose you are getting ready for the fair now. Please don't work so hard like you have been doing. I really hope everything goes well and tell all the students that I wish them luck. Who was elected sponsor [of the senior class. Gladys was the other sponsor.] in my place?

Darling, are you getting my letters? I've written several times but have received no answer from you. This place is so large that I'm afraid the mail doesn't leave very often.

There is too much static going on in this room – I can't even think. I'm terribly in love with you and miss you more and more each day. You must write as soon as you can. If I don't write every day or two, please don't think anything of it because sometimes there isn't time – and I mean just that.

All my love to you sweetheart. Write soon.

Love – Mac

Harry was getting a big dose of basic training in the army. He signed his letters "Mac" as that was his nickname used by family and friends. He shouldn't have worried about receiving letters because after a slight delay in the beginning, he began receiving at least one a day and sometimes more. By December, Harry had completed all of the work and tests that he needed to advance to bombardier school, and he was just waiting for orders so he could leave Maxwell. He wrote the following letter in mid-

December, but his situation had changed. He was no longer in the army just training for a possible war which might not happen. The war had arrived. On December 7, 1941, the Japanese attacked Pearl Harbor in the Hawaiian Islands without any previous declaration of war. In return and within two days, the United States issued a formal declaration of war with Japan, Germany, and Italy. Although by this time the country had been gearing up in case of formal hostilities, preparations would now begin in earnest. The stimulus the economy needed to pull out of the Depression had arrived. No one was celebrating, however, because the war had to be won, and the cost was going to be very high.[4] Gladys sat at home on that Sunday listening to the radio as the reports began pouring in of the destruction and casualties at Pearl Harbor, and she was crying so hard she could hardly listen because she knew what this would mean.

Tuesday night

Hello sweetheart,

How is everything at home? Did you have a good day at school? If you have any static from those kids, you tell them that I'll skin them alive when I get back. Are you planning to have a Christmas tree at the school? (Interruption – a fellow just poked his head in the door and said, "Give her my love and also a kiss for me." He's a pretty good guy so I'm sending you his love.) You should endeavor to make Christmas merrier than usual this year because it will be barren for some.

Had some news that was hard to take today. Received a letter from Berryhill and he was sailing on the President Garfield from San Francisco for an unknown destination. Somehow, I couldn't help but feel a little remorseful because we've been as close as brothers and I fear I won't be seeing him again. He was always pretty lucky, and he may get through all right though. His business isn't so dangerous.

On reading the paper, I noticed that a pilot friend of mine that I knew in California was killed in Sunday's fighting in the Hawaiian Islands. Too bad – he didn't have much of a chance in this war. His name was Markley, first on the list.

What does your brother plan to do now that war has started? If he knows when he's well off, he'll choose some branch of the service and join because the draft army is hell through and through.

Well, sugar baby, this Christmas holiday business is rather uncertain now. As the situation stands now, we don't get furloughs, passes or even open post on the weekends. Perhaps, if we move to some other training center, they'll relax a little and let us off for a few days Christmas. Let's hope for the best.

How's my honey feeling tonight? Probably if I ever get back to Iowa Park, the people will think a sand storm is coming because I intend to make some racket. I'll be so glad to get back, better tell Mrs. Apple to reinforce the front door because I'm liable to run through it, I'll be so anxious to see you.

Darling, always tell me about everything you do and everything that goes on out there in Iowa Park. Life is a little empty for us guys over here and I do so enjoy thinking about the fun and good times back there. Write to me and remember not to worry about this war business. It isn't so bad as most people think.

All of my love.

Yours.
Mac

The worst part of the war was losing friends, and Harry was already being put in that position. It would take its toll on his normally outgoing personality. That Christmas Harry sent Gladys a special Christmas present – an engagement ring which was the best he could afford. He wasn't going to be there to put it on her finger, but he wanted the security of knowing that she was wearing his ring. He also sent her a picture of himself in his uniform about which he wasn't too thrilled , but he thought it would do. He thought he was very close to getting travel orders for bombardier school, and he was right. On Christmas Day, 1941, he arrived in Albuquerque, New Mexico, to start the next phase of his training.[5]

Gladys and Harry planned to get married after his next phase of training was completed and he had earned his wings. Flying high in the blue New Mexico skies and practicing bombing runs was sheer joy for Harry after his weeks of being confined to a barracks and a classroom in steamy hot Alabama. He still had class work to do, but the flying was what he truly enjoyed. Being the bombardier, he had a front row seat behind the glassed-in nose of the plane, and the view was magnificent. It was the most care-free flying of his career. Although he was stationed at Kirtland Airfield, his quarters for this phase of training were in the El Fidel Hotel in Albuquerque, so he had come up some in the world after the barracks of Maxwell Airfield. As was the case at Maxwell, he had many funny stories to write to Gladys about how the bombardiers spent their down time. He quickly developed the skills of eye-hand coordination which were so vital to bombardiers, and he knew that he had finally found work that he could do well. His training here lasted about ten weeks.[6]

Around March at midterm Gladys had regretfully changed her teaching position to one at the high school in Maydelle because an opportunity came up for her to do so. Gladys and Mac had discussed their situation and decided it might be best for her to live with her parents while she waited for him to complete his tour of duty in the war, even though Gladys hated to leave the position she loved at Iowa Park. Although she would make less money teaching in Maydelle, she could save money while living at home and could be there to help her aging parents.

After the ten-week training at Albuquerque, Harry earned his wings and his commission as a lieutenant, and he was given a short leave before he had to report to Geiger Field in Spokane, Washington. There he would become part of a flight team which would train together and be assigned a plane for missions. Harry's short leave was all the time that Harry and Gladys needed to have a wedding at Iowa Park in front of their friends and students. He had already told her that they would not have much notice, so she was ready when he called on April 1rst and drove to Iowa Park from Maydelle that night. She notified her friends that she was there and to get ready for the wedding. On April 2nd of 1942 at high noon in order for the entire school to attend, Harry married Gladys. The First Baptist Church was packed, the senior class sat in the reserved seats, the senior boys were ushers, and the high school glee club sang. Gladys' roommate played the wedding music and the ladies of the church decorated with redbud sprays. After the ceremony, the high school boys lined up to kiss the bride, rice was thrown, and the car was decorated. It was a wonderful day and a lasting memory and didn't take months to plan!

Harry and Gladys Wedding Day

Afterwards Harry and Gladys went on a short trip to visit his parents near Waco, Texas, and then Harry left for Spokane, Washington.[7]

Upon arrival in Spokane and after Harry's bomb group was formed, he was relieved to discover he would be flying in the new Flying Fortress B-17 aircraft, the biggest and the best-armed planes the army had at that time. They would be a great improvement over the planes he had been flying in training. Gladys taught another month at Maydelle to end the school year and received the following letter from Harry before arrangements could be made for her to join him for a short honeymoon.

Saturday morning

Hello sweetheart,

How are you this morning? It's a fine morning out here – just the right kind for flying. In fact, I'm doing something this morning that I've never done before – writing to my wife while up in the air. I'm only going along for the ride this morning, not dropping any bombs. Therefore, there's nothing for me to do but sit here in the nose and watch the beautiful scenery. Thought I might write to you while I'm doing it.

Here we are – up about 6000 feet and travelling about 200 miles per hour. The country is beautiful – green forests, snow-capped mountains and millions of lakes of all sizes. Gee but it's wonderful – wish you were here beside me to enjoy it. We have plenty of room up here. The navigator and I are the only ones in this compartment. We have a table to write on and plenty of space to walk around in.

How is everything at home, hon? Guess you'll be glad when school is out. Wish I knew for sure where I'd be in a month so that we could begin planning for you to come to see me. Maybe I'll be in Salt Lake City for a while (two weeks) and perhaps I can arrange to have you come there. However, that is only an idea of mine as I don't know when or where we leave or where we're going. I'll do what I can.

Are you feeling better after your sick spell? Always thought I'd be with you to take care of you after we were married but I guess that was another funny idea that didn't come true.

Darling, I guess this is all for now. Write to me soon. The cross country trip may yet come to pass and I'll see if we make it. All my love to my darling.

Your Mac

For all of his life, Harry would love to fly, even after his harrowing war time experiences. It quickly got in his blood. Arrangements were finally made, and Gladys was to go to Spokane on the train to be with Harry for a two week honeymoon. After the honeymoon spent in Spokane at a local hotel and doing some sightseeing, Gladys returned home by way of California where she stayed for an extended visit with her family, especially her sister Floyce who was expecting a baby. This was a very enjoyable time for Gladys with lots of sightseeing in Los Angeles and long gab sessions with her siblings.[8] After Gladys had departed for California, Harry did a lot of flying around the country with short assignments to Muroc Dry Lake, California; Alamogordo, New Mexico; Louisville, Kentucky; Hartford, Connecticut; and finally Holyoke, Massachusetts, where he was stationed before making the long flight to England. At the first stop, Muroc Dry Lake, he was close enough to be with Gladys and her family in California for a weekend which was fun for all of them, except Gladys and Harry had to go through saying goodbye again.[9]

All of this hopping around and the preparation of the plane for the trip to England took several months. Harry's letters to Gladys during this time were constantly trying to reassure her about his future, but in fact, he really didn't know what he would be facing. The army had provided him with a tour of the United States, however, and it was something a man who had never been out of Texas really appreciated. Finally the orders came for the trip to England, and Harry was flying off literally into the wild blue yonder. The telegram he sent to Gladys was short but chilling. "We are going. Will write later. Goodbye. All my love – Mac"[10] It was time for Gladys to start praying in earnest.

Floyce had her baby on July12, 1942, and Gladys received the above telegram from Harry on July 25 while she was still at Floyce's house. The baby was named Robert Charles Leaverton, thereafter known as Bobby in the family.[11] After Floyce was able to function fairly well, Gladys was ready to make the long trip home to Maydelle. As she rocked along on the train home, she had plenty of time to think about all that had happened in the past few months and the changes in her life. She had given up the idea of returning to her beloved Iowa Park and gone home to East Texas, but Iowa Park would always provide happy memories for her and for Harry. It was where they met and married and where they had made lifelong friends. It had represented the height of her teaching career and would always hold a special place in her heart.

22

World War II

During 1942 and 1943 the war became an everyday reality for most Americans both at home and overseas. Factories went into full production to supply the armaments, airplanes, ships, and land vehicles that were needed to fight the war. Technological inventions were created to meet the new needs of the army (including the army air corps) and navy. Women in the United States went to work in numbers never seen before because the men had departed to swell the ranks of the fighting force needed to win the big battles of the war. Women also served in the military in much higher numbers than in World War I. Not only did the war help pull the United States out of the Great Depression, it stimulated new growth in industry, technology, and business. Every effort was thrown into the war, and every citizen was expected to do his or her part, whether it was buying war bonds, volunteering with the Red Cross or the USO [a new organization founded during WWII to support the troops], rationing food and other vital items, or maintaining victory gardens. It was all about winning the war. The Japanese military had referred to the United States as a "sleeping giant," and now the giant was awake and moving at a ferocious pace.[1] Clyde Crume wrote this letter home in February of 1943.

Dearest Mom and Dad,

I guess you thought I wasn't going to write, but I have been working so hard that I just haven't had time. They have really been putting us through the mill. Most business they have ever seen. We work sixteen hours both ways. So my little rear end is dragging my tracks out.

Clyde Coming Home from Work

I was out at Floyce's yesterday and read your letter. Awfully sorry about you having another stroke, Dad. You just take it easy and you will be alright.

We have had two or three pretty bad snow storms over the mountains since we came back, but we shouldn't have very much more bad weather, I hope.

I got another deferment the other day. It is up July 24th.

We enjoyed Gladys and Mac's being with us. Sorry they couldn't be with us again before they left. I suppose we should be glad we saw them at all.

I certainly wished that I could have stayed longer Christmas, but we were in a whirl all the time that we were gone. I suppose it was quiet after we left. Does Art know when he is leaving? Tell him the hunting knife he sent me was a honey!

Bobby is just as onery as a little heathen, but he is a pretty cute boy.

That food was certainly good Christmas. I never ate so much in my life.

We deadheaded over here (Barstow, California) today on the caboose, and we were banged around so I didn't get much sleep. So I gotta hit the hay and get a little rest before I get called.

When you see Aunt Minnie and Uncle Lester, tell them we sincerely appreciated the help coming back. Tell Aunt Minnie I wanted to have a long talk, but it will have to wait until time isn't rushed.

I hope you can get the radio fixed soon, but parts are hard to get to fit anything now. Maybe this war will hurry up and come to an end soon. At least we can all hope for the best.

Well, I have to hit the bed. I will not wait so long to write from now on. All of you be good and take care of yourselves.

Tell all hello!

Love always.

Your son – Clyde

Clyde was getting along well with the railroad work. However, the sheer amount of work that he was doing was an indication of the activity of the war years. Not only did goods have to be transported by railroad, but also troops had to be moved about the country from various training facilities and stations. He was deferred by the military and was waiting to volunteer for the service until he could determine what his situation was. It should be noted here the role that the railroad played in American history and in the Crume family. The railroad had helped to reconstruct the country after the Civil War and open up the West to settlement. It had provided tremendous profits for some and employment for many over the years, and it helped the unemployment situation to a certain degree in the Great Depression. It played a vital transportation role in the World Wars and in peacetime as well.

However, the negatives were present as well. The owners/chief executives of the railroads were not always above corruption and graft, the railroads were voracious in destroying competition and swallowing up small towns, and the workers who built the railroads and operated them had a very hard job with few safety regulations.[2] Still, one of the railroads provided employment for Gus Crume, and others supplied employment for two of his sons and a son-in-law during the Depression when jobs were hard to come by. The work was often brutal, but it was still work that paid something. Many of the railroad's abuses were eventually addressed in future years, and federal regulation helped to correct some of the problems. In many ways, the railroads' period of dominance and success was curbed by the rise of the airline industry, the interstate highway system, and the trucking industry after World War II.

Clyde also mentioned in the above letter shortages in parts to repair electronics. This was not the only item which was in short supply. Almost everything was. American citizens learned to live with ration books for many of their necessities such as food and gasoline, and for most, luxuries were very hard to find. It was a different world for some, but it was one that most of the American people had been trained for by the deprivations of the Depression. Going without was nothing new. In a different part of the Western Hemisphere, Art was in Las Mercedes, Venezuela in 1943. He wrote the following letter home.

June 12, 1943
Dearest Mom and Dad,

Your letter of May 24th came last Saturday nite and this is Monday morning, but this letter can't get out of Caracas until Thursday, I think, so you won't get it until sometime next week.

I am sure sorry to hear Dad is sick again and surely hope is much better by now.

Yes, I had a nice letter from Floyce and some pictures of them all. I have answered it quite a bit ago. I wrote you one about a month ago from Rincon Largo, but I guess it must have gotten lost. Am very sorry you did not get it as I had a $10.00 check in it. Anyway I wrote the bank last night to stop payment on it, so it won't matter. If the letter should finally come through dated May 3, don't try to cash the check, just tear it up.

I came over here the first of this month to drill our last well here in this field until after the war. I don't know what we will do after this well. We have material for one wildcat now and material enough bought to drill another wildcat and one more well in Rincon Largo. My time is up November 8 and I want to leave here about the first of December so I can be sure and be home for Christmas this year. I don't think I will come back here if I can possibly go any where else as I sure don't like Venezuela very much. If I can, I'd like to go to work in Old Mexico till after the war.

Brother Bogard and one of his associates sent me a tract about the Jews and a nice letter the other day. I haven't answered it as yet, but I think I'll send him about $5.00 to help a little in his work. My radio won't quite pick them up on long wave very distinct so I never hear them. I get a missionary station in up in Central America nearly any time on short wave.

Mom, I am inclosing a $15 check this time. If you need any money, get it from Cullen or Lester and let me know and I'll send you a check right back.

Dad, don't worry about me. I'll be seeing you one of these days either there at home or across the big divide. Thanks a lot for having been the man you are and the kind of Dad you have been to us kids. I'm sorry for all the heartaches I've caused you, and I know the others are also. I guess we just more or less took you for granted all our lives. But I know none of us kids can ever forget the example of Christianity, good citizenship, and manhood you have always lived before us. I am in good health now but am very impatient for this hitch to get over so I can come home.

I've got to run along as its noon time and I go to work at three this afternoon. Hope this letter finds you all in good health and spirits.

Your son,
Art

Art was always glad to come back to the United States, and there were some places in the world that he liked better than others. His job had given him an opportunity to see many different countries and had also given him a world view that many in the United States did not have. In this he was fortunate. He remembered always where he came from and took the time to thank his father for being a good parent. All of the children were proud of their childhood and the way they were raised, and thanking their parents was something they were not hesitant to do, especially now that their father was living his last days.

Morris and Onah Crume in California

Morris and his family made the decision in 1943 to move to California, specifically Los Angeles. They may have been looking for a change of scene and were hoping to find work in the factories of the city. After arrival, Morris first worked in a beer factory and Onah worked as a seamstress, making wedding gowns. Over the years in California, Morris worked at several different companies, including defense plants, and Onah worked at wedding shops as long as her back permitted. They lived at Maywood which was next door to Huntington Park. Their son, Buster, was eighteen and a senior in high school when Morris and Onah moved to California. After he graduated, he enlisted in the Navy late in 1943. A few months later, he married Margaret "Margie" Ann Crawford in Huntington Park on February 28, 1944.[3]

Buster and Margie Crume

In late July of 1942, Gladys's husband Harry had flown to England with his combat crew in their newly-refurbished Flying Fortress B-17 aircraft. England turned out to be a pleasant interval before he received his orders for his final tour of duty assignment in the war. With a name like McAdams, he was in his element in the British Isles. He managed a few short flight trips to Scotland, but most of his time was spent in England where he was stationed outside of London at a base near Chelveston. Not all of his time had to be spent on his training missions. He had some free time to explore the countryside and the city of London where he visited the Tower of London, Buckingham Palace, the Houses of Parliament, and most impressive to him, Westminster Abbey and the graves of all the great men.[4] With his background of being a social studies teacher, he was enjoying himself immensely. He wrote to Gladys the following letters during this period.

England – Sunday

Dearest Gladys,

Was very happy to receive a letter from you yesterday Darling. It was a little old but that couldn't be helped of course. I'm very anxious to hear from you and find out how everything is at home.

Here it is Sunday again. I used to always look forward to Sunday – to having a whole day with nothing to do but come to see you and ride around, waste time, take life easy. Those were the good days all right. I surely wish you could come here some time. Being interested in English literature, you would find many things to interest you. It seems as though everything has some historical background. I can hardly wait to get back to London so that I can see some more of the famous places. Am also planning to go up into the country formerly inhabited by Oliver Cromwell and his Roundheads.

Was interested to hear that Charlie Metz and Earle Denny had joined the navy. They were two of my favorites in Iowa Park and I'm glad to hear that they have joined up. Wish I could hear from Campsey and Elloise. You must give them my address as soon as you can.

There isn't much else to tell you today Honey. Everything is all right so far so don't worry about me. Keep writing to me as often as you can and tell me about everything that happens. It is possible that you won't get my letters as quick as I get yours but that can't be helped. All my love to you Darling.

Your Mac

Friday

Dearest Babe,

Have some time off today so I'll write to you again. Haven't received any letters from you yet, but I really don't expect any for a long time. It's rather difficult to get mail through.

There isn't much to do here except work. I have a bicycle issued by the government and can ride around a good bit. Usually go into a town here at night but there isn't much to do. I get quite a lot of fun out of going about over the country and looking at the old landmarks. Am thinking about going to church next Sunday to a church that was built before the Norman conquest. Have also seen George Washington's ancestral home.

Didn't know that yesterday was my birthday until last night. Had lost track of the time. Some friends and I went to a nearby inn and had quite a time drinking ale with the upper classes and playing ten pins with the commoners. They certainly have a caste system here. There's nothing else to tell you, Sweetheart, except that I love you. Everything is all right – good as it can be. Keep writing to me – maybe I will get a letter someday. All my love to you, Precious.   Your Mac

Harry was not one to sit on his bunk and feel sorry for himself. He was taking the opportunity to see the country and all its sights, even by bicycle. For years afterward he would remember those days of riding his bicycle down the narrow British roads between the hedge rows which lined each side. It was the calm before the storm and one of the gifts the army air corps gave him. For all of the things that the war took away from him, his chance to travel and see places in the world that he had only read about before was a priceless gift that would forever after give him a different world view. He was evolving from a small-town Texas boy into a man who had traveled the world and seen much of history in real time.

Whenever he changed locations, it would take a while for his mail to catch up with him, which was annoying but unavoidable. He had five choices for sending word back to the United States – actual letters which were usually fairly short and folded into small envelopes, telegrams for really short messages, post cards, the Red Cross messages which were also short and pretty impersonal, and V mail. V mail was instituted during WWII to reduce the weight and space required to ship the mail to thousands and thousands of soldiers. Letters were written on specially designed paper and envelopes which were then microfilmed, sent to a receiving station, blown up and printed and delivered to the recipient. Obviously, the letters had to be kept short. This system did save space and weight shipping the mail, but it was not used as much as regular letters which most people preferred.[5]

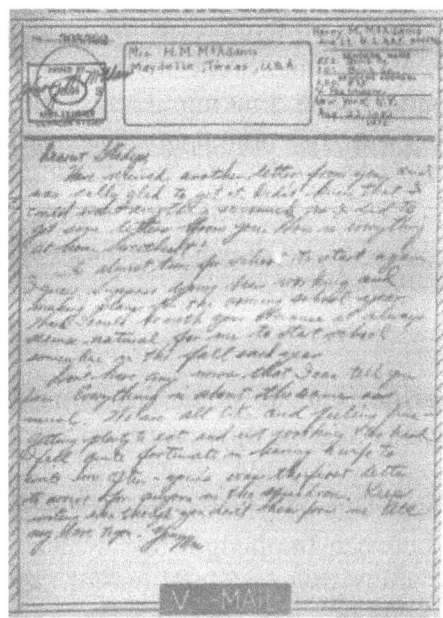

Harry did conduct some bombing missions into France while he was at Chelveston, but these were just the warm-up for the real action in his permanent theater assignment which turned out to be North Africa. The Allied forces command decided to invade Africa to create a second front from which to attack Germany and its allies and perhaps take some of the pressure off of England. Harry's 301st Division was the second division of Army Air Corps sent to Africa. He spent a year and a half at various bases in Algeria, he kept the same plane named the "Pegasus," and he served with basically the same crew, both air and ground, for most of his time in Africa. The Pegasus was eventually shot down, but he and his crew weren't on it at the time. Their new plane was the "Dirty Girty." He flew an impressive 59 missions, completed 50, and was decorated many times, his medals including the Distinguished Flying Cross, the most treasured medal for any airman.[6] He wrote many letters during his time in Africa, and his letters from Gladys helped to keep him sane.

While the war was going on, Gladys was at home with her parents in Maydelle, Texas, and teaching school at the local high school. It was a time for her to renew old friendships and enjoy the company of the people in the area. She even played cupid once by driving her step cousin, Evelyn, and her beau to a neighboring town to get married. The town of Maydelle gave Gladys a bridal shower while she was home which included a set of FiestaWare dishes, the newest rage.[7] Maydelle was a place of comfort for her while waiting and hoping for her husband to return. She tried to stay as busy as possible to keep from thinking of what could happen. She wrote newsy letters as often as she could, every few days, and they were a Godsend for Harry. She said of that period, "The anxious times were when I was at home listening to the radio news, reading the newspaper accounts of the Flying Fortress sorties, and haunting the post office for a letter (when one came, putting it under my pillow to read it over and over, together with the occasional telegrams)."[8]

Somewhere in North Africa
March

Dearest Gladys,

Do you get tired of waiting for letters from me? I suppose you do. Sometimes I have plenty of time to write and then again there are days in which all of my time is taken. Have just finished playing ball for a while and "Big Tom" Thayer and I are here in our pup tent talking over the day's work and old times. We have a candle tonight so that we aren't hampered by darkness.

The past few days I've been working hard and have had many exciting moments. However, according to the battle orders for tomorrow, our crew is off and we'll get a rest – for which I'm very thankful.

The weather is getting better – no more snow and rain. We have managed to get some boards with which we made walls for the tent. Makes the tent warmer and keeps the water from running under. Our food is getting better. More supplies are coming to us up here and we are able to get eggs and tangerines from the Arabs. Guess times are getting better but they damn sure looked doubtful for a while.

For my work so far, I'll probably receive the air medal four times or its equivalent – the air medal with three oak leaf clusters. Don't have them yet but am supposed to get them under the present orders. The Distinguished Flying Cross is almost in my hands so don't be surprised if I get that too.

Don't know when I'll be home. I've been holding up fairly well so far, but sometimes I feel very tired and wish for a nice quiet place somewhere. Guess I'd give most anything for a room with lights and heat where I could bathe once more and shave and lie in a bed. Next, I guess I'd like something to eat – most anything would be good. Do you think that would be asking too much when I come home?

Most of the boys are still here and doing all right. Rather doubt if their folks are going to recognize some of them or not because they've changed some. I feel like I'm getting along as well as any of them so don't worry about me.

Guess I'll have to get in my blankets now because the cold is coming. Keep writing to me and I'll write when I have the chance.

All my love - Mac

North Africa
May 21, 1943, Friday

Dearest Gladys,

Have a day with nothing to do so I'll write. Perhaps you think I'm lazy about writing and I really am. Guess I could write more often but somehow I have difficulty in thinking of anything these days. Weak-minded I guess. Most days, there is no time but I was taken off the battle order today for a minor illness. It's the first time that I haven't gone over when I was assigned to go. Would have gone anyway but Les (Major Holman) said no.

This is the time of the month that your school will be out. Guess you're glad and will get a good rest. What are you planning to do this summer? Suppose visiting relatives will take up a good bit of the time. Needless to ask, you were re-elected [to a new school term in the fall], I suppose. I used to worry about this at this time every year, but my worries were always groundless. How are your folks and my folks? Am glad that the warm weather is here because they will all feel much better.

Have been to all the captured territory and seen many interesting sights. The Tunis area was most interesting. Cannot tell about the conditions there but will say that they were mute evidence of good work on our part. On El Corsina Airdrome, I found some souvenirs and some unopened Italian mail. This is some of the stationary that I found in one of them. Being without paper myself, I decided to use it. Gee, but it felt good to fly over those places without getting the hell knocked out of us. That place was hot before the war moved on.

Have six oak leaf clusters to my air medal now and am recommended for another for a special job. Medals are not interesting like they were for a while. This is Ace Madeley's first anniversary and he is trying to write a letter to Eloise. It's hard to think of anything that one can say. Thayer is here and still flying, but Dempsey is in the hospital again with ear trouble. Don't know if he'll get well or not. Looney is O.K. and still going. Most of the others are here and we've had some new men to fill in the holes.

We've had a little social life lately. There is a big stone grainary here and we have dances occasionally. Get nurses from the American and British hospitals which are numerous around here. Provides an occasion to get "hepped" up on champagne, wine or beer and gives us something to think about for a change.

Our female dog has made her debut into dog society this week and I've never seen such a mess of dogs in my life. One night I had my gun out ready to clean house but couldn't for fear of hitting someone. Have had to chase her out of the tent along with all of her boy friends. It's a damn funny thing to me that every place we land, there is not anything to be seen anywhere, but within an hour, there are flocks of dogs and Arabs everywhere. Damned if I know where they come from.

How are our friends from Iowa Park? Ever hear from them? Of all my time overseas, I've never met anyone that I knew at home. Write to me often.

Best love to you,
Mac

Most of Harry's letters did not describe any of his missions or places where he was based until after some time had passed. This was because of the censorship on his letters by the people in charge of that or sometimes perhaps by himself. Still, some of the flavor of his life was seeping through the lines of his messages home. He was seeing some magnificent country, different people in different lands with different customs, and he was living under harsh conditions in the desert. His missions were often brutal, and many times he was fortunate to escape alive. One of his medals was the Purple Heart, and he earned it. The glass covered nose of the B-17 was great for sight-seeing, but not such a good thing when other planes were trying to shoot at anything in the plane that moved.

On one occasion a news reporter was available to write about his mission when the Dirty Girty landed at its home base, and when Harry sent the account home, Gladys sent it to the Dallas News to print. The account detailed the part that the bombardiers played in the vicious battle for Kasserine Pass in Tunisia where the Anglo-American forces met the German general, Rommel. Both sides took a severe beating, but the Allied Forces continued to push until the German forces were removed from Africa, and the Mediterranean Sea was open to Allied shipping and air power. After the article appeared in the Dallas paper, Harry became rather famous at home in East Texas. The copies of the newspaper were read until they were worn out in both Maydelle and Lorena, Harry's home town.[9]

By the end of 1943, Harry knew that it was time to return to the United States. He was very thin from lack of good nourishment, depleted of energy, and was losing the concentration he needed to go on missions. He had already stayed in the field longer and conducted more missions than most airmen, and even though there were comrades that he hated to leave behind, he was done, emotionally, mentally, and physically. He was eligible for a transfer home to the States whenever he was ready, so he accepted the transfer, and two of his crew members decided to go home with him. They began the long trip to the United States, hitchhiking rides on various aircraft from Africa to South America until finally Harry arrived in Dallas, Texas, in December of 1943 – a great Christmas present for his family. He went to the Baker Hotel where his brother was the general auditor, and his brother's eyes teared up just looking at him.[10]

The Crume family happened to be having a family reunion that Christmas in Maydelle to celebrate Gus and Nora's fortieth wedding anniversary. All of the children were home for the occasion, and as events in the near future would reveal, it would be the last time they would all be together. Gladys and her brother Morris went to pick up Harry and brought him back to Maydelle to face normal life in America, the fun and happiness of a family all together for the first time in a long time. The Crumes did not know quite what to make of a returning war hero, especially one who looked as worn out as this one did, but they welcomed him home. Gladys was ecstatic and so grateful to have Harry back that she didn't care what he looked like. Harry was exhausted and a bit confused by his surroundings, not able to transition back to ordinary life that quickly. He was still living in a war zone in his mind, and it was hard for him to understand how people could be happy and celebrating. It was surreal. After a few days, he began to feel a little more human, but it would be weeks before he felt normal again, and he would never again be the man he was before the war.[11]

After Christmas and a visit with Harry's family in Lorena, Texas, outside of Waco, Harry and Gladys reported to Santa Monica, California, for a complete physical for Harry and two weeks of R&R (rest and relaxation). They were able to visit with Gladys's California family some while they were there. After California, they returned to Texas to Midland for a short stay and some navigational training and then Harry was sent to Hobbs, New Mexico, for his next duty station. He was a Captain in the Army Air Corps by now and was to be a training officer at the base at Hobbs for new crews learning to fly bombing missions.

Gladys had been on leave from her teaching job at Maydelle during the California trip, but turned in her resignation when Harry got his orders for Midland, Texas. For the time being she was content to just be a wife.[12] Harry had returned to the States in one piece, but as Gladys would later say, he was a different man. Upon his return, he had nightmares, and for many years he would not talk about the war. In his last years he finally began to talk about it with his children and even wrote about it in his autobiography, but the things he had seen and done had irrevocably changed him to a more serious, less happy-go-lucky person. He still enjoyed laughter, singing, dancing, and playing the piano, but these things took a back seat to commitment, drive, and focus on building a future with Gladys. So many men had not come back, and he had. He was not about to waste his second chance.

In March of 1944, while Gladys was traveling around Texas with Harry, Floyce wrote home from California.

424 Lloyd
Bakersfield
March 27, 1944

Dearest Mom and Dad,

Monday morning and Charles is called to go to work, and I'm in a hurry, but wanted to drop you a line. We are all fine – still haven't heard anything from Morris.

I don't know what to do about coming home. I'm really not able, but guess I'm more able to do than you are. I just thought I'd come regardless if you needed me bad enough. I'll wait a little while and see how you get along.

Charles, Bobby, and Floyce Leaverton

Bobby is fine – talks more all the time.

Mother Leaverton wrote that Mr. Hudson died.

Clyde is working on a job out of Barstow for a week or so. He is fine – had a sore throat last week. I don't know how he'll come out on this new draft business.

I'm glad Gladys got to come home. If only it wasn't so far, I wouldn't wait a minute, but I do know what a hard trip it is and if I got there and was sick, I wouldn't be any help.

I'll write again in a few days. Try to take care of yourselves and I'll write again in a few days.

Lots and lots of love,
Floyce

It was obvious that Floyce was worried about her parents. Gus was probably not doing well and possibly Nora was sick as well. Their living conditions were not the best for people their age. Floyce was too far away to make a trip home often with a small child, so she was trying to gauge how badly she was needed by her folks. As it turned out, she was correct to be worried. Things were not going well at home, and they would come to a head in just nine days' time. Time was slipping away for one very dear family member.

Gus and Nora Crume 1943

Coping with Endings

In the spring of 1944 around Easter time, Samuel Augustus Crume, the seemingly invincible head of the Crume family, was slowly but surely coming to the end of his life, his health ravaged by strokes and heart problems. On April 5, 1944, he passed away quietly at home with his wife Nora by his side.[1] His final words were, "See that beautiful light!" He had gone as he lived, led by the light. As it turned out, his father, Silas Moses, had seen a bright light on his death bed as well. His service was held at the Pleasant Grove Baptist Church, and he was buried at Pleasant Grove Cemetery with the rest of his family. The Crume row had now grown to being two rows. His eulogy was written into the minutes of the 1944 area-wide Baptist church conference. Among other things it said:

> His unending Christian life shall remain a benediction to his family, and to his church, for he served them to the extent of his ability, not only with time, thought, and spiritual endeavor, but he was ever ready to give, and give freely, of the worldly possessions he had accumulated in this life. He was truly a good man; without a doubt he was God's servant. The Christian love of his big heart leaves a glow in our spirits to the end of our lives.[2]

Gus had remained the same friendly, out-going person that he had been as a small boy, sitting on the front fence in front of his parents' stage stop in Pine Town, Texas. He never knew a stranger, spoke to everyone no matter their background, and he was an active member of every community in which he ever lived. He was a hard worker who loved what he did – a natural farmer. His most obvious characteristic, though, was his belief in a higher power that would provide for all of his needs. Both he and Nora had been raised with this belief and kept it close to their hearts all of their lives. It wasn't just words or quoting scripture with them; it was a way of life. It was their life.

Gus Crume 1944

From the following letters it looks as though Floyce and Bobby came from California for the funeral and to be with Nora. Art and his wife may have also been at the funeral because they were in the United States. Gladys and Harry were probably at Midland, Texas, but Harry, at least, was under military orders and may not have been able to come. Gladys, however, may have come alone. Clyde wrote from California that he could not be there.

April 6, 1944

Dearest Mom and all,

Just received the message and regret the passing. We must console ourselves that it is for the best, but sometimes it is so hard to see it in that light. I know that he would want it that way.

I am writing on the caboose and I doubt whether you can read this at all.

I wanted to come home so badly, but it seemed utterly impossible. The army is staring me in the face and I am working out of Barstow on an outside job and could not get released.

Well, there is so much to say, but I have no words to express what I feel. All of you are there together to reason things out. Write and tell me what you want to do or plan to do. If there is anything I can do, let me know and I will do it at once.

I did not get to see Floyce as the message was delayed.

We are at the Mojave Oil Yard and there is some switching to do, so I will close. Write me and tell me everything. I will write a letter then.

Love – Clyde

Houston, Texas
Monday morning,
April 10, 1944

Dear Mom, Floyce and Bobby,

We got home O.K., found the kids just fine only Chub [Arthur's stepson] and wife had to leave about 8:30 last night so he had to be in New Orleans this morning to service one of their ships.

Well, I guess if you have had time to look around, you see we had our usual luck of leaving things, such as my suit and Jap's best pair of hose. If you find anything else, just hang on to it until I can get up there.

I hope everything is O.K. with you and Mom. Please take it easy and don't work so hard. Floyce, you must rest up a lot also. I'll be up as quick as I can get things cleared up around here which I think will be about next Saturday week. Give my love to Aunt Ella and Aunt Betty. I'll be seeing you soon.

Love – Art

Art and Jap were in Houston on leave from work with the oil companies at the time of Gus's death, but that situation was quickly due to change. Art had gotten a job with a new oil company and would be leaving the last of May for the Middle East. Over the years his home base in the United States had usually been Houston, and his wife spent time there when she could not be with him on the jobs overseas. As it turned out, May 24, 1944 found him in New York City, and without his wife.

May 24, 1944
New York City

Dear Mom,

Here I go I guess. We are supposed to leave New York tomorrow for Virginia and will catch a troop transport ship in the same convoy that Chub and Billy are in. I don't know how or whether I'll get to see them or not.

We are supposed to land on the coast of Africa and will be flown in from there, but I do not know how far we go. For the present we have a mail service from the Army. I haven't had any more fever and I sure hope I don't.

Mama, take good care of yourself. Don't try to work too hard and if you can, get Annie or Pearl to stay with you, and I'll feel a lot better.

We shall probably be about two to three weeks on the way so you can write about the 5th or 10th of June. Give my best regards to Aunt Ella and Aunt Betty and regards to all the rest.

If you need anything in the way of money, you write Jap and beginning in August she can send it. She will send you ten dollars each month anyway as soon as it starts coming in.

Bye now. Take care of yourself.

Your loving son,
Art

All the children were worried about their mother, but she was also worried about them. It was the middle of a world war, and here her son was leaving to go where the fighting was much closer than in the United States. Her youngest son was due to be drafted at any time, but was planning to join the navy before the army inducted him into service. She had gotten one son-in-law back safely from the war, but his life was far from settled, and her daughter was hopping from place to place at his side. Her daughter in California was not in good health most of the time. Morris was settled in California, but her grandson Buster was in the navy. And she now had to learn how to live alone after all those years of married life.

Throughout the month of May while Art was getting ready to leave, Clyde was moving in two directions at the same time and was not certain which direction would finally be the one he took. He had taken his physical for the Navy and the Navy had accepted him for duty.[3] He was also studying for the conductor's position with the railroad and was up for the promotion on June 10. He was making plans to sell his car and most of his possessions if he was drafted or called for duty with the Navy. He wrote the following letter home at this time.

May 18, 1944

Dearest Mom,

Well, I received your letter and thought I would drop you a few lines to let you know I am O.K. Floyce got back in one piece, but she was really wore out. Bobby was right in his glory and talked about cows, etc.

I am called up for the conductor examinations, and I will take the promotion June 10. I am writing the book and studying every spare moment. I don't know whether I will still be here or not, but you can't tell. I have not heard any more from the draft board.

How is everyone there? I suppose it is pretty there about now. Surely would like to be there. Is there any news around the place?

Boy, this war has gotten everyone about scared out. They do not know which way to jump. All but me – I just sit tight and relax. Every day is another day the war will be over.

Have you heard from Gladys? I suppose she is living the life of Riley – her and the Army half. Has Arthur gone as yet? I suppose he is anxious to shove off.

If you ever need anything, just write and I will send it. I am putting everything in my car and squaring everything up. I have got to go now, so be good and write.

Love – Clyde

As Clyde noted in this letter, the war was playing havoc with people's lives. They didn't know how to plan anything because they never knew where they would be next, what they would be doing, or who they could count on to be there with them. Even though Clyde was trying to be relaxed about his situation, it still must have been nerve-wracking. However, he was soon to be released from decision making and uncertainty, but not in the way that he thought. About ten days after the above letter was written, he went on a picnic with some friends beside the Kern River in a park at Bakersfield. The river was almost at flood stage at the time from the mountain snow melt. In spite of the cold water, Clyde decided to wade out into the water after lunch and try swimming. He crawled up on a large rock in the river and stood up. Suddenly he just collapsed without making a sound and slipped into the river. He quickly disappeared with the swift current. In just a few minutes, his life was snuffed out, leaving his friends and later his family in bewildered shock. Morris telegraphed the family and later wrote this letter:

Sunday

Dear Mother,
 This is the hardest letter I ever wrote. We have spent the day on the river with all the police and officials, but we have had no luck. Mama, it is hard to tell you this but his body may never be found until September or October as the river is at flood stage and the huge rocks and boulders are so thick his body is lodged under one of them. This makes four or five that have drowned in the river and they have found only three of them. I am trying to tell you how things are, so you will understand.
 Floyce is fine. I will be here a few days and if nothing happens, will go home and wait as there is nothing any one can do. Please don't worry as Floyce and I talked last night – he has gone to Dad. Would like so much to be with you, talk to you, but can't come unless we find Clyde. They were on a picnic and he waded out in the water and he was standing there and suddenly he just sank over as if to sit down, then just disappeared. Mama, he is better off than to face this war. He was going to go next week, so think of it that way.
 I prayed to Jesus to just let me have his body so as to give him a good burial. Maybe it will be found tonight. If not, his

spirit has gone to the home above. Tell Gladys to be brave and look ahead as we will do all we possibly can. We had just got to Floyce and had Buster and Marge with us, so we called his room for him to come out. Then they told us the grave news. It nearly got us both, but we have faith that it was done through the Lord's will. That is all we can satisfy ourselves in knowing that all things are done for the good of the Lord.

Well, Mama, we will keep you in touch with everything and do all we can. Love to you so much.

Morris

Apparently, by some fortunate stroke of luck, Gladys was home with her mother when all of this happened, so Nora was not alone. Letters from the California family flowed back and forth trying to make the arrangements that needed to be made. Morris and Floyce took charge of the situation and kept those in Texas informed. All of Clyde's things were sold to pay off his debts and bury him. Most would have been sold anyway if he had gone into the Navy. The paperwork was started to obtain his insurance and pension. The worst problem was recovering the body so a funeral could take place. Clyde had been a popular young man, and his friends were helping to support his family, calling and coming by. Even the railroad supervisors had been very kind and attentive. However, everyone in the family was staggered by this loss, especially since it came so quickly after Gus Crume's death. Clyde had been the baby and so close to his family. As Floyce put it, "I'm nearly crazy, but I'm doing the best I can."[4] Art was still in transit to the Middle East when he got the news and sent the following V mail.

June 26, 1944

My dear mother,

Hi Mom, how are you feeling by now? Much better I hope and trust. Well, Mom, I'm still traveling and I have no idea when we shall arrive at the job but hope to be there by the first week in July.

Is Gladys still with you? I guess by the time I get on the Island, I will know about Clyde's death and all the particulars in regards to it. I tried to do all I could for you to help make it as easy as possible. I guess he will help keep Dad company till we get there. We couldn't all go on here forever and I don't think I want to. I've seen a lot of guys I knew over here but none from home.

Mom, I'm feeling fine and seeing some real interesting things that I have read about in history. Some time I can tell you all about it I hope.

Art in the Persian Gulf

When you write the kids, tell them I'll write as soon as I can. Take good care of yourself cause we all still need you.

Your loving son,
Art

The date of Art's V mail was June 26, 1944, which meant a very significant event had taken place in the war earlier in the month, but no one in the Crume family really had time or energy to keep track of the fighting in France because of the current personal nightmare they were living through. On June 6, 1944, the Allied Forces massed in England invaded the European continent at a place called Normandy, France. Normandy would forever after be known for the battles that took place there on its beaches and cliffs which cost thousands of lives in one day, but which would mean the beginning of the end for Nazi Germany. Without France as a buffer, Germany was much more vulnerable and on the defensive. It would remain so until the war was finally over.[5] What did Gladys's husband Harry think about this? He, like everyone else, was glad about the success of the invasion, but he had no regrets about not being there to take part in it. He was probably more interested in the fighting still taking place in Italy and Sicily where he had served and knew men who were still in the fight. He had paid his dues and was content to stay where he was until he could map out a future for himself and Gladys.

All through June and into July, things did not change in the search for Clyde's body. Floyce continued to make headway on some of the paperwork and the selling of Clyde's possessions, but she had to take some time out to go to the hospital and have surgery on her arm. It had gotten to the point where she could not lift it above her head. The old broken arm injury from the car wreck in her youth would occasionally need attention with more surgery to remove scar tissue. The arm had picked this low point in the family's existence to cause problems again. Floyce wrote a letter to Gladys and Mac after she finally got out of the hospital.

Bakersfield, California
June 28, 1944

Dearest Glad and Mac,

I surely did appreciate your letter, and whenever I get to thinking I'm not worth a s--- I'll get it out and read it and say my sister thought I was pretty nice once. ha

I am really glad to be at home again. They had to open my arm and scrape the bone again, so I'm pretty weak, but I feel like I'll be well when it heals up. My posterior end looks like a pin cushion all right, but it is about to get back to normal. Mac, if it hadn't been for you, I would have sent for Glad, but I thought if I did, you would probably go to Reno, and I know no court would refuse you a divorce under the circumstances. I am like you – I nearly have heart failure every time the telephone rings or some stranger comes to the door. I can do a good bit with one arm and have some help from a little neighbor girl.

Mama will have Clyde's insurance, railroad retirement, and the $150.00 from the Burial Association. I still haven't found a policy, but we know it was paid up, and I don't think there will be any trouble about it. I don't think any of this will be paid though until his body is found or death established by law.

I had the nurses and both the other patients in my room crying when I came out from underneath the gas. I kept begging them to do something for my baby brother, that I didn't care what happened to me as long as they would help him. I was feeling sorry and praying for you, Mom, Dad, Bobby and Charles – everybody but myself, as usual. I was crazy – that makes the 7th time!

Lots of love – Floyce

About a month after the above letter was written, Nora had decided to make the trip to California to try to help Floyce while she was recovering from the surgery on her arm. Clyde's body had still not been recovered, and perhaps she wanted to see what was being done. After she arrived at Floyce's home, she wrote the following letter to Gladys and Mac.

July 24, 1944

Dearest children,

Was glad to get your letter. I had a nice trip all the way. I was the only old lady on the train. It was a soldier troop train with some wives and mothers traveling to be with soldiers. I had to explain where and why I was going, and all around my seat heard. There were four soldier boys from the North that had a seat across from mine. Now they really was nice all day and sometimes all four sit and talked with me. When they were out, the ladies would stop and talk awhile. We would meet in the restroom and as Bobby says "comb our hairs."

On Thursday we sat on sidings waiting for trains to pass one place and counted five of those big long troop trains waiting for another to come in before they could move on. They wired for another engine and we was late. It left out so we finally got into Barstow at two o'clock. Stayed there until about nine the next morning – no air, no water, everyone burning up. They got another engine, and we hit the breeze. My those mountains were sights to be seen. I thought of the song, "She'll Be Coming Around the Mountain When she Comes." My right foot ankle and leg up to my knee just wouldn't walk Thursday night. I just made it to bed. It was late Friday morning before anyone stirred out. Porter taken the beds up, and I had to wear my house shoes to the rest room. I changed before we started out to Bakersfield.

My foot isn't well yet. I can walk pretty good, but my foot feels dead. I'm hoeing Floyce's backyard for exercise. Her arm is healing up very well, but she is still running the temperature. I keep begging her to go to bed while I'm here, but she won't. I still have that weakness in my back. I guess I always will. The river is going down now. Mrs. Terry had Floyce and Bobby and I out for dinner. I talked with Terry quite a bit about Clyde. He said Clyde had cramps or a heart attack – that there wasn't anything bothering Clyde. I'm praying that his body will be found while I'm here. It may be wrong, I don't know yet why I come. But somehow the Lord brought me. Sometimes I do very well, then it's all back. The meeting is going on at home this week. You be sure to write Hazel and send the rent. I will write Cullen too to pay the light bill. He sent my pension yesterday. I will have to go get it cashed today. Well, I must get up and clean up. I could talk a lot about so many things. Write soon.

Love – Moms

Gus Crume's fears at the time of his first stroke in 1941 that Nora would be left with no means of support proved to be unfounded. The railroad or the new Social Security Program did provide her with a pension after Gus died in 1944. They either made a special case of her situation or perhaps the rules for pensions changed in the years between Gus's stroke in 1941 and when he died in 1944. In 1935 the Railroad Retirement Board came into being which was a federal agency that operated similarly to Social Security, only for railroad workers. Railroad workers, in turn, did not receive Social Security benefits. This plan started providing benefits for surviving spouses in 1946. Because Nora was receiving benefits in 1944 when Clyde died, the retirement progam she used may not have been through the railroad, but through Social Security instead. Social Security began in 1935, but may not have offered benefits for surviving spouses until after 1941.[6] Nora was also to receive whatever was left of Clyde's insurance and retirement money after his bills and his burial expenses were paid.

As for Nora's strange problem with her leg and foot, it may have been that Nora suffered a blood clot in her leg from riding the train for such a long distance without moving around or it could have been a slight stroke. She had a history of high blood pressure issues. Apparently the problem eventually solved itself.

Nora felt she had come to California for a reason and not just to help Floyce while she was recovering from her surgery. About the middle of August, the reason revealed itself. The river had finally gone down enough, and a fisherman spotted what was left of Clyde's body. Positive identification was difficult as there was so little left, but the police felt certain that the body was Clyde's. About a week later, a funeral was held with a large number of his friends and associates attending.[7] Nora got to see her boy decently buried and also how many people cared for him and thought highly of him. Somehow she felt better and was ready to go home. She weathered the long train ride back to Texas and was glad to be back home among her friends and familiar surroundings. The rest of the family got on with their lives also, but it was with heavy hearts for a long time. Floyce had always been a caretaker for Clyde when he was alive, and she continued to do things for him through the long summer of his death. She finally found a measure of peace through a dream that she had. She saw Clyde with another man in a room. They were wearing long, gray railroad slickers and rain hats. Clyde was standing by a table with a signal lantern in his hand and he said, "Don't grieve for me. I am so happy in my work here."[8] She could finally let him go.

The year of 1944 had brought the Crumes much sorrow, but a brighter time was on the horizon. The war ground on with large battles which cost many lives such as the Battle of the

Clyde Crume 1944

Bulge, but the Allies were winning it, one step at a time. There was hope as the new year began that it would soon be over and America could take advantage of the many new advances that the war had brought in medicine, science, and the economy. A new age of prosperity was coming.

Gus Crume's Family

October 8, 1944
Sunday

Dear Grandmother,

Just a line to tell you I haven't forgot you. We have been so busy on this ship. We hardly have time to sleep. We stand four hour watches and then work between watches. I stand some watches in the engine room and is it hot! The sweat runs all the time. Well I didn't get seasick when we were out. I haven't been home in about six days. I am about twenty miles from home now, but can't get off the ship. How is things in Maydelle? I would really like to be there. I could sleep for a week without getting up.

Today sure doesn't seem like Sunday for we are working like the devil. I have a twelve to four watch today and twelve to four watch tonight. Is anyone staying with you now? How is the church services now? I sure wish I could be there for one. How is Aunt Ella and Uncle Willie? Tell them hello. I guess Dad is doing fine in the café now. I won't get to eat up the profit this time. I would like to get away from the States now so we could get back sooner, if we get back. I guess Cullen is still getting rich at the store. Marge [Buster Crume's wife] is going back east in November. She will probably be down to see you. There sure is a lot of electrical equipment on this ship, so it keeps nine electricians pretty busy, especially when we are sailing.

I sure would like to see one of those East Texas nights, with the moon shining through the pine trees. We get pretty good food and sleeping quarters on the ship, although the bunks are a little crowded.

I must close now and go on watch. Write very soon.
With love. Your grandson   Bus
Samuel E. Crume
W.S.S. Banner
Fleet Post Office
San Francisco, California

This letter to Nora from her grandson, Buster, rambled on from one subject to another, but did manage to keep Nora informed about her grandson's life in the navy. He obviously loved her and East Texas probably because he had spent quite a bit of time with her and his grandfather when he was a youngster. His parents, Morris and Onah, eventually escaped the stress of the Los Angeles freeways and moved back to Haskell, Texas, the area of Texas where Morris had lived during high school and where Onah grew up. He had a café business there, a nice home, and he and Onah stayed at Haskell the rest of their lives. He lived to be seventy-four, and he, like many in his family, suffered from heart problems in his last years. Onah lived to be eighty. Buster and Marge ran a filing station business for years, beginning in Los Angeles and continuing in Abilene, Texas, after they moved to be near Buster's folks. They had two children, and after Marge died in 1986, Buster retired from the filing station and worked for several banks. He lived to be seventy-three and eventually died of cancer.[1]

Art continued to work for oil companies in South America and the Middle East. He worked himself hard when he was drilling wells, carried a lot of responsibility and did not have much help. In his letters he often complained of not being able to rest, and slowly the work took its toll. He died at the early age of 47 of a heart attack on an oil rig in South America. Jap, his wife, and his stepchildren continued to live in the Houston area after his death.[2] He was still thinking of others until the day he died, making plans for taking care of his mother in her old age, and showing concern for his brother and sisters. His death was one more blow for Nora to have to somehow absorb. One letter he wrote to his sister Gladys from South America in late 1945 revealed the life he typically led.

Creole Petroleum Company
Jusepin Camp
Caripito, Venezuela
Dear Sis and family,

Hi folks! How are you doing by now? I will try and answer our most welcome letter of some weeks ago. Sure glad to get it but as usual I'm very lax in answering.

We have had a revolution down here since I received your letter and for some two weeks we had no mail service or communication of any kind. Now though things have resumed their regular course. The revolutionists gained control of the government, but so far I can't see much change in the general run of things to what they were. If the reforms that are planned are put through, it should help things here a bit. I am afraid though that this will be another typical latin revolt and do no good at all.

Art in the Last Years

Thanks a lot for Jimmy's picture – seems to look a bit like Dad across the eyes maybe. Gladys, I have written Mom, in fact my last letter told her of my change in address and enclosed a check for her. So far I haven't heard from her any more. I've had my nose to the grindstone since I came down this time. I had to buy a place in Houston in order to have a home. It took all I could rake and scrape to swing the deal. I hope Jap can come down by February 1. If so, I shall be able to resume my regular contribution to Mom. If she doesn't, I shall anyway. I am supposed to get a house at that time and truly hope we can. I hope to be able to put in a tank and bathroom for Mom on my vacation.

What are your plans? Does Mac intend staying in the army or will he be up for demobilization soon?

I have had a day off today but go out this p.m. Hope I can write Floyce tonight on the job. I've owed her a letter longer than you. Will try and mail this before I go out.

Honey, this is about the best I can do for now. Will truly try and do better next time. Write when you can.

Love to you all.

Art

Floyce and Charlie continued to work in Bakersfield, California, for many years until they could retire, Charlie from the railroad and Floyce from her secretarial work at a local church. They died two years apart, and both lived until almost eighty years of age. Floyce suffered from some of the same illnesses as her mother before she died. Their son Bobby grew up, lived through one tour of duty in Viet Nam, and worked as a representative for a pharmaceutical company until he retired. He married Jan Moser in 1971, but had no children.[3]

Gladys and Harry did get out of the active Army Air Core at the end of the war, and Harry decided to go into the radio station business in Hobbs, New Mexico, where he was last stationed. He partnered with another man who owned several stations, he managed the station in Hobbs, and he became well known for his play-by-play broadcasts of the local high school football and basketball games. He became a reservist in the new U.S. Air Force, commanded the local reserve unit, and rose to the rank of Lt. Colonel before he retired from the Air Force. Hobbs was a primitive ranching town when Gladys and Harry first came there with dirt streets and few places to live, but oil was discovered and the town grew to become a city of 30,000 people within twenty-five years. Harry's radio station grew with the town, and he stayed in business for close to fifty years, contributing to the growth of his community by serving in leadership positions on various boards and his tireless support of education and children's activity programs. During his last years in business, he got into politics, became a New Mexico state senator, and served two six-year terms in the state legislature where he was highly regarded and accomplished much for southern New Mexico.[4]

Gladys never went back to her teaching career after she left it at Maydelle during WWII. Once she and Harry were settled in Hobbs, she had two children, James (Jim or Jimmy) and Diane, but a major heart attack in 1953 meant she could not return to teaching. She became a stay-at-home mom, raised her children, taught a Sunday School class of high school girls at church, worked in the PTA and various clubs, and took up genealogy as a past-time. She attended many of the high school sports events where Harry was announcing the games on the radio, and she was able to be with him during his sessions at the state legislature. She enjoyed it all. She died at the early age of sixty-one from a combination of illnesses including her weak heart. After several years, Harry married again to Barbara Andrews Ripley in 1976, and their marriage ended with Harry's death on January 3, 2008, at the age of 91. When he died, the flags of New Mexico flew at half mast, and he was honored by many, as he was in life.[5]

After Nora returned to Texas after burying her son, Clyde, in California, her children built her a small house at Maydelle. Her sister-in-law, Ella, lived next door in a similar house. For several years her children and grandchildren visited her and she visited them, but she always wanted to return home to Maydelle. As the years went by, she had a harder time living alone. She began to suffer from dementia, and she was frequently ill. After Art died, she could barely go on, so the remaining family members found a nursing home near Maydelle to give her the care

Lanora Crume Last Years

that she needed. She did not live long after that, dying in 1954, just two years after Art, at the age of seventy-seven. She was laid to rest beside Gus at Pleasant Grove.[6] She had lived a long, hard life but a good one. Sometimes her willpower was the only thing that kept the family going. She was educated, intelligent, and determined, qualities that sustained her as she sought to raise her children. She never had much in the way of worldly possessions, but she had the love of her family, a purpose in living each day, and a life devoted to being led by a higher power than her own. She had what was important to her, and she knew it.

Of all of Gus Crume's children, the one who perhaps inherited the most characteristics of Silas Moses was Gladys. The drive, ambition, and energy which were so typical of him were the characteristics that were the most prominent in Gladys. She was the only one of Gus's children to complete a college education and reach the goal that she had set for herself of becoming a teacher. In that career she kept pushing to be better and take on more challenges as was evidenced by her move to a better position at Iowa Park, Texas. Unfortunately her health did not keep up with her ambitions and she was severely limited in what she could do. However, even after her health failed, she continued to reach out for new opportunities. Her work in genealogy was ground-breaking as no one else in her family line had bothered to keep track of the Crume family passage through time or to publish findings. She was not a steward of the land, but she had the characteristics of one - great strength of purpose and determination.

It is striking to note the prevalence of heart disease in this Crume family and the Crume families that preceded it. Gus, Nora, Art, Gladys, Morris, and possibly Clyde all suffered from some form of it, and it caused their deaths in most cases, sometimes at an early age. In the previous generations, Silas Moses definitely had problems with stroke and sudden blindness, as did his father before him. Perhaps others in those generations and the generations before had heart disease and did not know it. If it can be proven that diseases run in families through heredity, the weakness in this Crume line would have to be the heart. It is ironic in a way because spiritually they were people with overly healthy hearts.

Another characteristic of this Crume family which was universal was laughter. If ever there was a family that loved to laugh, it was the Gus Crume bunch. It might be assumed through looking at what the family endured that the opposite might be the case, but it wasn't so. They loved to joke, play practical jokes, tell funny stories, tease each other, and in general, find the brighter side of life. It was one of the things that made the family so attractive to other people and so loved. Perhaps it was one of the great gifts the family could offer to others when money was not available. It certainly was a gift they gave themselves, even on the darkest days.

Gus Crume's Family Loved to Laugh

Cherokee County remained a farming, ranching, and timber industry county into the modern age. Although the Crume name was no longer present, descendants of the family were still living there. The Pleasant Grove Missionary Baptist Church and Cemetery remained active, and Maydelle was a small but viable town. Gus Crume's first home in Maydelle still stands and has been modernized over the years. The Texas State Railroad continues to operate, in recent times as a tourist train ride between Rusk and Palestine, and the State Parks in the area provide camping

Pleasant Grove Missionary Baptist Church Cemetery
The Crume Rows

and fishing opportunities. Pine Town, Java, and Gent are completely gone, but signs have been erected for Java and Gent to mark their location. The old Rusk to Palestine road can still be traveled. Rusk remains the county seat, but Jacksonville is the largest city. [7]The event of note for the area since the year 2000 arrived was the Columbia space shuttle explosion in 2003. A wide swath of debris spread across the county, especially the area where Pine Town used to peacefully reside in the pines.[8] Quite a difference one hundred and forty-four years can make! Over all, time has been kind to the place where two generations of Crumes found a home and built a life for themselves.

When Nora married Gus Crume, she united three great family lines – the Crumes, the Fergusons, and the Jordans. They were all people of the land, respecting it, cultivating it, living off of it, speculating with it, and loving it. It was simply a part of them. Throughout the long Crume line, the love of the land was a persistent force, an abiding influence passed from one generation to another, and even though Gus and Nora's children did not become farmers, they still loved the farm and the land. Their farm childhood lived on in their memories all the days of their lives, somehow, their good memories outweighing the nightmare of the Dust Bowl and the relentless poverty. Gladys once wrote about the farm life.

I think the best time on the farm is twilight. The sun would be nearly gone, just beautiful colors across the western sky. We would do the evening chores and romp with our dog, Pal. There were the sounds of children and dogs from neighboring farms and our own farm animals as they had their evening meal. Then we went inside for our own meal, the dark came down, the stars came out, and all was very, very quiet and peaceful down on the farm.[9]

Living History

"So, Mom, the Crumes started out as big shot land owners with lots of acres of land and ended up after two hundred years with a house and a lot in town." Typical of a teenager, I summed up the family history rather succinctly. I was perched on the arm of a chair in the den listening to my mother talk about her family's experiences once again.

"Well, actually they started out with nothing in the beginning, but I guess the rest of what you said was true of our family line. I don't know what happened to all the other Crume family lines. Perhaps there were some of them that stayed with farming or ranching as a way of life," Mom allowed. "The pull of the land was always strong with this family."

"If this happened to our family line and many others, why did agriculture survive and remain important in the United States?" I wondered.

"Over two hundred years' time and a growth in population, things change. In the beginning of the country, it was possible for many people to own land, and they were interested in that and in making a living that way. Over time, as the population grew and adverse farming conditions developed, fewer people stayed on the land. New technology brought about new careers as well. The people moved to the cities and swelled the population there. However, you only have to get in an automobile and drive around the country to see that every state in America has huge tracts of land being used for some form of agriculture. The reason for this is that conditions in the United States are ideal for producing food -- the weather, the land, and the water supply. It makes sense that this would still be a big industry for our country, but the changes occurred in the number of people farming or ranching and in the way they took care of the land and made it produce for them. The Great Depression made quite a difference in this regard."

"Wow! Mom, the Crume story reads like an American History text. From the colonial period in America to World War II and even farther if you keep tracking. It's all there."

"Yes, if you look closely at their lives, you will see American history playing out as you have read about it in school. It makes us realize that our national history was actually the everyday lives of our ancestors. They lived history and were a part of history, although they didn't always realize it at the time. If asked, they would have said their lives weren't very important. If people would consider their lives today as living history, it might make them want to be more careful what they say and do." Mom never hesitated to make a point when she had a chance – the old teacher coming to the fore once again.

"It's like that old saw. If you don't study history, you are doomed to repeat it," I guessed.

"Yes, but it is more than that. We also study history to find out about where we came from and who we are," Mom commented, and man, was she speaking from personal experience!

As a final thought, Mom speculated, "The Crumes were there for most of the great events in American history. To watch their march through time is to discover America's history through its people – not a bad way to go about it."

"Not bad at all," I whispered gently.

A Journey of Voices: Stewards of the Land 291

CRUME CEMETERY
Fairfield Corner, Breckinridge County KY

Cemetery Location

Layout of Cemetery Mound

Cemetery coordinates:
37 degrees, 40.458 minutes North
86 degrees, 17.326 minutes West

M = male
F = female

D. Gladow
Jan. 2010

Epilogue

Breckinridge County, Kentucky
October 2009

On a chilly, dreary autumn day that included a fine mist in the air, four people made their way slowly through a field of tall corn toward a raised, somewhat-cleared patch of ground. This day had been a long time coming, almost one hundred and fifty years, and the souls buried in the patch of ground up ahead had been patiently waiting all of that time to be rediscovered and remembered. The four individuals who were interested in this hallowed soil had parked their vehicles off the nearby paved road, had walked about one hundred yards, passing a farm pond on the way, had entered the field of corn, and were forcing their way through the tall stalks, trying not to step in any more mud than was absolutely necessary. It would have been easy to become disoriented walking in a field of corn stalks higher than a normal-sized person's head, so the group stayed close together until they reached their destination. The partially cleared ground had never been cultivated because the owners of this land had always known not to farm there, but it had been covered with tall grass, shrubs, and fledgling trees. There was one large tree on the site that was now only a remnant of what it had once been, but it helped to mark the spot.

One of the four people was an Abraham Lincoln family researcher from Elizabethtown, Kentucky, John Lay. At the request of two Crume family researchers from Kansas, Dean and Diane Gladow, he had discovered the burial site with the help of his friend Henry Morrison, a grave dowser or witcher; Shirley Pile, a Crume descendant who lived in the vicinity; Karen Schafer, the Breckinridge County, Kentucky, archivist; and Philip

Hudson, the owner of the land. John had then assumed the responsibility for clearing the cemetery ground so that it could be examined and its contents marked and mapped. John had brought with him on this visit to the cemetery Henry Morrison and the two Crume family researchers from Kansas, Diane Gladow being a direct descendant of the people possibly buried at the site and her husband Dean. John, although not a Lincoln descendant, had been doing research on the Capt. Abraham Lincoln family, first members of the Lincoln family to live in Kentucky. In 1803 a Crume had married one of Capt. Lincoln's daughters, Mary, uniting forever the destinies of the two families, so it was fitting that the interests of both families be represented in this investigation of the site.

Because rain was eminent, the group wasted no time. Henry witched or dowsed the graves with his swinging metal rods to determine their location and the gender of each person interred.

Crume Cemetery Surrounded by Corn Fields

He found thirteen graves, eight women and five men, one of whom was a small boy (The grave contained a male and was short in length). John planted metal wire stakes with pink engineering flags attached at the head and foot of each grave. Dean and Diane probed each grave carefully in search of tombstones. Four stones were found; two were headstones and two were footstones. After examining the stones carefully and even using cornstarch on one of them, the Gladows found no discernible marks on the stones although at least one of them was uneven and showed promise of carved letters. John nailed a handmade sign to the stump of the old tree that guarded the burial place. It read, "Crume Cemetery 5 men 8 women." Pictures were taken by two of the group to record the place, the day, the grave sites and the tombstones. Dean Gladow drove tall stakes into the ground at several places in the perimeter of the cleared area, and he identified GPS coordinates for the site.

As the clouds began to produce a weak drizzle, the four made their way back through the corn to their cars and departed the scene. It was not the end of a long search (for many people had searched for this cemetery over the years) but only another milestone in the journey to find and identify this place. Much work still remained to be done to prove that this small patch of ground contained the final remains of the pioneer Ralph Crume, Sr. and some of the members of his family, one of whom was Mary Lincoln Crume, the aunt of President Abraham Lincoln. After spending four or five days searching through Breckinridge County land records at the courthouse archives, Dean and Diane Gladow left for their home in Kansas, carrying with them copies of over sixty land deeds.

Over the next few months, the documents were catalogued and mapped, and slowly the land deeds began to form a logical progression of land ownership that started with the present and traveled backward to approximately 1810. Working with a present-day aerial map of the land where the cemetery sat and the descriptions of the various Crume land plots, Dean was able to draw diagrams of the land plots to the aerial map's scale and fit the plots together like a jigsaw puzzle, showing conclusively that the Crume Cemetery was sitting on what had been Crume land up until 1886 when the land was sold out of the family. Because no one had been buried there since shortly before 1886, it was possible to say that the abandoned cemetery was the final resting place of thirteen members of the Ralph Crume, Sr. family, a family and a cemetery that had been missing for decades. As well, it was possible to create a map of the Ralph Crume Sr. family lands, known as Crume Valley, a wide swath of land that swept across Fairfield, Kentucky, comprising over 1500 acres.

The only remaining work to be done was to decide who was buried in this place by eliminating those who could not be there. This involved making a list of three generations of the Ralph Crume Sr. family which also included some of Philip Crume's family (Ralph Sr.'s father) and carefully checking each one of the family members with census and other records to determine when and where they died. After eliminating those who had moved to other places before they died and those who most probably were buried in other places, the number of possible family members was still not conclusively thirteen - the number of grave sites discovered by the grave dowser - but it was close.

As a part of this process of looking for evidence that would identify the people buried in the cemetery, Diane Gladow began to study on the computer the pictures of the two large grave markers that had been found at the cemetery site. A process of looking at close views of the markers and zooming in began to reveal letters carved into the stone. Recognizable letters were the initials RC and RC Jr. on one of the stones. The other stone seemed to have indistinct letters to be studied as well. The RC and RC Jr. carvings were conclusive evidence, along with the land document study, that Ralph Crume Sr. and Ralph Crume Jr. were buried in the cemetery. Their wives were more than likely present as well, according to the dowser's determination of females buried in the cemetery.

Further examination of the grave markers would be needed to see if more initials would be revealed, but the evidence discovered up to that point rather conclusively indicated that Mary Lincoln Crume, wife of Ralph Crume Jr. and aunt of President Abraham Lincoln, was indeed buried in the cemetery. As concluding activities for the project, Dean and Diane composed a report about the cemetery, complete with maps and diagrams, and distributed it to various libraries, archives, and persons interested in the Crume and Lincoln families.[1] A sign was also designed by Dean Gladow and installed at the Fairfield, Kentucky, intersection by John Lay, the Gladows, and Philip Hudson to commemorate the Crume land and cemetery.

It had taken a year of concentrated work by a group of Crume and Lincoln family researchers and Breckinridge County archivists to finally find the final resting place of the Ralph Crume, Sr. family and Mary Lincoln, a goal that had been illusive up to that point. Not only would this complete the search for the early Crume family in Breckinridge County and their land, but it completed the search for the final resting places of the first two

Lincoln generations in Kentucky, Capt. Abraham Lincoln, his wife Bersheba (or Bathsheba), and their children Thomas (father of President Abraham Lincoln), Josiah, Mordecai, Mary and Nancy. Mary was the last member of those two generations to be found. Although people who lived in the neighborhood, such as Shirley Pile, knew there was an old cemetery located somewhere on Philip Hudson's land which contained Lincoln descendants, perhaps the cemetery had just been waiting patiently to reveal itself to the right group of interested people who would positively identify it. What was lost for so many years had been found, and a circle had been completed for the Crume and Lincoln families.

Author's Notes

Because I knew personally many of the people in this book, it was especially poignant for me to read their letters and listen to their stories. I learned much about people that I thought I knew very well. I also was able to verify stories that I had heard as a child and almost forgotten. I found many things to be proud of and also, inevitably, a few to cry over, but putting this book together and telling these people's story was a personal journey which I enjoyed very much and from which I ultimately derived a great amount of satisfaction.

In this book, unlike the first one in the series, I decided to provide family charts. They help the reader to keep straight the many people in the book, and they provide vital statistics about the individual people so that less of that material has to be included in the text of the book. The charts are by no means complete. There is much more information about each of Philip Crume's sixteen family lines, and if the reader is interested, he or she can contact me. This book is confined to my direct line of Crumes, for the most part, to prevent having a book of such large proportions as to be difficult to read.

The maps included in the book were drawn by Dean Gladow, using the original land documents as a source. This work consumed a large part of the research for the book. Another part of the research involved the tracking down of old family stories to check their credibility. There is still work to be done in that area, but Crume descendants will notice as they read this book, new information which was compiled from that research. Follow the endnote markers to find sources, and feel free to contact me for more information.

At times, the letters in the book were edited for spelling, punctuation, and sentence structure to increase readability. They were also edited for length as the Crumes tended to ramble and repeat themselves when they wrote. Some scans of the old documents and letters are provided for readers who enjoy handwriting study and/or deciphering old written sources.

The bibliography/notes pages at the end of the book probably do not include all of the multitude of public documents, research material from genealogists, Bible records, obituaries, cemetery records, etc. which went into the research for this book. The author tried to include as many as possible. I am indebted to many libraries/archives across the country for their generous help. A special thank you goes to the many genealogists/family researchers who have helped with this project. Many of their names appear in the source notes. Without your help, this book would not be as complete as it is. Thanks so very much.

Because a project of this nature is never truly complete, anyone who is seeking more information about the Crume families or who would like to contribute to this story is welcome to contact me. The mystery of the Crume immigrant to America still remains to be solved conclusively. Who was Daniel Crume and what happened to him? Was he the immigrant to America or was his father or was his son? I, as well as others, will be working for a while longer on the Crume story to see if we can find out.

Finally, I wish to thank some special people, my proofreaders/editors. In writing a book and looking at the words for hours at a time, the author can reach a point at which he/she cannot see areas which need improvement. For that reason, I have at least two people (sometimes more) read each of my books to give me their input. So, thank you to Lucy Geoghegan, Nancy Methvin, Dean Gladow, and Jim McAdams for your insight and help.

Lastly, I have to say that I could not have written this book without the assistance of my mother's research records and memoirs and Lucy Geoghegan's vast collection of Crume information. So many times when I had questions or needed eye witness accounts, I found the answers and the accounts in my mother's collection of materials. This collection was invaluable since she was no longer living to answer my questions in person.

So thanks, Mom, for being a writer, a recorder, and a researcher. You made this book possible, and because you weren't able to write it yourself, I am proud to be your scribe. Thanks as well to Lucy who answered my questions and ferreted out what seemed like reams of material from her collection that I could study to make my Crume story more complete and accurate. My memories of her generosity, good humor, and sharp recall of facts will live as long as I do.

Family Charts
Generation One

Philip Crume Family
Born August 9, 1724
Died April 20, 1801

Married Sarah Withers (Weathers) December 23, 1749
Born December 25, 1729, Died January 9, 1787

Children:
1. Ralph Crume Sr.   12 Dec 1750 – 3 Feb 1828
    Mary "Polly" Riggs Crume
2. Philip Withers Crume   11 Aug 1752 – 8 May 1823
    Sarah "Sallie" Trot
    Son Jesse wrote his diary in 1859.
3. Susanna Crume   10 July 1754 – 14 July 1829
    Eleazer Birkhead
4. Mary Crume   15 March 1756 – 1817
    Abraham Birkhead
5. Daniel Crume   27 January 1758 – after 1827
    Mary Dodson
    Mary Lincoln (common law perhaps, no public documents)
    Hannah Springer Askins
6. Jesse Crume   16 January 1760 –16 Sept 1824
    Elizabeth Collins
    Jane Cyphers
7. Elizabeth Crume   19 April 1762 – Before 1810
    James Harrell
8. William Crume   2 April 1764 – 4 Nov 1795
    Mary Thomas
9. Moses Crume   27 Feb 1766 – 1 April 1839
    Sarah Marks
    Ann Morehead
10. Isaac Crume   17 March 1768 – 7 Feb 1791
    unmarried

11. Sarah Crume   11 March 1771 – prior to 1820
    George Marks
12. Eunice Crume   7 Dec 1776 – 15 July 1857
    Michael Klinglesmith

Married Anna Barret September 9, 1788
Born December 19, 1769, Died December 27, 1848

Children:
13. John Crume   26 Nov 1789 – 8 Dec 1865
    Elizabeth Cotton
    Elizabeth Wood
14. Margaret "Peggy" Crume   14 June 1791 – 5 Dec 1876
    John Ridgeway
15. Nancy Crume   20 Dec 1792 – 30 April 1854
    Charles "Brick" Jordan
16. Keziah Crume   17 Feb 1795 – 19 Dec 1866
    James Howey
17. Squire Crume   17 July 1798 – 27 Dec 1860
    Sarah Ann "Sally" Cotton

Squire was the only child born in Kentucky. All the rest were born in Virginia.

Anna Barret Crume married Jacob Marks December 20, 1804

Children:
1. Thomas Marks   5 March 1807 – 14 Sept 1876
   Lydia Howey
2. James Marks   19 Oct 1808 – 29 November 1876
   Jane Howey
3. Elizabeth Marks   17 Aug 1810 – 14 Oct 1827
   unmarried
4. William Marks   21 March 1812 – Feb 1851
   Catherine Greer

Anna Barret Crume Marks married Rev. William Morris
around 1819-20

Children: None

Generation Two

Ralph Crume, Sr. Family
Born December 12, 1750
Died February 1829

Married Mary "Polly" Riggs August 4, 1772
Born 1750-1754, Died before 1839

Children:
1. Charles Crume   Born in 1775, Died after 1850
    Mary Snelling
2. Rachel Crume   Born on 16 July 1773, Died after 1860
    Benedict Lucas
3. Sarah Crume   Born ca 1777, Died between 1850 - 1860
    Levi Horsley
4. Ralph Crume Jr.   Born 16 July 1779, Died between 1830 - 1832
    Mary Lincoln
5. William Crume   Born 27 May 1783, Died 31 Aug 1812
    Susannah Lavernia Jones
6. Mary "Polly" Crume   Born around 1785, Died after 1850
    Thomas Pile
    James Ruckman
7. Silas Crume   Born unknown, Died before 1832
    unmarried
8. John Crume   Born around 1794, Died in 1875
    Permelia Shrewsbury Bratcher

Generation Three

Ralph Crume, Jr. Family
Born July 16, 1779
Died between 1830-1832

Married Mary Lincoln August 5, 1801
Born between 1775 - 1776, Died between 1830 - 1832

Children:
1. Ann Crume   Born in or before 1804, Died unknown
    Charles Hoskinson
2. William Cox Crume   Born January 1804, Died after 1883
    Mary Susannah Hoskinson
    Mary Ann Lucas Norris
3. Ralph Lincoln Crume   Born 1809, Died after 1890
    Mary Brumfield
    Rebecca Ann Carr

Generation Four

Dr. William Cox Crume Family
"Dr. Billy"
Born January 1804
Died after 1883

Married Mary Susannah Hoskinson February 7, 1825
Born 1806, Died between 1830-1832

Children:
1. Silas Moses Crume   Born 14 Dec1825, Died 23 March 1912
   Nancy Catherine Williams
   Sarah Lucinda Sherman
2. John Daniel Crume   Born 1827, Died around 1863
   Jane Nottingham
   Julia Ann Butler
3. Ann Crume   Born 1828-1830, Died between 1831-1837
   unmarried

Married Mary Ann Lucas Norris July 27, 1837
Born abt. 1805, Died after 1883

Children:
1. Eliza Jane Crume   Born 1 May 1838, Died 12 January 1917
   William Hall Hudson
2. Ralph Mark Crume   Born 23 April 1840, Died 25 March 1902
   Mary Thomas Crume
3. Susan Mary Crume   Born 7 April 1843, Died 22 July 1929
   John Berry Tucker
4. James F. Crume   Born between 1845-1846, Died 5 April 1852
   unmarried

Two stepchildren from Mary Ann Norris
1. William Norris
2. Harriet Norris

Generation Five, Paternal

Silas Moses Crume Family
Born December 14, 1825
Died March 23, 1912

Married Nancy Catherine Williams February 6, 1853
Born November 29, 1831, Died October 14, 1876

Children:
1. John William Crume   Born 25 December 1853,
    Died 26 February 1912
    Sarah Sherman
2. Thomas Anthony Crume   Born 18 September 1855,
    Died 9 November 1875
    unmarried
3. Susan Cole Crume   Born 9 November 1857,
    Died 19 February 1862
    unmarried
4. Mary Elizabeth Crume   Born 9 November 1857,
    Died 8 September 1928
    Alexander Acker
5. James Richard Crume   Born 5 November 1859,
    Died 27 August 1925
    Mollie Elizabeth Stewart
6. Ada Belle Crume   Born 28 August 1861,
    Died 22 January 1931
    John Thomas Ferguson
7. Samuel Augustus Crume   Born 21 August 1864,
    Died 5 April 1944
    Elizabeth Isabel (Lizziebeth) Crawford
    Lanora "Nora" Belle Ferguson
8. Sarah "Sally" Jane Crume   Born 23 February 1870,
    Died 1 July 1894
    Seborn Tankersley

**Married Sarah Lucinda Sherman October 1, 1878
Born abt. October 1833, Died September 1880**

Children:
1. Ida Mae Crume   Born 5 December 1879, Died 21 August 1926
   William Merrell Stewart

Generation Five, Maternal

John Finley Williams, Sr. Family
Born August 5, 1797
Died May 24, 1848

Married Mary Vernon February 14, 1822
Born December 26, 1804, Died January 28, 1881

Children:
1. Samuel Best Williams   Born 29 January 1823,
    Died 15 October 1865
    Rachel Taylor
2. Elizabeth Williams "Aunt Betsey"   Born 24 July 1824,
    Died 11 December 1893
    James Kendall
3. James Henry Williams, Sr.   Born 22 March 1826,
    Died 05 November 1902
    Amanda Wiseheart
4. Anthony Williams "Tony"   Born 28 February 1828,
    Died 20 February 1858
    unmarried
5. Frances Williams "Fanny"   Born 28 January 1830,
    Died 08 August 1898
    David Vanmeter
6. Nancy Catherine Williams   Born 29 November 1831,
    Died 14 October 1876
    Silas Moses Crume
7. Thomas Williams   Born 01 February 1834,
    Died 13 January 1863
    unmarried
8. Richard Williams   (infant)   Born 28 November 1836,
    Died 24 November 1837
    unmarried
9. Mary Jane Williams   Born 14 December 1838,
    Died 11 February 1899
    Henry R. Smith

10. John Finley Williams, Jr. "Uncle Jack" Born 10 May 1841,
    Died 15 March 1925
    Catherine B. Kennedy
    Son was Anthony "Tony" Vernon Williams.
11. Sarah "Sally" Williams   Born 26 January 1845,
    Died 07 May 1892
    Orla C. Stanfield

Generation Five*, Maternal
*Daughter in Generation Six, Second Wife in Generation Six

Rev. John Thomas Ferguson Family
Born March 5, 1844
Died April 14, 1916

Married Margaret Jane Jordan   October 12, 1865
Born February 18, 1842,   Died April 30, 1902

Children:
1. David L. Ferguson   Born 14 August 1866   Died Before 1881
    unmarried
2. John D. Ferguson   Born 4 October 1868   Died 1889
    unmarried
3. K. Danny Ferguson   Born 31 July 1870   Died Before 1881
    unmarried
4. Thomas Floyd Ferguson   Born 29 April 1875
    Died 8 May 1930
    Willie Mae Lively
    Son was Julius Alton Ferguson.
5. Lanora Belle "Nora" Ferguson   Born 20 February 1877
    Died 29 January 1954
    Samuel Augustus Crume
6. James Walter Ferguson   Born 24 September 1878
    Died November 1959
    Victoria Bishop
7. William Hugh "Willie" Ferguson   Born 9 December 1883
    Died 8 May 1946
    Lou Ella "Ella" Featherstone

Married Ada Belle Crume   October 1902
Born August 28, 1861,   Died January 22, 1931

Children:
1. Harold A. Ferguson   Born 16 September 1903
    Died 5 December 1973
    Maudie Clarice Hampton

Generation Six, Paternal

Samuel Augustus "Gus" Crume Family
Born August 21, 1864,
Died April 5, 1944

Married Elizabeth Isabel "Lizziebeth" Crawford January 16, 1890
Born December 11, 1871,
Died September 30, 1895

Children:
1. Ernest Elmer Crume, Sr.   Born 2 February 1891,
    Died December 1966
    Bertha Lee Stidham/Moore
2. Jewel Luther Crume   Born 2 August 1893,
    Died 5 March 1895
    unmarried
3. Infant son Crume   Born 26 September 1895,
    Died 26 September 1895
    unmarried

Married Lanora Belle "Nora" Ferguson November 19, 1903
Born February 20, 1877,
Died January 29, 1954

Children:
1. James Arthur Crume   Born 2 September 1905,
    Died 20 January 1952
    Beatrice Moore Bayley
2. Samuel Morris Crume   Born 11 November 1907,
    Died 5 August 1981
    Onah L. Day   Son was Samuel Elvis "Buster" Crume.
3. Lura Gladys Crume   Born 28 December 1912,
    Died 1 December 1972
    Harry Mayhew McAdams
4. Floyce Mae Crume   Born 21 January 1915,
    Died 3 December 1993
    Charles A. Leaverton   Son was Robert C. "Bobby."

5. Clyde Martin Crume   Born 9 September 1919,
   Died 27 May 1944
   unmarried

Notes and Sources

Chapter 3

1. Augusta County, Virginia Court Record Order Book 1, p. 168 (Cited in Cecil O'Dell, Pioneers of Old Frederick County, p. 490).
2. Frederick County, Virginia Land Deeds, Surveys, Warrants, 1749. Survey by John Bayless 2 September 1749, Warrant 15 August 1749.
3. County descriptors for Orange, Augusta, Frederick, Dunmore, Shenandoah, and Warren in Virginia. USGenWeb sites. www.usgenweb.com. Accessed 2012.
4. Arthur McClinton, ed. The Fairfax Line: A Historic Landmark including "The Fairfax Line Thomas Lewis's Journal of 1746." New Market, VA: The Henkel Press, 1925; Edinburg, VA: Shenandoah County Historical Society, 1990.
5. Orange County and Frederick County, Virginia Land Records. Pioneers of Old Frederick County, Virginia by Cecil O'Dell. Marceline, Missouri: Walsworth Publishing Company, 1995.
6. Philip Crume Family Bible. London: Thomas Baskett and the Assigns of Robert Baskett, 1759. Copy of family records by Orrie B. Kellogg on July 6, 1933 from a transcript in the files of Dr. L.G. Crume done by Dr. Crume's uncle, a Philip Crume. Sarah Withers name is often seen as Sarah Margaret Withers or Margaret Sarah Withers. There are currently no sources available which prove conclusively that Margaret was ever a part of Sarah's name. Her mother's name was Margaret, but the Philip Crume Bible record lists only the name Sarah for Sarah Withers.
7. Philip Crume Family Bible. See #6 above.
8. "A Brief History of the French and Indian War." The Philadelphia Print Shop, Ltd. 2012. The Philadelphia Print Shop, Ltd. Accessed 7 February 2012. http://www.philaprintshop.com/frchintx.html. Reference listed from Seymour I. Schwartz. The French and Indian War. 1754-1763. The Imperial Struggle for North America. Edison, NJ, 1999.
9. "A Brief History of the French and Indian War." See #8 above.
10. "A Brief History of the French and Indian War." See #8 above.
11. Thomas Crump, Abraham Lincoln's World (New York and London: Continuum, 2009) Pages 1-2.

12. Northern Neck Grants M, 1762-1765. Page 66. Frederick County. 7 October 1762.
13. Philip Crume Family Bible. See #6 above.
14. Northern Neck Grants O, 1767-1770. Page 57. Frederick County. Northern Neck Grants Q, 1775-1778. Page 108. Dunmore County. Philip Crume Family Bible. See #6 above.
15. Philip Crume Family Bible. See #6 above.
16. Crume family records. Lucy Geoghegan research collection. Nelson County Public Library. Bardstown, Kentucky. 2009-2010.
17. "The History of the Daniel Boone Wilderness Trail." The Daniel Boone Wilderness Trail Association. 2006. The Daniel Boone Wilderness Trail Association. Accessed 13 April 2011. www.danielboonetrail.com/history.php
18. "The History of the Daniel Boone Wilderness Trail." See #17 above.
19. "The Washington County Virginia Surveyors Record 1781-1797." Page 16. Philip Crume, 180 acres on the head of a small branch of the Clinch River, Commissioners Certificate, 25 March 1783, and 400 acres on the north side of the Clinch in New Garden, 4 September 1782, same document and page number.
20. "Indian Atrocities Along the Clinch, Powell and Holston Rivers of SW Virginia, 1773-1794." p. 131. Emory L. Hamilton. Published online. Accessed 10 March 2011. http://www.rootsweb.ancestry.com/~varussel/indian/63.html
21. Russell County Virginia Deed Book 2 Grantor Index (1795-1798). Philip and Ann Crumes of Shenandoah County Virginia to Henry Smith 180 acres. 1 August 1797.
22. John M. Blum, Bruce Catton, Edmund S. Morgan, Arthur M. Schlesinger, Jr., Kenneth M. Stampp, and C. Vann Woodward. The National Experience. New York: Harcourt, Brace & World, Inc., 1963. Page 103.
23. The National Experience. Page 103. See #22 above.
24. "The French and Indian War 1756-1763." USHistory.org. 1995. Independence Hall Association. Accessed 31 March 2012. http://www.ushistory.org/Declaration/related/frin.htm.
25. "Revolutionary War Records, Section IV." Virginia in the Revolution and War of 1812. CD-Rom Disk Family TreeMaker 121. Accessed 15 June 2008.
26. "Revolutionary War Records, Section IV." See #25 above.
27. Letter from Mrs. William Henry Sullivan, Jr. of the Daughter of the American Revolution Library in Washington, D.C. affirming Philip Crume I is listed on the DAR Patriot Index, page 167,

along with the record from the court of Shenandoah County Virginia which listed his help for the patriot cause in the American Revolution. 1967.
28. DAR letter in regards to Philip Crume I, Patriot. See #27 above.
29. "Register of Virginians in the Revolution (alphabetical)" Virginia in the Revolution and War of 1812. CD-Rom Disk Family TreeMaker 121. 15 June 2008.
30. The Road to Independence: Virginia 1763-1783. Virginia State Department of Education. Project Gutenberg E-book. 2009. http://www.gutenberg.org/files/30058/30058-h/30058-h.htm#western
Accessed 4/25/2012.
31. Crume Family Records. Lucy Geoghegan research collection. See #16 above.
32. Northern Neck Grants R, 1778-1780. Page 250. Northern Neck Grants S, 1780-1788. Page 47.
33. Deed Book C, page 375. Shenandoah County, Virginia. 20 February 1781. 400 acres.
34. Deed Book 18, page 81. Frederick County, Virginia. 29 January 1779. Ralph Withers to grandson Philip Crume Jr. 140 acres.
35. "Shenandoah Valley." Wikipedia. Accessed 14 May 2011. http://en.wikipedia.org/wiki/Shenandoah_Valley
36. The Road to Independence: Virginia 1763-1783. See #30 above.
37. John W. Wayland. A History of Shenandoah County, Virginia. Strasburg, Virginia: Shenandoah Publishing House, 1927. Page 745. Marriage record.
38. Thomas Crump, Abraham Lincoln's World. Page 3. See #11 above.
39. Virginia State Land Office, Jefferson County, Kentucky Military District, Book U, P. 142, #666. Philip Crume, 1000 acres on the north side of the Beech Fork, 2 Dec 1785.
40. Virginia State Land Office, Jefferson County, Kentucky Military District, Book Z, p. 158, #70. Daniel Crume 500 acres on the south side of the Beech Fork, 2 Dec 1785.
41. Virginia State Land Office, Nelson County, Kentucky Military District, Book 2, p. 389, #182. Philip Crume, 201 acres on the south side of the Beech Fork, 18 May 1790.
42. "Virginia Treasury Warrants" Virginia Treasury Warrants Home Page. 2012. Kentucky Land Office, Kentucky Secretary of State. Accessed 1 April 2012.
http://sos.ky.gov/land/nonmilitary/virginia/ "Virginia Treasury Warrants." Message Board on Land and Tax Records.

Ancestry.com
http://boards.ancestry.com/topics.researchresoources.land-tax/201.1/mb.ashx   Accessed 5/17/2011.
43. Philip Crume Family Bible. See #6 above.
44. Shenandoah County Virginia Marriage Records. Shenandoah County, Virginia Website. GenWeb. 2001-2008. Accessed 24 April 2010. http://www.vagenweb.org/shenandoah/ Marriage Register #1 - 1772-1853. Woodstock, Shenandoah County, Virginia. Moses Crume to Sarah Marks and Sarah Crume to George Marks.
45. Crume Family Records. Lucy Geoghegan research collection. See #16 above.
46. "Rev. Moses Crume." Centennial History of Butler County, Ohio 1905. Pages 987-988.
47. Letter from Dr. William Robert Crume of Gratia, Ohio to Dr. George P. Crume. March 22, 1928. Dr. George Crume discounted the flatboat story.
48. A Pictorial History of Bardstown and Nelson County. D-books Publishing Inc. 2000. Page 39.
49. "Rev. Moses Crume." See #46 above.
50. Shenandoah County Virginia Minute Book Court Records 1781-1785. March 1784 session.
51. A Pictorial History of Bardstown and Nelson County. See #48 above.
52. Jesse Crume family records. Brett Berry and Rick Crume private research collections. Some of Rick Crume's records are online.

Chapter 4
1. Incidents in the Life of Jesse Crume. 1859-1864. Unpublished personal diary of Philip Crume Sr.'s grandson written late in Jesse's life. There may possibly be a complete copy that may be accessed in the Lucy Geoghegan research collection of Crume records at the Nelson County Public Library at Bardstown, Kentucky.
2. Marriage bond 28, 29 August 1788. Shenandoah County, Virginia. Also Philip Crume Family Bible. See #6, Chapter 3 above.
3. Philip Crume Family Bible. See #6, Chapter 3 above.
4. Marriage Register #1 1772-1853. Shenandoah County Clerk's Office. Woodstock, Virginia.
5. Deed Book I, Page 615. 8 September 1795. Shenandoah County Clerk's Office, Woodstock, Virginia.

6. Will Book 5, page 261. Frederick County Clerk's Office. Winchester, Virginia. Incidents in the Life of Jesse Crume. See #1 above. Diary gives a birth date of 1 September 1680 for Ralph Withers and says he lived 108 years. It may have been 109 years according to the date of the will.
7. Deed Book 18, page 81. 29 January 1779. Frederick County Clerk's Office, Winchester, Virginia.
8. Deed Book F, page 134. 6 December 1785. Shenandoah County Clerk's Office, Woodstock, Virginia.
9. Will Book 5, page 261. See #6 above.
10. Philip Crume Family Bible. See #6, Chapter 3 above.
11. Will Book D, pages 34-35. 28 May 1791. Shenandoah County Clerk's Office, Woodstock, Virginia. Returned and recorded at a court held on 30 June 1791.
12. Thomas Crump. Abraham Lincoln's World. Page 4. See #11, Chapter 3 above.
13. Philip Crume Family Bible. See #6, Chapter 3 above.
14. Crume Family Records. Lucy Geoghegan research collection. See #16, Chapter 3 above. Census records for Nelson County, Kentucky 1800 and 1810.
15. Incidents in the Life of Jesse Crume. See #1 above. Letter from Jesse W. Crume of Taylorsville, Kentucky. 9 March 1928. Jesse W. Crume was the grandson of Jesse Crume and lived with him when he was small.
16. Dean and Diane Gladow research trip to Pennsylvania, Virginia, and Kentucky. June 2011.
17. Deed Book I, page 479. 13 October 1794. Deed Book L, page 308. 15 October 1794. Shenandoah County Clerk's Office, Woodstock, Virginia. Deed Book I, page 615 for William Marks' land.
18. Incidents in the Life of Jesse Crume. See #1 above.
19. Letter from Jesse W. Crume of Taylorsville, Kentucky. 9 March 1928. Jesse W. Crume was the grandson of Jesse Crume and lived with him when he was small.
20. Zadok Cramer. The Navigator. Pittsburgh: Cramer, Spear & Eichbaum, 1811. Pages 43-45. This was a guide to navigating the Ohio and Monongahela Rivers among others. Available online at the Library of Congress site, American Memory, under the heading The First American West: The Ohio River Valley 1750-1820. Redstone Old Fort is discussed under the name of Brownsville, Pennsylvania.
http://memory.loc.gov/award/icufaw/cbf0003/0005v.jpg

21. Zadok Cramer. The Navigator. Pages 76-90. See #20 above.
22. Zadok Cramer. The Navigator. See #20 above. Discussion of Maysville, pages 106-107. Jean Calvert and John Klee."Washington - The First County Seat." The Towns of Mason County - Their Past in Pictures. Maysville, Ky: Mason County Public Library. Pages 8-9.
23. Zadok Cramer. The Navigator. See #20 above. Discussion of Lexington, pages 106-108.
24. Incidents in the Life of Jesse Crume. See #1 above.
25. Executors and Guardians Bonds 1792-1803. Page 59. Nelson County, Kentucky. 18 March 1796. Bond appointing Moses Crume guardian of the children of William Crume and Mary Thomas Crume the executrix of the estate. Deed Book 7, pages 272-273. Nelson County, Kentucky.29 December 1797.
26. Incidents in the Life of Jesse Crume. See #1 above.
27. Dean and Diane Gladow research trip to Bardstown, Kentucky. 2011.
28. Letter from Jesse W. Crume of Taylorsville, Kentucky. 9 March 1928. See #19 above.
29. Incidents in the Life of Jesse Crume. See #1 above.
30. Incidents in the Life of Jesse Crume. See #1 above.
31. Orrie Beam Kellogg. "Memoirs of Squire Crume Family Life." 1982.
32. Orrie Beam Kellogg. See #31 above.
33. A.H. Redford, Methodism in Kentucky. Excerpted in The Kentucky Pioneer Genealogy and Records. Vol. 6, No. 1, 1985. Page 3.
34. Letter from Jesse W. Crume of Taylorsville, Kentucky. 9 March 1928. See #19 above.
35. William R. Langford Map of Kentucky Counties. Whiskey Hollow was apparently also referred to as Still-House Hollow. Crume Family Records. Lucy Geoghegan research collection. See #16, Chapter 3 above.
36. Thomas Crump. Abraham Lincoln's World. Page 23. See #11, Chapter 3 above.
37. Thomas Crump. Abraham Lincoln's World. Page 23. See #11, Chapter 3 above.
38. Dean and Diane Gladow research trip to Bardstown, Kentucky. 2009.
39. Crume Family Records. Lucy Geoghegan research collection. See #16, Chapter 3 above.
40. Philip Crume Family Bible. See #6, Chapter 3 above.

41. Philip Crume Sr. Will. Will Book A-1, page 470-475. Nelson County, Kentucky.
42. Virginia Census Records for 1775 in Dunmore County, Virginia and 1783 and 1785 in Shenandoah County, Virginia. The First Census in 1790, Shenandoah County, Virginia Heads of Households.
43. Letter from Jesse W. Crume of Taylorsville, Kentucky. 9 March 1928. See #19 above.
44. Incidents in the Life of Jesse Crume. See #1 above.

Chapter 5
1. Our American Heritage Library. http://mymilitaryhistorypages.bravehost.com/Boone.html
2. 1790-1792 Tax Lists for Nelson County, Kentucky
3. The Daniel Boone Wilderness Trail Association. "History of the Wilderness Trail." 2006. www.danielboonetrail.com/history.php. Accessed 15 April 2011.
4. Our American Heritage Library. See #1 above.
5. John Lay. "An Overview of Abraham Lincoln's Ancestry." Self-published. 2006. Book available at the Hardin County History Museum and through John Lay. Source material in the book may be found in The Lincolns on Mill Creek by Gerald McMurtry, Two Centuries in Elizabethtown and Hardin County 1776-1976 by Daniel McClure and a wealth of literature on the Lincoln family. The book primarily concerns the Capt. Abraham Lincoln family.
6. Brumfield, Berry, Lincoln, Crume Family Records. Lucy Geoghegan research collection. See #16, Chapter 3 above. Census records for Hardin County 1840-1880. John Lay research collection. Brumfield/ Nall Family Records.
7. Crume Family Records. Rick Crume and Brett Berry private research collections. See #52, Chapter 3 above.
8. Philip Crume Family Bible. See #6, Chapter 3 above.
9. Deed Book 2, pages 157-158. Nelson County, Kentucky for the power of attorney. Deed Book 7, page 264-272. Eleven deeds to the children of Philip Crume, Sr. dated either 28 December, 29 December, or 10 September of 1797. One of the deeds was to Benedict Lucas, a grandchild-in-law, perhaps taking the place of Isaac who had died in Virginia. There was no deed for Elizabeth Harrell, and there were two deeds for Moses. Philip later in a codicil to his will gave the piece of land deeded to Abraham Birkhead to Philip's son Daniel - no reason was given. Four

deeds went to Richard Parker for his work in dividing the land. Parker's deeds are recorded on pages 1-4 in Deed Book 7 and dated in August and September of 1796. No reason is known for why Parker got more land than each of Philip's individual children, even more than Ralph who helped with the division.

10. Will Book A-1. See #41, chapter 4 above.
11. Dean and Diane Gladow Research trip to Bardstown, Kentucky, 2011.
12. Dean and Diane Gladow Research trip to Bardstown, Kentucky, 2011.
13. Mary Thomas Crume Family Records. Lucy Geoghegan research collection. See #16, Chapter 3 above. The following land deeds concerning the same piece of property prove the second marriage of Mary Thomas Crume and the whereabouts of the family. Deed Book 7, page 272 on 29 December 1797. Deed Book 11, p. 20 on 24 August 1810, and Deed Book 14, page 194 on 17 March 1820. Nelson County, Kentucky Marriage record on 16 January 1798 for Samuel and Mary Horsley.
14. Hasty and Davis Family Records. Lucy Geoghegan research collection. See #16, Chapter 3 above. See other records through the private research collections of Jack Jeffries and Claudia Hasty Whitaker.
15. Daniel Crume Family Records. Lucy Geoghegan research collection. See #16, Chapter 3 above. Marriage record at Washington County, Kentucky in 1801.
16. Land Records in Butler County, Ohio, and Dearborn County, Indiana. Census records in 1820 in Dearborn County, Indiana. The History of Decatur County Indiana. 1915. page 138.
17. Washington County Historical Series. Orval W. Baylor. Article 41, May 17, 1934. "The Crumes of Campground." The article has several errors but was correct concerning Moses Crume's early religious activities.
18. Deed Book 6, page 349. Nelson County, Kentucky. 1805. Deed Book 13, page 192. Nelson County, Kentucky. 1806. Tax List 1806, Butler County, Ohio, page 4.
19. Minutes of the Annual Conferences of the Methodist Episcopal Church 1839-1845. Volume III. New York: T. Mason and G. Lane, 1840. Obituary pages 52-53. "Rev. Moses Crume."
20. "Rev. Moses Crume."Centennial History of Butler County, Ohio 1905. Pages 987-988.

21. The Descendants of the Rev. Moses Crume and Sarah Marks of Butler County, Ohio, 1766-1994. Compiled by Rick Crume. August 16, 1994.
22. Minutes of the Annual Conferences of the Methodist Episcopal Church 1839-1845. See #19 above. Indiana Miscellany. Rev. William C. Smith. Indiana 1867. "Chapter XIX Rev. Moses Crume." Pages 145-147.
23. "Scotch Irish Emigration to America." abstracted from The Scotch-Irish, A Social History by James G. Leyburn. Chapel Hill: University of North Carolina Press, 1962. www.homepages.rootsweb.ancestry.com/~mccle112/homepage/migrate.htm accessed online Accessed March 2011.
24."Scotch Irish Emigration to America." See #23 above.
25. Order Book, Nelson County, Kentucky. 17 May 1788. Ralph Crume Sr. appointed captain of the Nelson County, Kentucky militia.
26. Deed Book 6, page 224. Nelson County, Kentucky. 16 March 1803. Ralph Crume and wife Mary sell to Cyrus Talbott 86 acres on Sun Fish Creek.
27. Deed Book B, pages 13-15. Breckinridge County, Kentucky. 7 June 1803. Ralph Sr. and Jr. buying land from William Hardin.
28. Marriage Records Washington County, Kentucky. 5 August 1801. Bond signed by Ralph Crume Jr. and Mordecai Lincoln.
29. Federal Census Records for Breckinridge County, Kentucky. 1810, page 305 or 164 and 1820, page 243. Ralph Crume Jr. head of household.
30. Crume Family Records. See #16 in Chapter 3 above. Marriage records for Nelson County, Kentucky. 20 December 1804. Jacob Marks and Anna Barret Crume.
31. Marriage records for Nelson County, Kentucky. 4 December 1802. Eunice Crume and Michael Klinglesmith.
32. Crume Family Records. See #16, Chapter 3 above.
33. Marriage records for Nelson County, Kentucky. 21 October 1807. Margaret Crume and John Ridgeway.
34. Crume Family Records. See #16, Chapter 3 above.
35. Crume Family Records. See #16, Chapter 3 above. Anna Barret Crume family records.
36. Philip Crume Family Bible. See #6, Chapter 3 above.
37. Philip Crume Family Bible. See #6, Chapter 3 above.
38. Deed Book D, page 377. Breckinridge County, Kentucky. Bond agreed to on 31 August 1810. Deed recorded in 1818.
39. Philip Crume Family Bible. See #6, Chapter 3 above.

A Journey of Voices: Stewards of the Land 321

40. Marriage records for Nelson County, Kentucky. 26 March 1811. John Crume and Elizabeth Cotton.
41. John Crume Family Records. Lucy Geoghegan research collection. See #16, Chapter 3 above.
42. Age calculations from Federal Census 1810 Nelson County, Kentucky.
43. <u>Philip Crume 1724-1801 Family and Kentucky Land Records</u>. Lucy Geoghegan. Bardstown, Kentucky: Nelson County Public Library, 2010.

Chapter 6
1. Diane McAdams Gladow. <u>A Journey of Voices: Chasing the Frontier</u>. College Station, Texas: Virtualbookworm.com Publishing, 2010.

Chapter 7
1. <u>Deed Book C</u>, pages 22-23. Breckinridge County, Kentucky. 18 June 1810. Extract. Ralph Crume, Sr. from John Fentress.
2. Dean and Diane Gladow research trip to Breckinridge County, Kentucky. 2009.
3. <u>Deed Book B</u>, pages 13-15. Breckinridge County, Kentucky. 7 June 1803. Ralph Sr. and Jr. buying land from William Hardin.
4. <u>Deed Book C</u>, pages 22-23. Breckinridge County, Kentucky. 18 June 1810. Ralph Crume, Sr. from John Fentress. Land on the Clear Fork of the Calamese Creek. <u>Deed Book C</u>, page 24. Breckinridge County, Kentucky. 18 June 1810. Charles Crume from John Fentress. Land on the North Fork of the Rough River. <u>Deed Book C</u>, page 25. Breckinridge County, Kentucky. 18 June 1810. Ralph Crume Jr. from John Fentress. Land on Calamese Creek. <u>Deed Book C</u>, pages 25-26. Breckinridge County, Kentucky. 11 January 1810. Charles Crume from John Fentress. Land on Clear Fork of Calamese Creek. <u>Deed Book C</u>, page 26. Breckinridge County, Kentucky. 18 June 1810. Levi Horsley from John Fentress. Land on Calamese Creek.
5. Lucy Geoghegan. <u>Philip Crume 1724-1801 Family and Kentucky Land Records</u>. Bardstown, Kentucky: Nelson County Public Library, 2010. Marriage records from Nelson, Breckinridge, and Hardin County Clerks.
Note about Silas Crume, son of Ralph Crume Sr.: There is only slight evidence that Silas ever existed. There are enough boy children for Ralph Sr. on the 1820 census for Breckinridge County to include him, but of course, no names to prove his

existence conclusively. He may have signed the 1829 dower settlement for Mary Riggs Crume, but there was a Silas, son of William W. Crume (who died in 1812 and left four orphans), who could have signed the document (See #1, Chapter 8). No other evidence has been found. He was definitely gone or not in the picture when Ralph Crume Sr.'s estate was settled and divided as discussed in the 1832 and 1842 documents (See #33 below).
6. Crume Family Records. Brett Berry private research collection. Other sources Rick Crume research collection and Lucy Geoghegan research collection, also Diane Gladow research collection on Charles Jordan's family.
7. Court Order Book 1, pages 246-247. Breckinridge County. 15 September 1817. Ralph Crume Jr. appointed guardian to four children of William Crume deceased. Court Order Book 2, pages 165 and 253. Court orders on 18 March 1816 and 17 November 1817 in regards to Ralph Jr. administering the estate of William Crume, the one in 1817 reporting on a piece of land of 160 acres purchased in the name of the children. The land purchase may have been begun by their father before he died.   Census records for Breckinridge County 1820.
8. Philip Crume Family Bible. See #6, Chapter 3 above.
9. The National Experience. See #22, Chapter 3 above. Pages 175-183.
10. Index to Compiled Service Records of Volunteer Soldiers Who Served During the War of 1812. Ancestry.com. Roll Box 50, Roll Extract 602.
11. Index to Compiled Service Records. See # 10 above. Brett Berry research collection, records on James Howey.
12. Index to Compiled Service Records. See #10 above. Philip Withers Crume Family Records. Rick Crume research collection, Brett Berry research collection.
13. Federal Census Records for Breckinridge and Hardin Counties 1810-1850. Approximate birth dates.
14. County Court Minute Book 3 (1818-1823). Page 142. Breckinridge County, Kentucky. 15 May 1820.
15. Crume Family Records. Gladys Crume McAdams research collection. Contact Diane Gladow.
16. Lincoln Family Records. Lucy Geoghegan research collection. See #16, Chapter 3. Also John Lay. Overview of Abraham Lincoln's Ancestry. See #5, Chapter 5 above.
17. Brown-Pusey House records. Elizabethtown, Kentucky. 2006.
18. John Lay. See #5, Chapter 5 above.

19. John Lay. See #5, Chapter 5 above. Many other Thomas Lincoln background sources.
20. Keziah Crume Howey Family Records. Brett Berry private research collection.
21. Squire Crume Family Records. Lucy Geoghegan research collection. See #16, Chapter 3 above.
22. John Crume Family Records. Lucy Geoghegan research collection. See #16, Chapter 3 above.
23. Lucy Geoghegan research collection. See #16, Chapter 3 above.
24. Lucy Geoghegan research collection. See #16, Chapter 3 above. In 2011 Lucy Geoghegan did an extensive study of Philip Crume's original cabin on Sunfish Creek and its exact location. She was able to pinpoint the location although the log home is no longer there.
25. <u>Deed Book E</u>, page 59. Breckinridge County, Kentucky. 25 October 1819.
26. 1820 Federal Census Record for Breckinridge County, Kentucky.
27. Rev. William Morris Family Records. Lucy Geoghegan research collection. See #16, Chapter 3. Breckinridge County, Kentucky land records dated 8 November 1815, two parcels of land on Buffalo Run, one from Nehemiah Board and one from David H. Moorman.
28. Dean and Diane research trip to Breckinridge County, Kentucky. 2009.
29. <u>Breckinridge County Kentucky Records, Volume I</u>. Page 50. 23 October 1805. Grand Jury indicted Ralph Crume along with others for assault. William Hardin Jr. was found not guilty by a jury of assault on Ralph Crume on 22 July 1806. Page 64. Same incident?
30. <u>Philip Crume Family Bible</u>. See #6, Chapter 3 above.
31. Ralph Crume Sr. Family Records. Rick Crume research collection. Some records are online.
32. Crume Cemetery Tombstone and Investigation. 2009. Report written in <u>Crume Families of North Central Kentucky.</u> Diane and Dean Gladow. Available at Nelson County Public Library and Breckinridge County Archives.
33. <u>Deed Book N</u>, pages 311-312. Breckinridge County, Kentucky. 22 October 1842. Sale of Ralph Crume Sr.'s estate.
34. There is no exact death date for Mary Riggs Crume. She was alive for the 1829 dower settlement (See #1, Chapter 8 above) and the 1830 census for Breckinridge County, Kentucky. It is possible she could have died by the 1832 settlement (<u>Chancery Court Book</u>

K, pages 485-486) of Mary Drane's suit against Ralph Crume Sr.'s estate because the slaves which were given to Mary Riggs Crume as a part of her dower settlement were sold by order of the 1832 court settlement. Her death is usually listed as anywhere between 1832 and 1839.
35. Cenus records on Crume family members 1830-1850 in Kentucky, Indiana, Illinois, and Missouri. Land purchases by family members from each other as outlined in the 1832 and 1842 court settlements on the Ralph Crume Sr. estate . See #33 and #34 above. John Crume Family Records. Diane Gladow research collection.
36. Rick Crume research collection. Census records for Breckinridge County, Kentucky 1840, Missouri 1850, and Texas. John Crume land sale records. Breckinridge County, Kentucky. 22 September 1842 (Deed Book N, pages 473-474).
37. Mary Crume Pile Ruckman Family Records. Census records for Breckinridge County 1830, Vermillion County, Illinois 1840, 1850. Estate documents for Ralph Crume Sr.
38. William Crume Family Records. Rick Crume research collection. Census records for Breckinridge, Hardin, and Edmonson Counties 1830, 1840, 1850. Estate documents for Ralph Crume Sr. and land sale documents from Breckinridge County, Kentucky.

Chapter 8

1. Deed Book I (as in Isaac), page 43. Breckinridge County, Kentucky. 30 March 1829. Dower settlement for Mary Riggs Crume. Ralph Jr. signed the document. 1830 census for Vermillion County, Indiana.
2. Marriage record/bond for 7 February 1825 in Hardin County, Kentucky.
3. Hoskinson Family Records. Fannalou Guggisberg research collection. Marriage records for Hardin County (marriages performed by Rev. Hoskinson). Deed Book 2, page 291. Hardin County, Kentucky. 3 December 1855.
4. Federal census for Vermillion County, Indiana 1830. Silas Moses Crume Bible Record. Recorded between 1870-1875.
5. Federal census for Vermillion County, Indiana 1830. Ralph Crume, Sr. estate settlement documents 1832 and 1842. See #33 and #34, Chapter 7 above.
6. Federal census for Vermillion County, Indiana 1830.
7. Marriage bond/record in Hardin County, Kentucky. 10 November 1831. Permission given by Mary Crume's guardian, William

Washington Crume. Mary chose William to be her guardian on 19 September 1831 (Court Order Book 6, Pages 47-48). She married a few months later. These events would have taken place while Ralph Crume Jr. (her former guardian) was in Vermillion County, Indiana, or in the process of returning back to Breckinridge County. Her brother James B. Crume switched his guardian to John Skilman Jr. on 19 January 1829 (Lincoln Kinsman, #42, page 6) which would have fit with Ralph Crume Jr. leaving Kentucky to go to Vermillion County, Indiana. These dates of guardian change do not agree, either because one was in error or Mary's record was not filed until later or Mary waited to change her guardian until 1831.

8. Tax Records for Vermillion County, Indiana in 1830 and 1835.
9. U.S. Government Land Patent. Document # 8528, Accession/Serial # IN1040___.210. Vermillion County, Indiana W1/2SE, Sec 11, TN 16-N, RG 9-W.
10. Vermillion County Indiana - History and Families. 1988. "Ferries." Chapter 12. Pages 57-58. The author confused Ralph Crume Jr. and Ralph Lincoln Crume.
11. Chancery Court Book K, Pages 485-486. Breckinridge County, Kentucky. 18 October 1832. Thomas Drane and wife vs. Ralph Crume Sr. estate.
12. Circuit Court Book 10, Pages 488-489. Breckinridge County, Kentucky. 23 April 1842. Final partition of the estate of Ralph Crume Sr. discussing who of the heirs had sold their shares and to whom. Chancery Court Book K, Pages 485-486. See #11 above.
13. Chancery Court Book K, Pages 485-486. See #11 above.
14. Crume Cemetery Report. Crume Families of North Central Kentucky. Dean and Diane Gladow. See #32, Chapter 7 above. Cemetery records of Mill Creek Cemetery at Ft. Knox, Hardin County, Kentucky. Ralph Lincoln Crume Family Records. Lucy Geoghegan research collection. See #16, Chapter 3 above.
15. Chancery Court Book K, Pages 485-486. See #11 above.
16. Crume Family Records. Lucy Geoghegan research collection. See #16, Chapter 3 above. The 1830 federal census record for Vermillion County, Indiana shows Susannah Crume alive. She could have returned to Kentucky with her husband and his parents and died shortly thereafter, or she could have died in Vermillion County, but all family records have her death occurring from 1830-1832. She was not mentioned in the 1832 court document for Ralph Crume Sr.'s estate. The exact date of her daughter's death is not known, but she is not included in the 1840 census for

Breckinridge County, Kentucky, in the William C. Crume household.
17. Deed Book 6, page 214. Vermillion County, Indiana. 20 August 1836. Ralph Lincoln Crume selling his land to Charles Hoskinson.
18. Deed Book L, page 51. Breckinridge County, Kentucky. 29 September 1835. Ralph L. Crume mortgage to Harry Jennings and Stanley Singleton, merchants at Hardinsburg, Kentucky.
19. Deed Book 5, Page 467 or 9 or 4. Vermillion County, Indiana. 1 August 1837. Charles Hoskinson to Eliphalet Allen.
20. Deed Book 2, Page 291. See #3 above.
21. Marriage record for Ralph L. Crume and Mary Brumfield. Hardin County, Kentucky. 1 July 1837. #335 in the marriage book.
22. Land Rental Agreements between Ralph Lincoln Crume and Samuel Haycraft for the years 1843 (Deed Book N or M, Pages 469-470), 1844 (Deed Book U or V, Pages 189-190), 1847 (Deed Book W, Pages 445-446), 1849 (Pages 341-342), and 1850 (Pages 185-187). Hardin County, Kentucky.
23. Meryl S. Justin. "The Entry of Women into Medicine in America: Education and Obstacles 1847-1910." Pages 1-2. Accessed 13 July 2007. http://campus.hws.edu/his/blackwell/articles/womenmedicine.html.
24. "Mountain Medicine: Healthcare in the 1800's." http://home/att/net/~mman/Medicines.htm Accessed 13 July 2007.
25. Incidents in the Life of Jesse Crume. See #1, Chapter 4 above.
26. Marriage records for Breckinridge County, Kentucky. 27 July 1837. William C. Crume and Mary Ann Lucas Norris. Family record from Eliza Jane Crume Hudson written before 1917. Supplied to Gladys Crume McAdams by Eliza's granddaughter, Verna Fitch, in 1960. Gladys Crume McAdams research collection. Contact Diane Gladow.
27. Crume Family Records. Lucy Geoghegan research collection. See #16, Chapter 3 above.
28. Federal Census for Hardin County, Kentucky, 1850. Middle names of daughters determined by other family records including newspaper articles and court records. Breckinridge County Kentucky Records Vol. 4. See #7, Chapter 9 below.
29. Will Book 1, pages 89-90. Breckinridge County, Kentucky. November 1837 probated. William Morris will.

A Journey of Voices: Stewards of the Land 327

30. Equity Court Record. #86. Meade or Nelson County, Kentucky. 9 May 1856. Suit by William Marks against the estate of Anna Crume Marks Morris asking for compensation for caring for Anna in the short period of time before the land in Breckinridge County, Kentucky, was sold and she moved to Nelson County to live with John and Squire Crume. The suit found in favor of the Crumes.
31. Deed Book N, pages 311-312. Breckinridge County, Kentucky. 22 October 1842. Sale of Ralph Crume Sr.'s estate.
32. Marks Family Records. Lucy Geoghegan research collection. See #16, Chapter 3 above.
33. Deed Book N, Page 461. Breckinridge County, Kentucky. 16 October 1843. Sale of 510 acres to Philip Thurman from the Marks family.
34. Crume Family Records. Lucy Geoghegan research collection. See #16. Chapter 3 above. Tombstone inscription at Poplar Flat Cemetery.
35. 1850 Federal Census Record for Meade County, Kentucky. Calculation, along with his age, when Silas Moses moved to Meade County to live with the William Marks family.
36. Breckinridge County, Kentucky tax record. 1848 and 1850.
37. Silas Moses Crume Family Records. Gladys Crume McAdams research collection. See #15, Chapter 7 above.
38. 1850 Federal Census Record for Breckinridge County, Kentucky.
39. 1850 Federal Census Record for Breckinridge County, Kentucky. Francis T. Ingmire. Breckinridge County Births. St. Louis, Missouri: Ingmire Publications, 1983. "Adeline Crume."
40. Francis T. Ingmire. Breckinridge County, Kentucky Death Records. St. Louis, Missouri: Ingmire Publications, 1983. Page 16. " Jane Crume."
41. Breckinridge County, Kentucky Births. See #39 above. "Adeline Crume." John D. Crume Family Records. Gladys Crume McAdams research collection. See #15, Chapter 7 above.
42. Breckinridge County, Kentucky Death Records. See #40 above. Also official Kentucky Death Records.
43. Marriage records for Breckinridge County. Book B (1855-1858). 25 September 1857. John D. Crume to Julia Ann Butler. Greenberry Butler bondsman. Recorded in Breckinridge County Kentucky Records Volume 2. Library catalogue #GEN976.9854C772.
44. John D. Crume's death date comes from the fact that Julia, his second wife, remarried in March of 1864 and his children were given a guardian of Ralph Marks Crume in December of 1865.

One land record where the heirs of John Daniel Crume are verifying the sale of his land after his death lists his death date as 7 February 1857 (2 Feb 1886, <u>Deed Book 41</u>, pages 482-483), but this is in conflict with the 1860 census for Breckinridge County, Kentucky and John's marriage to Julia Butler.
45. Breckinridge County Marriage Records. March 1864. "Julia Crume." <u>Breckinridge County Kentucky Records Volume 4.</u> Ralph Marks Crume appointed guardian for Susan A. Crume, Moses Crume, and Mary C. Crume 5 December 1865.
46. John D. Crume Family Records. Gladys Crume McAdams research collection. See #15, Chapter 7 above.

Chapter 9
1. Orrie Beam Kellogg. "Memoirs of Squire Crume Family Life." 1982.
2. <u>Deed Book T</u>, page 248. Breckinridge County, Kentucky. 11 March 1851. Philip Thurman to Dr. William C. Crume. 122 ½ acres.
3. Francis T. Ingmire. <u>Breckinridge County, Kentucky Deaths.</u> St. Louis, Missouri: Ingmire Publications,1983. Page 3. " James F. Crume." Also official Kentucky Death records.
4. 1850 Federal Census for Breckinridge County, Kentucky. Ralph Lincoln Crume Family Records. Diane Gladow research collection.
5. Mill Creek Baptist Church Cemetery Records. Ft. Knox, Hardin County, Kentucky.
6. Marriage record #429. Hardin County, Kentucky. Ralph L. Crume and Rebecca Ann Carr. 12 January 1852.
7. <u>Breckinridge County Kentucky Records, Volume IV.</u> Library Catalogue #GEN976.9854C772. 19 March 1855. John D. Crume appointed guardian for Ann Mary Thomas Crume and Nancy Lewis Crume. William Tilley, bondsman. 1860 census for Hardin County, Kentucky. Luther J. Nall household.
8. <u>Newspaper Abstracts of Breckinridge County, Kentucky.</u> Pages 133-134. Wednesday, May 14, 1890. List of those exempt from paying county taxes for 1890 and 1891.
9. "Lincoln's Cousin Dies at Age of 83 in Missouri." <u>Denver Post</u>. 6 March 1931. Marriage certificate for Ralph Marks Crume and Mary T. Crume. 31 August 1865. Breckinridge County, Kentucky. Minister John Rhodus.
10. Francis T. Ingmire. <u>Breckinridge County, Kentucky Marriages.</u> St. Louis: Ingmire Publications, 1983. Page 49. 18 September 1861.

William H. Hudson to Eliza Jane Crume. And Page 53. 19 December 1861. John B. Tucker to Susan Mary Crume.
11. Family record from Eliza Jane Crume Hudson written before 1917. Supplied to Gladys Crume McAdams by Eliza's granddaughter, Verna Fitch, in 1960. Gladys Crume McAdams research collection. Contact Diane Gladow.
12. Family record from Eliza Jane Crume Hudson. See #11 above. Family records for John B. Tucker family. Gladys Crume McAdams research collection. See #11 above.
13. Military and pension records for Ralph M. Crume. Company F, 27th Volunteer Infantry from Breckinridge County, Kentucky. Entered the service of the Union in 1861, discharged 1865.
14. Francis T. Ingmire. Breckinridge County, Kentucky Marriages. St. Louis, Missouri: Ingmire Publications, 1983. 31 August 1865. Ralph M. Crume to Mary T. Crume. See #9 above.
15. Civil War Soldiers Service Records. Roll Box 000386, Roll Ext 0006 for Union troops. Roll Box 000377, Roll Ext 0003 for Confederate Troops. Ancestry.com CD-Rom Disk. 2000/2002.
16. The War of the Rebellion: A Compilation of the Official Records of the Union and Confederate Armies. The Civil War CD-Rom. Guild Press of Indiana, Inc. Series 1, Volume XX/2 (S#30) Correspondence, Orders, and Returns Relating Specially to Operations in Kentucky, Middle and East Tennessee, North Alabama, and Southwestern Virginia from November 1, 1862 to January 20, 1863.
17. Orrie Beam Kellogg. "Memoirs of Squire Crume Family Life." 1980.
18. Letter from Jesse W. Crume of Taylorsville, Kentucky. See #19, Chapter 4 above.
19. "Perryville." CWSAC Battle Summaries. National Park Service American Battlefield Protection Program. http://www.nps.gov/history/hps/abpp/battles/ky009.htm. Accessed 9/26/2010.
20. William R. Langford Map of Kentucky Counties. 1960. Various Civil War places are indicated on the map. Gladys Crume McAdams research collection. Contact Diane Gladow.
21. Bardstown, Kentucky visitors' brochure. Bardstown-Nelson County Tourist and Convention Commission. 2009.
22. "Letter to President Abraham Lincoln from Mrs. Susannah Weathers." Copy of the original. Abraham Lincoln Presidential Library. Springfield, Illinois. http://www.alplm.org/home.html
23. The War of the Rebellion. See #16 above. Also see #30 below.

24. Orrie Beam Kellogg. See #17 above.
25. Letter from Jesse W. Crume of Taylorsville, Kentucky. See #19, Chapter 4 above.
26. Letter from Jesse W. Crume. See #19, Chapter 4 above.
27. The War of the Rebellion: A Compilation of the Official Records of the Union and Confederate Armies. The Civil War CD-Rom. Guild Press of Indiana, Inc. Series 1, Volume XV. May 15 - June 17, 1862. Operations in the Shenandoah Valley. #1-8, 12, 14-18, 21-22, 25-30, 32-33, 36, 38-39. Ralph Withers' land at Front Royal as shown on map in Philip Crume Family of the Shenandoah Valley, Virginia by Dean and Diane Gladow. Self-published. 2011.
Over the years researchers have tried to prove that the Crume family lived in Prince William County in the beginning of their years in Virginia using the Manassas Civil War story, but no record has been found of them there and the story itself had a mistaken location in it.
28. The War of the Rebellion. See #27 above. The Battle of Kernstown, Virginia. 1864. #18, 1, 6, 8, 9, 10.
29. Diane McAdams Gladow. A Journey of Voices: Chasing the Frontier. College Station, Texas: VirtualBookworm.com Publishing, 2010.
30. "Breckinridge County History." Wikipedia. en.wikipedia.org/wiki/Breckinridge_County,_Kentucky Accessed 5/23/2012.
31. Letter from Mrs. Eva M. Silvers, descendant of Susan Mary Crume Tucker, to Mrs. Barney Crume. 1960. Gladys Crume McAdams research collection. See #15, Chapter 7 above.
32. Deed Book 31, pages 78-79. Breckinridge County, Kentucky. 22 September 1875. William and Mary Crume to Ralph Marks Crume. 122 ½ acres.
33. Deed Book 33, pages 313-314. Breckinridge County, Kentucky. 4 December 1878. Ralph M. Crume and Mary T. Crume to Hartwell B. Basham. 122 ½ acres. There was no deed returning the land to Ralph M. Crume and wife. The Bashams never made any payments for the land and moved to Edmonson County, so the land reverted to the Ralph Crumes.
34. Newspaper Abstracts of Breckinridge County, Kentucky. November 1883. "The Court of Claims column, Fourth Day."
35. Deed Book 40, pages 237-238. Breckinridge County, Kentucky. 27 July 1886. Ralph M. Crume and Mary T. Crume to George P. Duncan. This sale took the land and the cemetery out of the

Crume family for the last time. The land can be traced to the present day with deeds in the Breckinridge County Archives and County Clerk's office. The line of owners was George P. Duncan, J.H. Dodson, R. C. Sharp, R.C. Sharp heirs, Silas Hudson, L.H. Hudson, Philip Hudson, and the current owner, Philip Hudson II. See report on the Crume Cemetery and Crume Valley, Crume Families of North-Central Kentucky by Diane and Dean Gladow, April 2010, available through authors and the Breckinridge County Archives.

Chapter 10

1. Gaius Marcees Brumbaugh. Revolutionary War Records. Lancaster, Pennsylvania: Lancaster Press, Inc. 1936. Pages 598-599. John Netherton's List of the Persons in Dunmore County, Virginia in 1775. Heads of Families in the First Census of the U.S. 1783. Page 65. Shenandoah, Virginia. The census shows Philip Crume with no black persons in the household.
2. 1860 Slave Census for Nelson County, Kentucky and Cherokee County, Texas.
3. Incidents in the Life of Jesse Crume. See #1, Chapter 4 above.
4. Philip Crume V Family Records. Brett Berry research collection.
5. "Invitation to an Abolitionist Meeting." Ralph Crume Jr. to David Hoskinson. Diane Gladow research collection.
6. Orrie Beam Kellogg. See #17, Chapter 9 above.
7. 1860 Slave Census for Nelson County, Kentucky. Squire Crume's Will. Will Book 10, page 532. Nelson County, Kentucky. 11 March 1861.
8. Will Book A-1, pages 470-475. Nelson County, Kentucky. 16 April 1801. Philip Crume I (as in one or the first) will.
9. Court records for Breckinridge County, Kentucky. 18 June 1821 and 17 September 1821. Assignment of dower property to Anna Marks Morris from the estate of Jacob Marks.
10. Court record for Breckinridge County, Kentucky. 27 October 1821. William Morris trying to emancipate the slave Charlotte belonging to his wife, Anna. Will Book I, pages 89-90. Breckinridge County, Kentucky. 9 August 1833. Probated 1837. Will of William Morris.
11. Inventory of personal property of Squire Crume in February of 1861 after his death.
12. The dates 1848 and 1849 have been proposed for Anna's death. The tombstone is now unreadable. 27 December 1848 is probably used most often. She was probably living with her son Squire

when she died, but she could have been with her son John. Anna Barret Crume Marks Morris Family Records. Lucy Geoghegan research collection. See #16, Chapter 3 above.

Chapter 11
1. Bernard Mayfield. "Pine Town and Java." <u>Cherokee County History.</u> Rusk, Texas: Cherokee County Historical Commission. 1986. Page 62.
2. 1850 Federal Census for Meade County, Kentucky.
3. John Finley Williams Family Records. Diane Gladow research collection.
4. Crume Family Records. Lucy Geoghegan research collection. See #16, Chapter 3 above. 1850 Federal Census for Meade County, Kentucky.
5. Marriage certificate from Meade County, Kentucky. 6 February 1853. Silas Moses Crume to Nancy Catherine Williams.
6. Gladys Crume McAdams. Family Memoirs. "Give to the World." Gladys Crume research collection. Contact Diane Gladow.
7. Williams Family Records. Diane Gladow research collection. 2009.
8. Bernard Mayfield. <u>Cherokee County History</u>. See #1 above. Page 62. Also Page 14 in <u>Cherokee County History.</u>
9. Original field notes of Silas Moses Crume on land located between Tail's Creek and One-Arm Creek in Cherokee County, Texas. Broome's part of the Wm. S. Box League survey. These surveys are dated 1859. Silas must have claimed the land when he first arrived and then gone through a long process of having it surveyed and then finally deeded to him.
10. Silas Moses Crume Family Bible Record. Silas Moses Crume family records. Gladys Crume McAdams research collection. Contact Diane Gladow.
11. "Cherokee County." <u>The Handbook of Texas Online.</u> Last updated 2006. Accessed 9 August 2007. http://www.tsha.utexas.edu/handbook/online/articles/CC/hcc10.html
12. Gladys Crume McAdams. Family Memoirs. See #6 above.
13. Silas Moses Crume Family Bible Record. See #10 above.
14. 1860 Federal Slave Census for Cherokee County, Texas.
15. Letter from Allie Belle Rogers to Gladys Crume McAdams. Contains a description of Silas Moses Crume's occupations and life on Tailes Creek. 1960. Gladys Crume McAdams research collection. Contact Diane Gladow.

A Journey of Voices: Stewards of the Land

16. Marti Attoun. "Gristmills." <u>American Profile</u>. 21-27 August 2011. Page 15. Might be available online at americanprofile.com.
17. "Pleasant Grove Missionary Baptist Church." <u>Tree Talk</u>. Vol 35, Issue 3. Spring 2010. Page 99.
18. Bernard Mayfield. <u>Vanishing Towns of Cherokee County, Texas.</u> Page 13.
19. Williams Family Records and Williams Cemetery Records. Diane Gladow research collection. 2009.
20. <u>Cherokee County History</u>. See #1 above. Page 62. Also Page 14 in <u>Cherokee County History</u>.
21. Letter from Allie Belle Rogers to Gladys Crume McAdams. See #15 above.
22. <u>Cherokee County History</u>. See #1 above. Also Page 14.
23. Ralph A. Wooster. "Civil War." <u>Handbook of Texas Online</u>. Published by the Texas State Historical Association. Accessed 24 May 2012.
http://www.tshaonline.org/handbook/online/articles/gdc02
24. "Civil War." <u>Handbook of Texas Online.</u> See #23 above.
25. Linda Ericson Devereaux and Kathryn Hooper Davis. <u>Cherokee County Texas in the Civil War.</u> Erickson Books. 2005. "Silas Moses Crume." This record supports the idea that Silas Moses's father, Dr. William Crume's middle name was Cox.
26. Williams Family Records and Williams Cemetery Records. Diane Gladow research collection. 2009.
27. <u>Cherokee County History.</u> See #1 above. Also Page 14.
28. Silas Moses Crume Family Bible Record. See #10 above.
29. Pleasant Grove Baptist Church Cemetery Records and Tombstone. Silas Moses Crume Family Bible Record. See #10 above.
30. Bernard Mayfield. <u>Vanishing Towns of Cherokee County, Texas.</u> See #18 above. Page 11.
31. <u>Cherokee County History</u>. See #1 above. Page 63.
32. Gladys Crume McAdams. Family Memoirs. See #6 above.
33. Gladys Crume McAdams. Family Memoirs. See #6 above.
34. <u>Cherokee County History</u>. See #1 above. Page 63.
35. Gladys Crume McAdams. Family Memoirs. See #6 above.

Chapter 12
1. <u>Deed Book I-2</u>, page 657. Cherokee County, Texas. 2 January 1879. William Herndon and wife to Silas Moses Crume. <u>Deed Book L2</u>, page 27. Cherokee County, Texas. 16 November 1871. Tidwell Ball to Silas Moses Crume.

2. Silas Moses Crume Family Bible Record. See #10, Chapter 11 above.
3. Bernard Mayfield. <u>Vanishing Towns of Cherokee County Texas.</u> Page 11 and 16.
4. Silas Moses Crume Family Records. Gladys Crume McAdams research collection. Contact Diane Gladow. Also Cherokee County, Texas Marriage Records.
5. Silas Moses Crume Family Records. See #4 above. Pleasant Grove Missionary Baptist Church Cemetery records and tombstone.
6. Silas Moses Crume Family Records. See #4 above. Pleasant Grove Missionary Baptist Church Cemetery records and tombstone.
7. Silas Moses Crume Family Records. See #4 above. Also Cherokee County, Texas Marriage Records.
8. Bernard Mayfield. "The Story of Pinetown." <u>Tree Talk</u>. Newsletter of the Cherokee County Historical Society. May 1990. Page 5.
9. Silas Moses Crume Family Records. See #4 above. Cherokee County, Texas Marriage Records.
10. Silas Moses Crume Family Bible Record. See #10, Chapter 11 above.
11. Silas Moses Crume Family Records. See #4 above. Pleasant Grove Missionary Baptist Church Cemetery records and tombstone.
12. "Java, Texas." <u>The Handbook of Texas Online.</u> Accessed 9 August 2007.
http://www.tsha.utexas.edu/handbook/online/articles/JJ/htj2.html
13. "Gent, Texas." <u>The Handbook of Texas Online.</u> Accessed 9 August 2007.
http://www.tsha.utexas.edu/handbook/online/articles/GG/hvg80.html
14. <u>Deed Book W2</u>, page 128. Cherokee County, Texas. 13 February 1889. S.M. Crume to R. A. McQueen. <u>Deed Book Y2</u>, page 214. Cherokee County, Texas. 17 October 1889. J.W. Crume to R.A. McQueen.
15. <u>Deed Book 5</u>, page 256 (perhaps 226). Cherokee County, Texas. 3 June 1891. Sarah J. Crume to R.A. McQueen.
16. Evelyn Bolton Ezell. "Aaron Crawford Family." <u>Cherokee County History.</u> See #1, Chapter 11 above. Page 220.
17. Marriage certificate for S.A. Crume and Elizabeth Crawford.
18. Samuel Augustus Crume Family Records. Gladys Crume McAdams research collection. Contact Diane Gladow.
19. Helen Wooddell Crawford. <u>The Saga of Cherokee County, Texas 1889-1908.</u> Volume 7, page 63. Newspaper article from <u>Cherokee County Banner</u> 13 December 1892. "The Cyclone at

Pinetown." The article states the cyclone actually occurred on 6 December.
20. Silas Moses Crume Family Records. See #4 above. Cherokee County Marriage Records.
21. Letter from Allie Belle Rogers to Gladys Crume McAdams. See #15, Chapter 11 above.
22. Samuel Augustus Crume Family Records. See #18 above. Pleasant Grove Missionary Baptist Church Cemetery records and tombstone.
23. Samuel Augustus Crume Family Records. See #18 above.
24. Original land deed. Cherokee County, Texas. 8 September 1894. Silas Moses Crume to Samuel A. Crume. 100 acres.
25. Silas Moses Crume Family Records. See #4 above. Pleasant Grove Missionary Baptist Church Cemetery records and tombstone.
26. Silas Moses Crume Family Records. See #4 above. Cherokee County, Texas Marriage Records.
27. Samuel Augustus Crume Family Records. See #18 above. Pleasant Grove Missionary Baptist Church Cemetery records and tombstones.
28. Original agreement with attorneys to represent S.M. Crume in a court action for unpaid taxes. They were to be paid in land. The court summons in District Court at Rusk, Texas, to answer the complaint of unpaid taxes by S.M. Crume and the heirs to the Roach estate, the parties in a land sale. November 1897.
29. Deed Book 21, page 587. Cherokee County, Texas. 4 May 1901. Lease. S.M. Crume to Texas Western Oil County
30. Silas Moses Crume Family Records. See #4 above. Cherokee County, Texas Marriage Records.

Chapter 13
1. "Maydelle, Texas." The Handbook of Texas Online. Accessed 9 August 2007.
http://www.tsha.utexas.edu/handbook/online/articles/CC/hcc10.html
2. "Maydelle, Texas." The Handbook of Texas Online. See #1 above.
3. Deed Book 6, page 61. Cherokee County, Texas. 21 December 1891. S.M. Crume to J.R. (S.?) Sherman.
4. Letter from Verna V. Fitch to Allie Belle Rogers. 1960. Gladys Crume McAdams research collection.
Contact Diane Gladow.
5. Ferguson and Jordan Family Records. Gladys Crume McAdams research collection. Contact Diane Gladow.

6. Ferguson and Silas Moses Crume Family Records. Gladys Crume McAdams research collection. Contact Diane Gladow. Cherokee County, Texas Marriage Records.
7. Federal Census for Cherokee County, Texas 1900.
8. Ferguson and Silas Moses Crume Family Records. See #6 above.
9. Ferguson Family Records. Gladys Crume McAdams research collection. Contact Diane Gladow.
10. Samuel A. Crume Family Bible Record. Gladys Crume McAdams research collection. Contact Diane Gladow. Anderson County, Texas Marriage Records. Marriage Certificate for Samuel Augustus Crume and Lanora Belle Ferguson.
11. Wedding Announcement in Palestine Herald newspaper. E.C. Rice. 19-20 November 1903.
12. "Matrimony." Echo newspaper. P.C. Shilling. 20 November 1903.
13. Gladys Crume McAdams. Family Memoirs. See #6, Chapter 11 above.
14. Gladys Crume McAdams. Family Memoirs. See #6, Chapter 11 above.
15. Deed Book 6, page 61. Cherokee County, Texas. 21 December 1891. S.M. Crume to J.R. (S.?) Sherman.
16. Cherokee County History. See #1, Chapter 11. Page 63.
17. Deed Book 47, page 10-12. Cherokee County, Texas. 25- 26 September 1908. S.M. Crume transferring his land in 50 acre plots to his children. Bank note for Velma Tankersley of $100 for when she came of age.
18. Deed Book 46, page 99. Cherokee County, Texas. 18 November 1908. J.W. Crume to S.A. Crume. Deed Book 39, page 481. Cherokee County, Texas. 18 November 1908. A.B. Ferguson to S.A. Crume.
19. Death Certificate 6416. Texas State Board of Health. Date of Death 23 March 1912. Silas Moses Crume.
20. Silas Moses Crume Family Records. See #4, Chapter 12 above.
21. Silas Moses Crume Family Records. See #4, Chapter 12 above.

Chapter 15
1. 1910 Federal Census for Cherokee County, Texas.
2. Samuel A. Crume Family Bible Record. Gladys Crume McAdams research collection. Contact Diane Gladow. Letter from Allie Belle Rogers to Gladys Crume McAdams. See #15, Chapter 11 above.
3. Samuel A. Crume Family Bible Record. See #2 above.

A Journey of Voices: Stewards of the Land 337

4. Samuel A. Crume Family Bible Record. See #2 above. Letter from Allie Belle Rogers to Gladys Crume McAdams. See #15, Chapter 11 above.
5. Gladys Crume McAdams. Family Memoirs. See #6, Chapter 11 above.
6. Karen Geerhardt Britton, Fred C. Elliott, and E.A. Miller. "Cotton Culture." Handbook of Texas Online. http://www.tshaonline.org/handbook/online/articles/afc03 Accessed 13 October 2011. Published by the Texas State Historical Association.
7. "Cotton Culture." Handbook of Texas Online. See #6 above.
8. Norman D. Brown. "Texas in the 1920's." Handbook of Texas Online. Accessed 13 October 2011. http://www.tshaonline.org/handbook/online/articles/npt01 Published by the Texas State Historical Association.
9. S.A. Crume Family Picture Album. The House at Maydelle. 1913. Gladys Crume McAdams research collection. Contact Diane Gladow. Gladys Crume McAdams. Autobiography. 1960. See #14, Chapter 15 below.
10. Gladys Crume McAdams. Family Memoirs. See #6, Chapter 11 above.
11. Samuel A. Crume Family Bible Record. See #2 above.
12. Samuel Augustus Crume Family Records. See #18, Chapter 12 above.
13. Gladys Crume McAdams. Family Memoirs. See #6, Chapter 11 above.
14. Gladys Crume McAdams. Autobiography. 1960. Never published, privately held. Gladys Crume McAdams research collection. Contact Diane Gladow.
15. "Cotton Culture." Handbook of Texas Online. See #6 above. The National Experience. See #22, Chapter 3 above. Pages 567-572.
16. Silas Moses Crume Family Records. See #4, Chapter 12 above.
17. The National Experience. See #22, Chapter 3 above. Pages 584-587.
18. Samuel A. Crume Family Bible Record. See #2 above.
19. Gladys Crume McAdams. Family Memoirs. See #6, Chapter 11 above.
20. "Cotton Culture." Handbook of Texas Online. See #6 above.
21. Gladys Crume McAdams. Family Memoirs. See #6, Chapter 11 above.
22. The National Experience. See #22, Chapter 3 above. Pages 615-616, 622-625.

23. Gladys Crume McAdams. Autobiography. See #14 above.
24. Dean and Diane Gladow research trip. 2003.

Chapter 16
1. Gladys Crume McAdams. Autobiography. See #14, Chapter 15 above. Gladys Crume McAdams. Family Memoirs. See #6, Chapter 11 above.
2. Gladys Crume McAdams. Autobiography. See #14, Chapter 15 above. Gladys Crume high school diplomas. Gladys Crume McAdams research collection. Contact Diane Gladow.
3. Gladys Crume McAdams. Autobiography. See #14, Chapter 15 above.
4. Gladys Crume McAdmas. Autobiography. See #14, Chapter 15 above.
5. Norman D. Brown. "Texas in the 1920's." Handbook of Texas Online. See #8, Chapter 15 above.
6. Norman D. Brown. "Texas in the 1920's." Handbook of Texas Online. See #8, Chapter 15 above.
7. Samuel A. Crume Account Book. 1923-1942. Gladys Crume McAdams research collection. Contact Diane Gladow.
8. Samuel A. Crume Account Book 1889-1896. Gladys Crume McAdams research collection. Contact Diane Gladow. Samuel A. Crume Account Book 1923-1942. See #7 above.
9. Samuel Augustus Crume Family Records. See #18, Chapter 12 above.
10. Gladys Crume McAdams. Autobiography. See #14, Chapter 15 above.
11. Gladys Crume McAdams. Family Memoirs. See #6, Chapter 11 above.

Chapter 17
1. Ben H. Procter. "Great Depression." Handbook of Texas Online. Accessed 27 October 2011.
   http://www.tshaonline.org/handbook/online/articles/npg01
   Published by the Texas State Historical Association.
2. "Poliomyelitis." Wikipedia.
   http://en.wikipedia.org/wiki/Infantile_paralysis Accessed 10/27/2011.
3. "Valedictory speech." Gladys Crume. Gladys Crume McAdams research collection. Contact Diane Gladow.
4. Gladys Crume McAdams. Autobiography. See #14, Chapter 15 above.

5. Gladys Crume McAdams. Autobiography. See #14, Chapter 15 above.
6. Gladys Crume McAdams, Autobiography. See #14, Chapter 15 above.
7. Ben H. Procter. "Great Depression" Handbook of Texas Online. See #1 above.
8. Samuel Augustus Crume Family Records. See #18, Chapter 12 above.
9. Gladys Crume McAdams. Autobiography. See #14, Chapter 15 above.
10. Gladys Crume McAdams. Autobiography. See #14, Chapter 15 above.
11. Gladys Crume Junior College Degree. Missionary Baptist College, Sheridan, Arkansas. 1930. Gladys Crume McAdams research collection. Contact Diane Gladow. Gladys Crume McAdams. Autobiography. See #14, Chapter 15 above.

Chapter 18
1. Ben H. Procter. "Great Depression." Handbook of Texas Online. See #1, Chapter 17 above.
2. "About the Dust Bowl." Modern American Poetry. Accessed 10/27/2011. http://www.english.illinois.edu/maps/depression/dustbowl.htm
3. Samuel Augustus Crume Family Records. See #18, Chapter 12 above. Gladys Crume McAdams. Autobiography. See #14, Chapter 15 above.
4. Katya Cengel. "Homecoming Tribute." The Courier-Journal. Features Section. Louisville, Kentucky. 24 May 2009. The Fort Knox Cemeteries Revisited.
5. Robert Leaverton Family Memories and Records. Diane Gladow research collection. 2011.
6. Gladys Crume McAdams. Autobiography. See #14, Chapter 15 above.
7. Oil leases from various companies. 1972-2007. Diane Gladow research collection and personal papers.
8. Gladys Crume McAdams. Family Memoirs. See #6, Chapter 11 above. Gladys Crume College Degree. North Texas State Teacher's College. Denton, Texas. 1936. Gladys Crume McAdams research collection. Contact Diane Gladow.
9. Gladys Crume McAdams. Family Memoirs. See #6, Chapter 11 above.
10. Samuel A. Crume Account Book. See #7, Chapter 16 above.

Chapter 19
1. Ben H. Procter. "Great Depression." <u>Handbook of Texas Online</u>. See #1, Chapter 17 above. "About the Dust Bowl." <u>Modern American Poetry</u>. See #2, Chapter 18 above.
2. Gladys Crume McAdams. Autobiography. See #14, Chapter 15 above.
3. Gladys Crume McAdams. Family Memoirs. See #6, Chapter 11 above.
4. Robert Leaverton Family Memories and Records. See #5, Chapter 18 above.
5. Samuel A. Crume Account Book. See #7, Chapter 16 above.
6. Samuel Augustus Crume Family Records. See #18, Chapter 12 above.
7. Robert Leaverton Family Memories and Records. See #5, Chapter 18 above.
8. Samuel Augustus Crume Family Records. See #18, Chapter 12 above.
9. Gladys Crume McAdams. Family Memoirs. See #6, Chapter 11 above.
10. Gladys Crume McAdams. Autobiography. See #14, Chapter 15 above.
11. Gladys Crume McAdams. Family Memoirs. See #6, Chapter 11 above.
12. "About the Dust Bowl." <u>Modern American Poetry</u>. See #2, Chapter 18 above. Donald Worster. "Dust Bowl." <u>Handbook of Texas Online</u>. Accessed 27 October 2011. http://www.tshaonline.org/handbook/online/articles/ydd01 Published by the Texas State Historical Association.

Chapter 20
1. This expression came from the story in the Bible about the man, Job, and all of his trials as God tested his patience and loyalty. He became very poor during God's testing period.

Chapter 21
1. Clyde Crume letters to his parents. 1940. Bakersfield, California. Diane Gladow research collection. 2011.
2. Gladys Crume McAdams. Family Memoirs. See #6, Chapter 11 above.
3. Gladys Crume McAdams. Autobiography. See #14, Chapter 15 above.
4. <u>The National Experience.</u> See #22, Chapter 3 above. Page 701.

5. Harry McAdams WWII letters and official orders. Diane Gladow research collection. 2011.
6. Harry M. McAdams. A Time to Recall: An Autobiography. 1990. Unpublished and privately held. Diane Gladow research collection. 2011.
7. Gladys Crume McAdams. Autobiography. See #14, Chapter 15.
8. Gladys Crume McAdams. Autobiography. See #14, Chapter 15.
9. Harry M. McAdams. A Time to Recall: An Autobiography. See #6 above.
10. Telegram from Harry McAdams to Gladys McAdams, his wife. 25 July 1942. Diane Gladow research collection. 2011.
11. Samuel Augustus Crume Family Records. See #18, Chapter 12 above.

Chapter 22

1. The National Experience. See #22, Chapter 3 above. Pages 701-702.
2. The National Experience. See #22, Chapter 3 above. Pages 409-411, 418-424.
3. Samuel Augustus Crume Family Records. See #18, Chapter 12 above. Samuel E. "Buster" Crume Family Records. 1998. Diane Gladow research collection. 2011.
4. Harry M. McAdams. A Time to Recall: An Autobiography. See #6, Chapter 21 above.
5. "V-Mail." Smithsonian National Postal Museum. Accessed 2/2/2012.
http://www.postalmuseum.si.edu/exhibits/2d2a_vmail.html
6. Harry M. McAdams. A Time to Recall: An Autobiography. See #6, Chapter 21 above.
7. Gladys Crume McAdams. Autobiography. See #14, Chapter 15.
8. Gladys Crume McAdams. Autobiography. See #14, Chapter 15.
9. "'Bombs Away' Over Kasserine." Dallas Morning News. Reprint of a letter sent to Gladys McAdams. 15 June 1943 (date of the letter, not the newspaper article). For the letter, access Diane Gladow research collection. 2011.   Harry M. McAdams. A Time to Recall: An Autobiography. See #6, Chapter 21 above.
10. Harry M. McAdams. A Time to Recall: An Autobiography. See #6, Chapter 21 above.
11. Harry M. McAdams. A Time to Recall: An Autobiography. See #6, Chapter 21 above.
12. Gladys Crume McAdams. Autobiography. See #14, Chapter 15.

Chapter 23

1. Samuel Augustus Crume Family Records. See #18, Chapter 12 above. Samuel Augustus Crume death record. Cherokee County, Texas. Texas Deaths, 1890-1976. Online database. Accessed 1 March 2010.
http://pilot.familysearch.org/recordsearch/start.html#start
2. John T. Watson and T.E. Acker. Committee of the 1944 Conference of the Baptist Church in Cherokee County, Texas. Written eulogy by the committee to appear in the minutes of the conference. 26 November 1944.
3. Clyde Crume letters to family. 1944. Diane Gladow research collection. 2011.
4. Floyce Leaverton letter to Gladys and Harry McAdams. 1944. Diane Gladow research collection. 2011.
5. The National Experience. See #22, Chapter 3 above. Page 711.
6. "History." Railroad Retirement Board. Accessed 3 June 2012.
www.allgov.com/Agency/Railroad_Retirement_Board
Amendments to pay benefits to spouses and dependents. www.rrb.gov/general/handbook/chapter1.asp   Accessed 3 June 2012.
Social Security Program. History.
www.ssa.gov/history/1940.html   Accessed 3 June 2012.
7. Crume Letters from June - August 1944. Diane Gladow research collection. 2011.
8. Letter from Floyce Leaverton to Gladys McAdams. August 1944. Diane Gladow research collection. 2011.

Chapter 24

1. Samuel E. Crume Family Record. 1998. Diane Gladow research collection. 2011.
2. Samuel Augustus Crume Family Records. See #18, Chapter 12 above. Harris County, Texas Death and Census Records.
3. Robert Leaverton Family Memories and Records. See #5, Chapter 18 above.
4. Harry McAdams Family Records. Diane Gladow research collection. 2011.
5. Gladys McAdams Family Records. Diane Gladow research collection. 2011.
6. Samuel Augustus Crume Family Records. See #18, Chapter 12 above.
7. Dean and Diane Gladow research trip. 2009.

8. News story concerning the Columbia space shuttle explosion in 2003. Accessed 1 June 2012.
http://lubbockonline.com/gallery/shuttle_columbia_debris/1.shtml
9. Gladys Crume McAdams. Family Memoirs. See #6, Chapter 11 above.

www.ingramcontent.com/pod-product-compliance
Lightning Source LLC
Chambersburg PA
CBHW060108170426
43198CB00010B/813